Contents

INTRODUCTION

THE SEX DISCRIMINATION ACT 1975

PART I DISCRIMINATION TO WHICH ACT APPLIES

Sex discrimination general

PART II DISCRIMINATION IN THE EMPLOYMENT FIELD

Discrimination by employers

Discrimination by other bodies

Special cases

THE POINT OF LAW

Discrimination Law Ex

London: The Stationery Office

A CIP catalogue record for this book is available from the British Library.
A Library of Congress CIP catalogue record has been applied for.

First published 2000

ISBN 0 11 702382 5

About the author

Colin Bourne a specialist in Employment and Discrimination Law is a barrister practising from the Chambers of Aidan Marron QC at 14 Toft Green, York YO1 6JT, www.yorkchambers.co.uk.

Disclaimer

This publication is intended to be a brief commentary on the Sex Discrimination Act 1975, Race Relations Act 1976 and Disability Discrimination Act 1995 and should not be relied upon by any party without taking further legal advice.

Printed in the United Kingdom for The Stationery Office Limited
TJ002999 C15 9/00 535726 19585

Part IV Other Unlawful Acts

Part V General Exceptions from Parts II to IV

Part VI Equal Opportunities Commission

Investigations

PART VII ENFORCEMENT

General

Enforcement in employment field

Enforcement of Part III

Non-discrimination notices

Other enforcement by Commission

Help for persons suffering discrimination

Period within which proceedings to be brought

PART VIII SUPPLEMENTAL

SCHEDULES

THE RACE RELATIONS ACT 1976

PART I DISCRIMINATION TO WHICH ACT APPLIES

Part II Discrimination in the Employment Field

Discrimination by employers

Discrimination by other bodies

Part III Discrimination in Other Fields

Education

Goods, facilities, services and premises

Part VII The Commission for Racial Equality

General

Codes of practice

Investigations

Part VIII Enforcement

General

Enforcement in the employment fields

Enforcement of Part III

Non-discrimination notices

SCHEDULES

DISABILITY DISCRIMINATION ACT 1995

PART I DISABILITY

PART II EMPLOYMENT

Discrimination by Employers

Enforcement etc.

Discrimination by other persons

Premises occupied under leases

Occupational pension schemes and insurance services

PART VIII MISCELLANEOUS

Discrimination Law Explained

INTRODUCTION

Discrimination law is changing, even as this book went to press, and further changes are already being considered whether to national law or by way of Directives from the European Union. This book states the law as it was in October 2000. Where, at the time of publishing, there is a date for the introduction of amendments or new provisions these are stated in addition to existing provisions.

The Human Rights Act 1998 is outside the scope of this work but it should be remembered that the provisions of the European Convention on Human Rights are to be incorporated into UK law by October 2000. Under Article 14 of the Convention, the right not to be discriminated against is wider than the present provisions of national law.

As is so often the case, each set of circumstances will need to be considered in detail before any firm conclusions can be reached about whether discrimination has occurred, will or is likely to occur. This book is not intended to be relied upon for detailed legal advice and specialist advice should always be sought before deciding on a particular course of action.

There are many terms which are used interchangeably in the Sex Discrimination Act 1975 and the Race Relations Act 1976 so parts of this book will cross-refer to other relevant provisions. Confusingly, although some of the same terms are used in the Disability Discrimination Act 1995 they do not bear the same meaning. For this reason the reader should assume that unless there is such a cross-reference to a similar provision in another Act, the provision set out does not bear the same meaning as elsewhere.

Sex Discrimination

Unlike other statutory anti-discrimination provisions, sex discrimination is covered not just by the Sex Discrimination Act 1975 but also by Directives from the European Union and by the Treaty of the European Union itself. Under Article 141 of the treaty (formerly Article 119) member states of the European Union are required to ensure that the principle of equal pay for male and female workers for equal work or work of equal value is applied. (The law on equal pay is a significant subject in its own right and is outside the scope of this work.)

The Treaty confers rights on all citizens of European Union member states and is directly enforceable. If a member state fails to implement any requirement under the Treaty a Claimant may rely on the Treaty itself to enforce the right in Courts and Tribunals. The Commission of the European Union may also issue Directives. This creates an obligation on the part of member states to make provision in their national laws to ensure that the right covered by that Directive is implemented. Unlike the Treaty, directives do not always have direct effect unless the person who claims that his or her rights have been infringed is claiming against the State itself or a body exercising statutory powers or existing by virtue of statutory provisions, for example the Health Service and Local Authorities. Where a person is not employed by such a body, if the national government fails to implement the requirements of a Directive, the person may make a claim against the State itself for failing to grant the rights required by the directive. Alternatively, if the provisions of a particular directive are clear and the present national law is capable of being interpreted so as to give effect to those provisions, courts and tribunals will interpret it in that way.

The Act works by ensuring that men and women are treated equally. This is not necessarily a guarantee that the outcome will be the same, merely that the opportunities afforded to men and women in employment, the provision of goods and services, access to qualifications etc. are not restricted by virtue of a person's sex.

The Act also outlaws indirect discrimination. Because of the way society is structured, even if equality of opportunity were to be guaranteed, treating men and women the same may result in a different outcome because of particular social disadvantages. For example, even after 25 years of anti-discrimination legislation, it is more common for women to work part-time than for men; it is more common for women to bear the primary responsibility for child-care, even for providing for care for elderly relatives, than it is for men. Imposing a requirement that employees should work full-time in order to gain access to certain benefits is likely, therefore, to have more of an adverse impact on women than on men.

The effect of a prohibition on indirect discrimination can be far-reaching. Even though particular social conditions apply, if women must be allowed to work part-time because they carry the primary responsibility for child-care, once women are allowed to work part-time, men can claim equality of treatment and be allowed to work part-time themselves.

However, this particular aspect of indirect discrimination is now provided for directly by Regulators (see the note to Section 1(1)(b) below.

Pregnancy and maternity leave gave the courts some difficulty in the early stages of anti-discrimination legislation until the European Court of Justice decided that the treatment of a pregnant woman was not to be compared to the treatment of a man unable to work through illness. It decided that, because pregnancy was not a condition that affected men, to discriminate against a woman, including dismissing her, because she was pregnant was direct discrimination and was unlawful. Detailed provisions about the treatment of pregnant women and those on maternity leave after the birth are now contained in the Employment Rights Act 1996.

There are circumstances in which restrictions having a disproportionate impact on one sex may be justified but those provisions will be dealt with at the appropriate point in the text.

The Sex Discrimination Act 1975

PART I DISCRIMINATION TO WHICH ACT APPLIES

Sex discrimination against women.

1.–(1) A person discriminates against a woman in any circumstances relevant for the purposes of any provision of this Act if–

(a) on the grounds of her sex he treats her less favourably than he treats or would treat a man, or

Section 1(1)

To be on the ground of her sex it is not necessary to show that the treatment was aimed at the complainant or even that the motive was discriminatory as long as the difference is because she was a woman (or a man). This applies even if the motive is a worthy one, for example to redress existing imbalance, unless it is covered by one of the exceptions in Part V of the Act.

A distinction between sex and race discrimination is apparent when a person is instructed to discriminate against another. If the person faced with an instruction to discriminate unlawfully on racial grounds against someone else refuses to do so, and is consequently dismissed, his dismissal is "on racial grounds". Unsurprisingly, this also extends to constructive dismissal where the employee instructed to discriminate resigns. This is not so if the instruction is to discriminate on grounds of sex since the Act states "on grounds of her sex" (that is the sex of the person complaining) whereas section 1 (a) of the RRA states "on racial grounds". The person dismissed would not be dismissed on the ground of his or her sex. In such circumstances it may be possible to argue that the person is being victimised for making a complaint about discriminatory practices, for which see section 4 below.

It is currently not unlawful to discriminate against a person on the ground of his or her sexual orientation but it has been decided that it is a breach of the Human Rights Convention, Article 8 (the right to respect for private and family life) to ban homosexuals from service in the armed forces. The Government has announced an intention to introduce a Code of Practice, i.e. not a legally enforceable right, against discrimination on these grounds although no time for implementation has been given.

The Act prevents discrimination on the ground of a person's gender or his/her marital status. It also protects those who are undergoing or have undergone gender re-assignment under the new section 2A.

Less favourable treatment includes omissions as well as acts. The loss of a choice of something reasonably thought to be of value is enough.

Pregnancy and maternity are obviously conditions that only affect women. A woman discriminated against on the ground that she is pregnant is therefore treated differently on the ground of her sex and she is not to be compared with a man who is incapacitated through sickness. This also applies to illness which is pregnancy-related but which continues after the period of maternity leave.

Detailed provisions for the protection of pregnant women and those on maternity leave are contained in the Employment Rights Act 1996 and are outside the scope of this work.

Sexual harassment is not specifically mentioned anywhere in the Act but there is no doubt that unwanted or unwelcome contact, behaviour or remarks of a sexual nature can amount to direct discrimination whether the conduct is that of a man towards a woman or vice versa. If the conduct is overtly sexual such that the person would not have behaved in that way towards a person of the same sex, no comparator is required. Remarks of a sexual nature may be discriminatory even if the same kind of comments are directed also towards male employees. The effect of such comments, although vulgar, would be much less likely to undermine the dignity of the man at work while having precisely that effect on a woman.

A single act, if sufficiently serious, can be enough.

This section uses the same terms as section 1 of the Race Relations Act 1976 (the "RRA") and cases on the principles set out decided under one Act are applicable to the other.

(b) he applies to her a requirement or condition which he applies or would apply equally to a man but–
- (i) which is such that the proportion of women who can comply with it is considerably smaller than the proportion of men who can comply with it, and
- (ii) which he cannot show to be justifiable irrespective of the sex of the person to whom it is applied, and
- (iii) which is to her detriment because she cannot comply with it.

Section 1(1)(b)
This is what is commonly known as indirect discrimination. The principles which apply are the same as those which apply to race discrimination and cases decided under the provisions of one Act apply to the corresponding provisions of the other.

Although the Act doesn't mention indirect discrimination specifically Article 2 of the Equal Treatment Directive does. It provides:

> *"For the purposes of the following provisions, the principle of equal treatment shall mean that there shall be no discrimination whatsoever on grounds of sex either directly or indirectly by reference in particular to marital or family status."*

This deals with the situation where, although men and women are treated differently, by reason of social conditions such as family responsibilities the effect of the treatment has a disproportionate impact on one group.

Even now, women are more likely to bear the primary responsibility for child care and looking after elderly relatives. Many who carry such responsibility work part time in order to do so. A requirement that such people should work full time therefore has a disproportionate effect on women and amounts to indirect discrimination. (Now, the rights of part-time workers are governed by the Part Time Workers (Prevention of Less Favourable Treatment) Regulations 2000, which prohibit less favourable treatment of part-time workers, so it is no longer necessary for a complainant to prove indirect sex discrimination.)

Similarly, the old requirement that before an employee could claim unfair dismissal he or she had to have 2 years continuous service was challenged on the grounds that women have more breaks in their career because of pregnancy or family responsibilities and are thus less likely to be able to qualify for the 2 year period.

The European Court of Justice decided that the requirement could be discriminatory but that it was for the national court to determine on the basis of statistical information available at the time the claim was made whether that requirement was discriminatory in the particular case. The House of Lords decided that the qualifying period was indirectly discriminatory but was objectively justified for reasons of encouraging recruitment by employers. A minority of their Lordships concluded that the provision was not discriminatory because the proportion of women who could qualify (68.9%) (was not considerably smaller) than the proportion of men who could (77.4%).

There is some doubt as to whether a 'requirement or condition' must operate as an absolute bar. Although this was the approach adopted in early cases decided under the Act, the words 'requirement' or 'condition' do not appear in the EU Equal Treatment Directive. For this reason it is probable that the provisions ought now to be operated more flexibly. If this proves to be the case, it is likely to have an effect on the operation of the same provisions under the RRA (section 1(1)(b)) because of the identical wording of the sections.

In order to show indirect discrimination a complainant must demonstrate that the proportion of women who can comply with that condition is considerably smaller than the proportion of men who can comply with it. In order to decide whether this is the case it is necessary to define a pool of workers for comparison. For a valid comparison the relevant circumstances of the one group must be the same or not materially different to the other.

Care must be taken in choosing the relevant pool because, if the wrong one is chosen and the disparate impact is not established, even if another pool for comparison would show a disparate impact, the claim will fail.

In order to provide the greatest chance of success in bringing a claim, it may be necessary to gather evidence in respect of a number of different pools for comparison and argue the case in the alternative.

Having identified the pool for comparison it is then necessary to go on to consider whether a considerably smaller proportion of the group to which the complainant belongs can comply with the requirement or the condition. This is usually calculated by calculating the proportion of men that can comply with the requirement and then looking at the proportion of women who can comply and comparing the two.

This is not simply a requirement to compare the number of men who can comply with the number of women; it may be appropriate to be selective. It could, for example, be right to limit the pool for comparison to candidates for promotion or for redundancy. Any limit on the pool must not be operated on criteria which are themselves discriminatory, for example, limiting candidates for redundancy to part-time workers or for candidates for promotion only to those who can work full-time, unless such requirements are justified on grounds which do not include sex.

This is a matter for the tribunal to determine on the evidence presented to it. The Tribunal's choice of the pool for comparison will not be disturbed on appeal unless such choice is perverse or is one which no reasonable tribunal would have made.

Since the Equal Treatment Directive requires that there shall be no discrimination whatsoever on grounds of sex it is unlikely that the tribunal will put too much emphasis on defining the word 'considerably'.

In the case involving the application of the 2 year qualifying period in order to claim unfair dismissal, the European Court of Justice decided that it was a matter for the national Court to decide and that the answer to the question would depend on whether the statistics are valid or they merely illustrate fortuitous or short-term phenomena. Provided that the evidence shows a persistent and reasonably constant difference over an extended period, it is likely that this will be sufficient to satisfy the test.

'Considerably smaller' may mean a difference of one or two where the pool for comparison is small; it may mean a difference of a few percentage points where the difference has been consistent over a long period of time but it may require greater statistical disparity where the difference is a recent phenomenon or has fluctuated over a period.

Having satisfied these tests, the complainant must then show that she has suffered a detriment in not being able to comply with the requirement or condition. It is sufficient for a detriment to be established that the person is merely denied an advantage rather than having to suffer a disadvantage.

Whether or not a person can comply with a requirement or a condition is something that has to be looked at from a commonsense point of view. Her claim will not fail merely because, in theory, she can comply but in practice she is unable to. So, when a single mother who is physically capable of working night shifts but faces considerable difficulty in making adequate child-care arrangements in order to do so, the requirement to work shifts is something with which she cannot comply.

Whether the requirement or condition is justifiable depends on striking a balance between the discriminatory effect of the requirement or condition and the needs of the person or body which applies that condition. So if the discriminatory effect of the measure far outweighs the needs of the employer in imposing the condition it is not likely to be justified. It will not be justified if the same effect could be achieved by a non-discriminatory route, provided that the alternative route is not disproportionately expensive or administratively burdensome.

(2) If a person treats or would treat a man differently according to the man's marital status, his treatment of a woman is for the purposes of subsection (1)(a) to be compared to his treatment of a man having the like marital status.

Sex discrimination against men.

2.–(1) Section 1, and the provisions of Parts II and III relating to sex discrimination against women, are to be read as applying equally to the treatment of men, and for that purpose shall have effect with such modifications as are requisite.

(2) In the application of subsection (1) no account shall be taken of special treatment afforded to women in connection with pregnancy or childbirth.

Discrimination on the grounds of gender reassignment

2A.–(1) A person ("A") discriminates against another person ("B") in any circumstances relevant for the purposes of–

(a) any provision of Part II,
(b) Section 35A or 35B, or
(c) any other provision of Part III, so far as it applies to vocational training, if he treats B less favourably than he treats or would treat other persons, and does so on the ground that B intends to undergo, is undergoing or has undergone gender reassignment.

(2) Subsection (3) applies to arrangements made by any person in relation to another's absence from work or from vocational training.

(3) For the purposes of subsection (1), B is treated less favourably than others under such arrangements if, in the application of the arrangements to any absence due to B undergoing gender reassignment–

(a) he is treated less favourably than he would be if the absence was due to sickness or injury, or
(b) he is treated less favourably than he would be if the absence was due to some other cause and, having regard to the circumstances of the case it is reasonable for him to be treated no less favourably.

(4) In subsections (2) and (3) "arrangements" includes terms, conditions or arrangements on which employment, a pupillage or tenancy or vocational training is offered.

(5) For the purposes of subsection (1), a provision mentioned in that sub-section framed with reference to discrimination against women shall be treated as applying equally to the treatment of men with such modifications as are requisite.

Section 2A
This section was introduced after the European Court of Justice decided that discriminating against a person because she had undergone gender re-assignment was discrimination on the ground of her sex.

Discrimination against married persons in employment field.

3.–(1) A person discriminates against a married person of either sex in any circumstances relevant for the purposes of any provision of Part II if–

(a) on the ground of his or her marital status he treats that person less favourably than he treats or would treat an unmarried person of the same sex, or

(b) he applies to that person a requirement or condition which he applies or would apply equally to an unmarried person but–

(i) which is such that the proportion of married persons who can comply with it is considerably smaller than the proportion of unmarried persons of the same sex who can comply with it, and

(ii) which he cannot show to be justifiable irrespective of the marital status of the person to whom it is applied, and

(iii) which is to that person's detriment because he cannot comply with it.

(2) For the purposes of subsection (1), a provision of Part II framed with reference to discrimination against women shall be treated as applying equally to the treatment of men, and for that purpose shall have effect with such modifications as are requisite.

Section 3

The tests are the same as those identified under section 1 dealing with discrimination against women.

See notes to section 1(1)(b) above for the interpretation of the phrases "considerably smaller", "justifiable" and "detriment".

Discrimination by way of victimisation.

4.–(1) A person ("the discriminator") discriminates against another person ("the person victimised") in any circumstances relevant for the purposes of any provision of this Act if he treats the person victimised less favourably than in those circumstances he treats or would treat other persons, and does so by reason that the person victimised has–

(a) brought proceedings against the discriminator or any other person under this Act or the Equal Pay Act 1970, or

(b) given evidence or information in connection with proceedings brought by any person against the discriminator or any other person under this Act or the Equal Pay Act 1970, or

(c) otherwise done anything under or by reference to this Act or the Equal Pay Act 1970 in relation to the discriminator or any other person, or

(d) alleged that the discriminator or any other person has committed an act which (whether or not the allegation so states) would amount to a contravention of this Act or give rise to a claim under the Equal Pay Act 1970,

or by reason that the discriminator knows the person victimised intends to do any of those things, or suspects the person victimised has done, or intends to do, any of them.

(2) Subsection (1) does not apply to treatment of a person by reason of any allegation made by him if the allegation was false and not made in good faith.

(3) For the purposes of subsection (1), a provision of Part II or III framed with reference to discrimination against women shall be treated as applying equally to the treatment of men and for that purpose shall have effect with such modifications as are requisite.

Section 4

This section corresponds to section 2 of the RRA.

The section is designed to protect a person who makes a claim that she has suffered discrimination on grounds of her sex. She is covered even if the claim is only made to the employer and no claim has been lodged at a court or tribunal. It also protects potential witnesses in discrimination claims and the employee is protected even if the employer only suspects that the person has done something in connection with the Act or intends to do so.

This protection applies, in a case brought by an employee against his/her employer, even after employment has terminated. So in a case where an employer refuses to provide a reference to a former employee merely because, during the employment, the employee made a complaint of discrimination, the refusal to provide such a reference amounts to victimisation.

Surprisingly, a complaint involving an allegation that a female police officer had been sexually assaulted by another officer while off-duty has been held not to be a protected act under this section. The incident had not occurred 'in the course of her employment' and the Chief Constable was not therefore vicariously liable so the act complained of was not capable of being an unlawful act under the SDA and she could not therefore be victimised for having made that complaint.

The protection against victimisation only applies if the allegation that discrimination has occurred is made in good faith. Although section 4(2) refers only to an allegation and appears to be confined to section 4(1)(d) it is likely that the defence will also be available if somebody had brought a claim in the tribunal which was not brought in good faith or where the evidence was not given in good faith.

Great care needs to be taken when dealing with somebody who has brought a claim, made an allegation or given evidence in a discrimination claim because the victimisation does not have to be a conscious act on the part of the person victimising. If the person is treated differently because the complaint was brought, even if there was no conscious intention to discriminate against them, they may succeed in a claim that they have been victimised under this section.

Interpretation.

5.–(1) In this Act–

(a) references to discrimination refer to any discrimination falling within sections 1 to 4; and

(b) references to sex discrimination refer to any discrimination falling within section 1 or 2, and related expressions shall be construed accordingly.

(2) In this Act–

"woman" includes a female of any age, and

"man" includes a male of any age.

(3) A comparison of the cases of persons of different sex or marital status under section 1(1) or 3(1), or a comparison of the cases of persons required for the purposes of section 2A, must be such that the relevant circumstances in the one case are the same, or not materially different, in the other.

PART II DISCRIMINATION IN THE EMPLOYMENT FIELD

DISCRIMINATION BY EMPLOYERS

Discrimination against applicants and employees.

6.–(1) It is unlawful for a person, in relation to employment by him at an establishment in Great Britain, to discriminate against a woman–

(a) in the arrangements he makes for the purpose of determining who should be offered that employment, or

(b) in the terms on which he offers her that employment, or

(c) by refusing or deliberately omitting to offer her that employment.

Section 6(1)

The only work excluded from these provisions is work which is done wholly or mainly outside Great Britain (see section 10). The definition under the Sex Discrimination Act (and the Race Relations Act) is wider than under the Employment Rights Act where an employee is covered for the protection under that Act unless he 'ordinarily works outside Great Britain'.

The meaning of employment is also wider than that in the Employment Rights Act. The definition is contained in section 82(1) and includes partners and the self- employed provided that the work is to be undertaken personally.

Provided that there is a legally binding contract to do the work, the wider definition may even include volunteers working for a charity, for example.

(2) It is unlawful for a person, in the case of a woman employed by him at an establishment in Great Britain, to discriminate against her–

(a) in the way he affords her access to opportunities for promotion, transfer or training, or to any other benefits, facilities or services, or by refusing or deliberately omitting to afford her access to them, or
(b) by dismissing her, or subjecting her to any other detriment.

Section 6(2)
The whole of the employment relationship is governed by this section from recruitment through to dismissal.

Only the Equal Opportunities Commission (or the Commission for Racial Equality in a race discrimination case) can make a complaint about an advertisement for a job. This is covered by sections 38 and 72 of the Act. An applicant may, however, complain that she has been disadvantaged, or has suffered a detriment, as a consequence of a discriminatory advertisement by reason that she has been excluded from those who may apply for the post.

Even if the advertisement is not discriminatory other aspects of the selection procedure including the interview may give rise to a complaint that an interviewee has been discriminated against. For this reason care should be taken about the structure of an interview and questions such as the arrangements the interviewee has made for child care during working hours if asked of female applicants should also be asked of male applicants.

A complaint will not fail by reason that the vacancy was not eventually filled. The detriment suffered by the complainant is the loss of the opportunity to be considered for the post.

It is also important to remember that indirect discrimination can arise in the recruitment process. In 1999 the Lord Chancellor appointed a special adviser without advertising a post and without carrying out a process of selection. He appointed someone well known to him. Two people complained that this amounted to the imposition of a requirement or condition that the successful applicant should be known to the Lord Chancellor. The evidence was that the Lord Chancellor in his close circle of friends had more men than women and it was held that this did amount to indirect discrimination.

One of the applicants succeeded in her claim that she had been discriminated against because she did have the necessary skills and experience to be considered for the post. The applicant who had claimed that she had been excluded by reason of her race did not succeed because she did not remotely have the necessary skills and experience and there was no chance that she would have been appointed. She, therefore, had suffered no detriment.

Although the words 'employed by him' appear to confine the protection to an act or omission during the currency of the employment, it has been held that this section also applies in certain circumstances after the employment has ended. The European Court of Justice has held that this protection can extend beyond the ending of the employment. A woman complained that her previous employer had refused to provide a reference because, while she was still employed by them, she had brought a claim of sex discrimination against them. The European Court of Justice held that the Equal Treatment Directive did extend beyond the date on which the employment was terminated and therefore section 6(2) had to be interpreted in order to give effect to the Directive. The woman concerned recovered substantial damages for the discrimination she had thus suffered.

(Although the provisions of section 4 of the Race Relations Act 1976 are in precisely the same words, the extended definition does not apply because there is no corresponding European Directive.)

It is advisable for an employer setting out to recruit staff to consult the Equal Opportunities Commission Code of Practice for the Elimination of Discrimination on the Grounds of Sex and Marriage which sets out a number of recommendations for good practice in recruitment and promotion. It is not legally enforceable but Tribunals will have regard to whether its provisions were followed or applied when considering a complaint of discrimination.

A similar Code, published by the Commission for Racial Equality, exists for the elimination of race discrimination in recruitment and selection.

Although set out slightly differently the terms used are the same as those in section 4(1) and (2) of the RRA.

(3) ... *Repealed*

(4) Subsections (1)(b) and (2) do not render it unlawful for a person to discriminate against a woman in relation to her membership of, or rights under, an occupational pension scheme in such a way that, were any term of the scheme to provide for discrimination in that way, then, by reason only of any provision made by or under sections 62 to 64 of the Pensions Act 1995 (equal treatment), an equal treatment rule would not operate in relation to that term.

(4A) In sub-section (4), "occupational pension scheme" has the same meaning as in the Pension Schemes Act 1993 and "equal treatment rule" has the same meaning given by section 62 of the Pensions Act 1995.

Section 6(4)

When the SDA was originally enacted benefits provided by occupational schemes were outside the scope of this Act and the Equal Pay Act. The Pensions Act 1995 introduced a provision which, in its language, mirrors the Equal Pay Act in relation to the benefits payable not just to the member herself but to her dependants. It also makes available the same defences to an equal pay claim, i.e. that the difference may be excused by genuine material factors which are not related to sex (the "GMF" defence). Any claims for equal benefits under a pension scheme must be brought against the managers and trustees of the scheme.

Pension schemes must now offer equal access to membership and must not discriminate in contribution levels or the provision of benefits subject to Section 64 of the Pensions Act 1995. This still permits account to be taken of the different ages at which men and women qualify for the state retirement pension and for different actuarial statistics to be used for the calculation of benefits.

Claims for access to pension schemes can be backdated to 1976 but claims for equal benefits under a pension scheme can only be backdated to service after 17 May 1990 because of a protocol which was attached to Article 141 of the Treaty (the right to equal pay). This may be subject to change because of a recent decision of the European Court of Justice which decided that the direct effect of Article 141 (equal treatment) may be relied upon from 1976 in appropriate circumstances. ***It is not possible in a work of this kind to convey the full complexity of this area of the law and specialist advice should be sought.***

(5) Subject to section 8(3), subsection (1)(b) does not apply to any provision for the payment of money which, if the woman in question were given the employment, would be included (directly or by reference to a collective agreement or otherwise) in the contract under which she was employed.

Section 6(5)
Reference to section 8(3) is now otiose since that sub-section was repealed by the SDA 1986 but the parliamentary drafting did not complete the job!

(6) Subsection (2) does not apply to benefits consisting of the payment of money when the provision of those benefits is regulated by the woman's contract of employment.

Section 6(5) & (6)
This is because such payments are covered by the Equal Pay Act 1970.

(7) Subsection (2) does not apply to benefits, facilities or services of any description if the employer is concerned with the provision (for payment or not) of benefits, facilities or services of that description to the public, or to a section of the public comprising the woman in question, unless–

(a) that provision differs in a material respect from the provision of the benefits, facilities or services by the employer to his employees, or

(b) the provision of the benefits, facilities or services to the woman in question is regulated by her contract of employment, or

(c) the benefits, facilities or services relate to training.

Section 6(7)

These provisions draw a distinction between the services provided to the woman as an employee and those provided to her, albeit by her employer, as a member of the public. If they are provided under the contract of employment, the complaint must be brought under sub-section (b) above; if it relates to those provided to members of the public generally, the complaint can only be brought in the county court under section 29.

See section 4(4) RRA.

Exception where sex is a genuine occupational qualification.

7.–(1) In relation to sex discrimination–

(a) section 6(1)(a) or (c) does not apply to any employment where being a man is a genuine occupational qualification for the job, and

(b) section 6(2)(a) does not apply to opportunities for promotion or transfer to, or training for, such employment.

(2) Being a man is a genuine occupational qualification for a job only where–

(a) the essential nature of the job calls for a man for reasons of physiology (excluding physical strength or stamina) or, in dramatic performances or other entertainment, for reasons of authenticity, so that the essential nature of the job would be materially different if carried out by a woman; or

(b) the job needs to be held by a man to preserve decency or privacy because–

(i) it is likely to involve physical contact with men in circumstances where they might reasonably object to its being carried out by a woman, or

(ii) the holder of the job is likely to do his work in circumstances where men might reasonably object to the presence of a woman because they are in a state of undress or are using sanitary facilities; or

(ba) the job is likely to involve the holder of the job doing his work, or living, in a private home and needs to be held by a man because objection might reasonably be taken to allowing to a woman–

(i) the degree of social or physical contact with a person living in the home, or

(ii) the knowledge of intimate details of such a person's life,

which is likely, because of the nature or circumstances of the job or of the home, to be allowed to, or available to, the holder of the job, or

(c) the nature or location of the establishment makes it impracticable for the holder of the job to live elsewhere than in premises provided by the employer, and–

(i) the only such premises which are available for persons holding that kind of job are lived in, or normally lived in, by men and are not equipped with separate sleeping accommodation for women and sanitary facilities which could be used by women in privacy from men, and

(ii) it is not reasonable to expect the employer either to equip those premises with such accommodation and facilities or to provide other premises for women; or

(d) the nature of the establishment, or of the part of it within which the work is done, requires the job to be held by a man because–
(i) it is, or is part of, a hospital, prison or other establishment for persons requiring special care, supervision or attention, and
(ii) those persons are all men (disregarding any woman whose presence is exceptional), and
(iii) it is reasonable, having regard to the essential character of the establishment or that part, that the job should not be held by a woman; or

(e) the holder of the job provides individuals with personal services promoting their welfare or education, or similar personal services, and those services can most effectively be provided by a man, or

(f) the job needs to be held by a man because of restrictions imposed by the laws regulating the employment of women, or

(g) the job needs to be held by a man because it is likely to involve the performance of duties outside the United Kingdom in a country whose laws or customs are such that the duties could not, or could not effectively, be performed by a woman, or

(h) the job is one of two to be held by a married couple.

Section 7(2)(a)–(h)

(a) The exclusion of physical strength or stamina in this subsection produces a curious result. An employer cannot insist that a strong man be required for the job but can insist that a strong person is required. The effect of this might be to create indirect discrimination because the proportion of men who can comply with that requirement is likely to be greater than the proportion of women who can comply. The case may then be defended on the grounds that the requirement or condition was justifiable.

(b) Under subsection (i) it might be thought reasonable that a man would object to having his inside leg measurement being taken by a woman. Such a case did come before an employment tribunal and it was held that this subsection did not provide a defence because there were other men employed by the employer who could have been called upon to do that part of the work so section 7(4) applied.

In subsection (ii), the obvious example of where this might apply is in the job of a lavatory attendant. In this increasingly European age, where lavatory attendants in other European countries are frequently female this subsection could come under attack. It may be that, in future, for this section to be relied upon the circumstances should be more restricted to cases involving advanced states of undress, changing facilities or, for example, showering.

(c) This covers accommodation whether temporary or permanent and is intended to deal with cases like oil rigs, lighthouses and other locations where living off the premises is not an option. It is not enough that the employer has only facilities for one sex; he must also prove that it is not reasonable for him to have to provide facilities for members of the other sex.

(d) This section is self explanatory but, as with subsection (c) it is not enough that the job is in a hospital or prison, it must be shown that the restriction applies to the particular part of the establishment where the employee is to work.

(e) It is not clear what circumstances this subsection will apply to in relation to sex discrimination. The corresponding section of the RRA, section 5(2)(d), although not identically worded has been applied in a case where a woman of Afro-Caribbean origin was appointed to a post in a child care centre in preference to a white applicant because the post required a personal awareness of Afro-Caribbean culture for the benefit of her charges. It may be that, in relation to sex discrimination, this section might apply where a person was called upon to provide counselling services in a situation where the establishment of a personal rapport between the counsellor and the person being counselled was essential to the success of the treatment.

(h) In this situation, where a married couple are being employed together, it may seem obvious that one has to be a woman and the other a man. In the light of the decision of the European Court of Justice concerning the service of homosexuals in the armed forces, this section may now be open to challenge on the grounds that it infringes Article No.8 of the Human Rights Convention (the right to respect for private and family life).

(3) Subsection (2) applies where some only of the duties of the job fall within paragraphs (a) to (g) as well as where all of them do.

(4) Paragraph (a), (b), (c), (d), (e), (f) or (g) of subsection (2) does not apply in relation to the filling of a vacancy at a time when the employer already has male employees–

(a) who are capable of carrying out the duties falling within that paragraph, and
(b) whom it would be reasonable to employ on those duties, and
(c) whose numbers are sufficient to meet the employer's likely requirements in respect of those duties without undue inconvenience.

Section 7(4)

(4) The " "genuine occupational qualification" " defence does not apply if it is possible for the employer to split the duties involved in the job so that some of those duties can be performed by other people already employed by the employer. See for example the note to subsection (2)(b) above

Section 7 generally sets out those circumstances where an employer might legitimately insist on employing a man, or alternatively a woman, for a particular job. Although the genuine occupational qualifications will be different when dealing with racial discrimination this section is set out in a similar way to section 5 of the RRA

Corresponding exception relating to gender reassignment

7(**A**).–(1) In their application to discrimination falling within section 2A subsections (1) and (2) of section 6 do not make unlawful an employer's treatment of another person if–

(a) in relation to the employment in question:
(i) being a man is a genuine occupational qualification for the job, or
(ii) being a woman is a genuine occupational qualification for the job, and
(b) the employer can show that the treatment is reasonable in view of the circumstances described in the relevant paragraph of section 7(2) and any other relevant circumstances.

(2) In subsection (1) the reference to the employment in question is a reference–

(a) in relation to any paragraph of section 6(1), to the employment mentioned in that paragraph;
(b) in relation to section 6(2)–
(i) in its application to opportunities for promotion or transfer to any employment or for training for any employment, to that employment;
(ii) otherwise, to the employment in which the person discriminated against is employed or from which that person is dismissed.
(iii) In determining for the purposes of subsection (1) whether being a man being a woman is a genuine occupational qualification for a job, section 7(4) applies in relation to dismissal from employment as it applies in relation to the filling of a vacancy.

Section 7(A)
The circumstances in which a genuine occupational qualification will apply are the same as those which apply in relation to discrimination on the grounds of sex. See however, the additional grounds in 7(B) below.

Supplementary exceptions relating to gender reassignment

7(**B**).–(1) In relation to discrimination falling within section 2(A)–

(a) section 6(1)(a) or (c) does not apply to any employment where there is a supplementary genuine occupational qualification for the job,
(b) section 6(2)(a) does not apply to a refusal or deliberate omission to afford access to opportunities for promotion or transfer to or training for such employment, and

(c) section 6(2)(b) does not apply to dismissing an employee from, or otherwise not allowing him to continue in, such employment.

(2) Subject to subsection (3), there is a supplementary genuine occupational qualification for a job only if–

(a) the job involves the holder of the job being liable to be called upon to perform intimate physical searches pursuant to statutory powers;

(b) the job is likely to involve the holder of the job doing his work, or living, in a private home and needs to be held otherwise than by a person who is undergoing or has undergone gender reassignment, because objection might reasonably be taken to allowing such a person–

(i) the degree of physical or social contact with a person living in the home, or

(ii) the knowledge of intimate details of such a person's life, which is likely, because of the nature or circumstances of the job or of the home, to be allowed to, or available to, the holder of the job.

(c) The nature or location of the establishment makes it impracticable for the holder of the job to live elsewhere than in premises provided by the employer, and–

(i) the only such premises which are available for persons holding that kind of job are such that reasonable objection could be taken, for the purpose of preserving decency and privacy, to the holder of the job sharing accommodation and facilities with either sex whilst undergoing gender reassignment, and

(ii) it is not reasonable to expect the employer either to equip those premises with suitable accommodation or to make alternative arrangements; or

(d) the holder of the job provides vulnerable individuals with personal services promoting their welfare, or similar personal services, and in the reasonable view of the employer those services cannot be effectively provided by a person whilst that person is undergoing gender reassignment.

(3) Paragraphs (c) and (d) of subsection (2) apply only in relation to discrimination against a person who–

(a) intends to undergo gender reassignment, or

(b) is undergoing gender reassignment.

Section 7(B)

This section merely provides the genuine occupational qualification defence in a case where a person is undergoing gender reassignment. Although the new section 2A is intended to outlaw discrimination on these grounds there are genuine circumstances where a person who is in the process of undergoing gender reassignment, or has undergone gender reassignment, might reasonably be excluded.

There are other general exceptions from liability under the Act and these are dealt with in Part V of the Act. Section 7 (and section 4 of the RRA) deal only with exceptions to liability in an employment context.

It should be noted that the defence of genuine occupational qualification is not available where the complaint is of discrimination against married persons and, of course, it is inappropriate where the complaint is one of discrimination by way of victimisation

Equal Pay Act 1970.

8.–(1)

Section 8(1)
Sub-section 1 amends the Equal Pay Act 1970, section 1 so as to allow claims for equal pay for work of equal value which provision was omitted from the original statute. The Equal Pay Act is outside the scope of this work and claims in relation to pay must be brought under that Act. Access to benefits, for example, membership of an occupational pension scheme, as opposed to the rate at which such benefits are paid or accrued, is covered by the provisions of the SDA

(2) Section 1(1) of the Equal Pay Act 1970 (as set out in subsection (1) above) does not apply in determining for the purposes of section 6(1)(b) of this Act the terms on which employment is offered.

(3) Where a person offers a woman employment on certain terms, and if she accepted the offer then, by virtue of an equality clause, any of those terms would fall to be modified, or any additional term would fall to be included, the offer shall be taken to contravene section 6(1)(b).

Section 8(3)
A woman cannot make a claim for equal pay unless she is in the same employment as her chosen comparator. This provision allows a woman to claim that she has been offered employment on less favourable terms even though she does not become an employee. She can, however, compare her pay and benefits to those paid to a predecessor or to a successor in the same employment – it does not have to be at the same time.

(4) Where a person offers a woman employment on certain terms, and subsection (3) would apply but for the fact that, on her acceptance of the offer, section 1(3) of the Equal Pay Act 1970 (as set out in subsection (1) above) would prevent the equality clause from operating, the offer shall be taken not to contravene section 6(1)(b).

Section 8(4)
If there is a 'genuine material factor' (a "GMF" defence) which explains the difference and that factor is not the difference of sex the claim will not succeed. In other words, the employer has the same defence against a potential employee as he would have against an existing employee.

(5) An act does not contravene section 6(2) if–

(a) it contravenes a term modified or included by virtue of an equality clause, or
(b) it would contravene such a term but for the fact that the equality clause is prevented from operating by section 1(3) of the Equal Pay Act 1970.

(6) *omitted*

Section 8(6)
This section introduced further amendments to the Equal Pay Act

(7) In its application to any discrimination falling within section 2A, this section shall have effect with the omission of sub-sections (3), (4) and (5)(b).

Section 8(7)
This has the effect of ensuring that gender reassignment related claims of discrimination come under this Act and not the Equal Pay Act 1970.

Discrimination against contract workers.

Section 9
This section corresponds to section 7 of the RRA although, unlike section 7 RRA, there is no exclusion for contract workers not ordinarily resident in Great Britain or where the training provided is to provide skills which are intended to be exercised wholly outside Great Britain.

9.–(1) This section applies to any work for a person ("the principal") which is available for doing by individuals ("contract workers") who are employed not by the principal himself but by another person, who supplies them under a contract made with the principal.

(2) It is unlawful for the principal, in relation to work to which this section applies, to discriminate against a woman who is a contract worker–

(a) in the terms on which he allows her to do that work, or
(b) by not allowing her to do it or continue to do it, or
(c) in the way he affords her access to any benefits, facilities or services or by refusing or deliberately omitting to afford her access to them, or
(d) by subjecting her to any other detriment.

(3) Subject to sub-section (3A), the principal does not contravene subsection (2)(b) by doing any act in relation to a woman at a time when if the work were to be done by a person taken into his employment being a man would be a genuine occupational qualification for the job.

Section 9(3)
In normal employment circumstances a worker supplied by an agency to a principal employer is regarded as an employee of the agency. This section prevents principal employers from discriminating against workers provided to them by agencies on the grounds of their sex.

The grounds on which discrimination is prohibited are the same as for direct employees and the "genuine occupational qualification" defence is also available.

(3A) Sub-section (3) does not apply in relation to discrimination falling within section 2A.

(3B) In relation to discrimination falling within section 2A, the principal does not contravene sub-section (2)(a), (b), (c) or (d) by doing any act in relation to a woman if–

(a) he does it at a time when, if the work were to be done by a person taken into his employment–
(i) being a man would be a genuine occupational qualification for the job, or
(ii) being a woman would be a genuine occupational qualification for the job, and
(b) he can show that the act is reasonable in view of the circumstances relevant for the purpose of paragraph (a) and any other relevant circumstances.

(3C) In relation to discrimination falling within section 2A, the principal does not contravene sub-section (2)(b) by doing any act in relation to a woman at a time when, if the work were to be done by a person taken into his employment, there would be a supplementary occupational qualification for the job.

Section 9(3A)–(3C)
Sub-sections 3A–3C make available to employers in relation to contract workers undergoing gender reassignment (or who have undergone it) the same defence as is available to them for direct employees.

(4) Subsection (2)(c) does not apply to benefits, facilities or services of any description if the principal is concerned with the provision (for payment or not) of benefits,

facilities or services of that description to the public, or to a section of the public to which the woman belongs, unless that provision differs in a material respect from the provision of the benefits, facilities or services by the principal to his contract workers.

Section 9(4)
As with section 6(7), this subsection draws a distinction between benefits facilities or services provided to the contract worker as part of the arrangements for their employment and those benefits facilities or services made available to them as an ordinary member of the public.

Meaning of employment at establishment in Great Britain.

10.–(1) For the purposes of this Part and section 1 of the Equal Pay Act 1970 ("the relevant purposes"), employment is to be regarded as being at an establishment in Great Britain unless the employee does his work wholly or mainly outside Great Britain.

(2) Subsection (1) does not apply to–

(a) employment on board a ship registered at a port of registry in Great Britain,
(b) employment on aircraft or hovercraft registered in the United Kingdom and operated by a person who has his principal place of business, or is ordinarily resident, in Great Britain;

but for the relevant purposes such employment is to be regarded as being at an establishment in Great Britain unless the employee does his work wholly outside Great Britain.

(3) In the case of employment on board a ship registered at a port of registry in Great Britain (except where the employee does his work wholly outside Great Britain, and outside any area added under subsection (5)) the ship shall for the relevant purposes be deemed to be the establishment.

(4) Where work is not done at an establishment it shall be treated for the relevant purposes as done at the establishment from which it is done or (where it is not done from any establishment) at the establishment with which it has the closest connection.

(5) In relation to employment concerned with exploration of the sea bed or subsoil or the exploitation of their natural resources, Her Majesty may by Order in Council provide that subsections (1) and (2) shall each have effect as if the last reference to Great Britain included any area for the time being designated under section 1(7) of the Continental Shelf Act 1964 or specified under section 10(8) of the Petroleum Act 1998, except an area or part of an area in which the law of Northern Ireland applies.

Section 10(5)
The words 'or specified under section 10(8) of the Petroleum Act 1998' were inserted by section 50, Schedule 4, paragraph 8(b) of that Act but have not yet been brought into force.

(6) An Order in Council under subsection (5) may provide that, in relation to employment to which the Order applies, this Part and section 1 of the Equal Pay Act 1970 are to have effect with such modifications as are specified in the Order.

(7) An Order in Council under subsection (5) shall be of no effect unless a draft of the Order was laid before and approved by each House of Parliament.

Section 10(7)
The note to section 6(1) makes clear that the scope of protection for employees under the Sex Discrimination Act, and the RRA is wider than that afforded under the Employment Rights Act 1996 so that a person who has a complaint of unfair dismissal and a claim of sex discrimination but who works only occasionally in the UK will be prevented from pursuing an unfair dismissal claim but will be allowed to proceed with the claim under the SDA.

This section corresponds to section 7 of the RRA.

Discrimination by other bodies

Partnerships.

Section 11
This part is intended to govern relationships where, although not directly between employer and employee, they govern access to employment.

11.–(1) It is unlawful for a firm, in relation to a position as partner in the firm, to discriminate against a woman–

(a) in the arrangements they make for the purpose of determining who should be offered that position, or
(b) in the terms on which they offer her that position, or
(c) by refusing or deliberately omitting to offer her that position, or
(d) in a case where the woman already holds that position–
  (i) in the way they afford her access to any benefits, facilities or services, or by refusing or deliberately omitting to afford her access to them, or
  (ii) by expelling her from that position, or subjecting her to any other detriment.

(2) Subsection (1) shall apply in relation to persons proposing to form themselves into a partnership as it applies in relation to a firm.

(3) Subject to sub-section (3A), subsection (1)(a) and (c) do not apply to a position as partner where, if it were employment, being a man would be a genuine occupational qualification for the job.

Section 11(3)

Corresponding to section 10 RRA, (although under the RRA there is a minimum requirement of six partners before the protection is available) the protection offered to employees and prospective employees is extended, by this section, to partners, applicants for partnership, those who wish to be considered in the formation of new partnerships and expulsion from partnerships.

The " "genuine occupational qualification" " defence is also available.

(3A) Sub-section (3) does not apply in relation to discrimination falling within section 2A.

(3B) In relation to discrimination falling within section 2A, sub-section (1) does not make unlawful a firm's treatment of a person in relation to a position as partner where–

(a) if it were employment–
 (i) being a man would be a genuine occupational qualification for the job, or
 (ii) being a woman would be a genuine occupational qualification for the job, and
(b) the firm can show that the treatment is reasonable in view of the circumstances relevant for the purpose of paragraph (a) and any other relevant circumstances.

(3C) In relation to discrimination falling within section 2A, sub-section (1)(a), (c) and, so far as it relates to expulsion, (d)(ii) do not apply to a position as partner where, if it were employment, there would be a supplementary occupational qualification for the job.

Section 11(3A)–(3C)

This is the standard defence available to employers in gender reassignment cases.

(4) Subsection (1)(b) and (d) do not apply to provision made in relation to death or retirement except in so far as, in their application to provision made in relation to retirement, they render it unlawful for a firm to discriminate against a woman–

(a) in such of the terms on which they offer her a position as partner as provide for her expulsion from that position; or
(b) by expelling her from a position as partner or subjecting her to any other detriment which results in her expulsion from such a position.

Section 11(4)

Equality of access to pension benefits is protected by this part.

(5) In the case of a limited partnership references in subsection (1) to a partner shall be construed as references to a general partner as defined in section 3 of the Limited Partnerships Act 1907.

Section 11(5)
Unlike section 10 RRA there is no minimum size of partnership.

Trade unions etc.

Section 12
Despite its heading, this section applies both to organisations of employees and of employers. It also applies to professional and trade associations.

12.–(1) This section applies to an organisation of workers, an organisation of employers, or any other organisation whose members carry on a particular profession or trade for the purposes of which the organisation exists.

(2) It is unlawful for an organisation to which this section applies, in the case of a woman who is not a member of the organisation, to discriminate against her–

(a) in the terms on which it is prepared to admit her to membership, or
(b) by refusing, or deliberately omitting to accept, her application for membership.

(3) It is unlawful for an organisation to which this section applies, in the case of a woman who is a member of the organisation, to discriminate against her–

(a) in the way it affords her access to any benefits, facilities or services, or by refusing or deliberately omitting to afford her access to them, or
(b) by depriving her of membership, or varying the terms on which she is a member, or
(c) by subjecting her to any other detriment.

(4) This section does not apply to provision made in relation to the death or retirement from work of a member.

Section 12(4)
Without this section protection from discrimination and access to employment might be rendered void if those seeking employment could otherwise be prevented from working by virtue of them being denied membership of an organisation which is a condition of employment. For this reason the section also covers organisations of self-employed people.

It should be noted that this section does not apply to death or retirement benefits.

With the exception of the provisions for death and retirement benefits, this section is the same as section 11 of the RRA.

Qualifying bodies.

13.–(1) It is unlawful for an authority or body which can confer an authorisation or qualification which is needed for, or facilitates, engagement in a particular profession or trade to discriminate against a woman–

(a) in the terms on which it is prepared to confer on her that authorisation or qualification, or
(b) by refusing or deliberately omitting to grant her application for it, or
(c) by withdrawing it from her or varying the terms on which she holds it.

(2) Where an authority or body is required by law to satisfy itself as to his good character before conferring on a person an authorisation or qualification which is needed for, or facilitates, his engagement in any profession or trade then, without prejudice to any other duty to which it is subject, that requirement shall be taken to impose on the authority or body a duty to have regard to any evidence tending to show that he, or any of his employees, or agents (whether past or present), has practised unlawful discrimination in, or in connection with, the carrying on of any profession or trade.

(3) In this section–

(a) "authorisation or qualification" includes recognition, registration, enrolment, approval and certification,
(b) "confer" includes renew or extend.

(4) Subsection (1) does not apply to discrimination which is rendered unlawful by section 22 or 23.

Section 13

Bodies which have the power to confer authorisation or qualification or some other form of certification which is necessary for a person to be able to work at a particular trade or profession are required not to discriminate on grounds of sex.

A body may be entitled to withhold the qualification or certification if it considers that, in the past the person or organisation has engaged in discrimination.

Subsection (4) avoids double liability arising under the other provisions mentioned.

For the corresponding provisions in relation to race, with the exception of sub-section (2), see section 12 RRA.

Persons concerned with the provision of vocational training

14–(1). It is unlawful, in the case of a woman seeking or undergoing training which would help fit her for any employment, for any person who provides, or makes arrangements for the provision of, facilities for such training to discriminate against her–

(a) in the terms on which that person affords her access to any training course or other facilities concerned with such training, or
(b) by refusing or deliberately omitting to afford her such access, or
(c) by terminating her training, or
(d) by subjecting her to any detriment during the course of her training.

Section 14(1)
The lack of access to training may also limit a person's ability to take up a particular employment or profession. This section outlaws discrimination by those providing the training in relation to access to the training or training facilities and the terms on which training is provided. See also section 13 of the RRA.

There are certain limited circumstances in which positive discrimination in the provision of training is allowed – see section 47 below (and section 38 RRA)

(2) Sub-section (1) does not apply to–

(a) discrimination which is rendered unlawful by section 6(1) or (2) or section 22 or 23, or
(b) discrimination which would be rendered unlawful by any of those provisions but for the operation of any other provision of this act.

Section 14(2)
This exclusion is to avoid overlap, or double liability, for educational establishments.

Employment agencies.

15.–(1) It is unlawful for an employment agency to discriminate against a woman–

(a) in the terms on which the agency offers to provide any of its services, or
(b) by refusing or deliberately omitting to provide any of its services, or
(c) in the way it provides any of its services.

Section 15(1)
Employment agencies are not allowed to refuse to take a person on by virtue of their sex or to provide services which are less favourable on the grounds of sex.

(2) It is unlawful for a local education authority or education authority or any other person to do any act in providing services in pursuance of arrangements made, or a direction given, under section 10 of the Employment and Training Act 1973 which constitutes discrimination.

(3) References in subsection (1) to the services of an employment agency include guidance on careers and any other services related to employment.

(4) This section does not apply if the discrimination only concerns employment which the employer could lawfully refuse to offer the woman.

Section 15(4)
Sub-section (4) makes available the "genuine occupational qualification" defence.

(5) An employment agency or local education authority, education authority or other person shall not be subject to any liability under this section if it proves–

(a) that it acted in reliance on a statement made to it by the employer to the effect that, by reason of the operation of subsection (4), its action would not be unlawful, and

(b) that it was reasonable for it to rely on the statement.

Section 15(5)
An agency will escape liability for acts of discrimination if it was mislead by the employer. In such a case there may be criminal liability for the making of the misleading statement – see subsection (6) below.

(6) A person who knowingly or recklessly makes a statement such as is referred to in subsection (5)(a) which in a material respect is false or misleading commits an offence, and shall be liable on summary conviction to a fine not exceeding level 5 on the standard scale.

Section 15(6)
The scale of fine is subject to change and applies to a wide range of criminal offences.

Manpower Services Commission etc.

16.–(1) It is unlawful for the Secretary of State to discriminate in the provision of facilities or services under section 2 of the Employment and Training Act 1973.

(1A) It is unlawful for Scottish Enterprise or Highlands and Islands Enterprise to discriminate in the provision of facilities or services under such arrangements as are mentioned in section 2(3) of the Enterprise and New Towns (Scotland) Act 1990 (arrangements analogous to arrangements in pursuance of section 2 of the said Act of 1973).

Section 16(1)
(1A) This subsection applies only in Scotland.

2. This section does not apply in a case where–

(a) section 14 applies, or

(b) the Secretary of State is acting as an employment agency.

Section 16(2)
This section deals with the provision for training related to unemployment for the purposes of equipping somebody to return to work. Subsection (2) is designed to avoid double liability under sections 14 and 15 above.

SPECIAL CASES

Police.

17.–(1) For the purposes of this Part, the holding of the office of constable shall be treated as employment–

(a) by the chief officer of police as respects any act done by him in relation to a constable or that office;
(b) by the police authority as respects any act done by them in relation to a constable or that office.

Section 17(1)
Police constables are not employees but office holders. Without this section police officers would be excluded from the protection of the Act. A person complaining of discrimination must bring their complaint against either the chief officer or the police authority, depending on who committed the unlawful act against the officer concerned.

(2) Regulations made under section 50, 51 or 52 of the Police Act 1996 shall not treat men and women differently except–

(a) as to requirements relating to height, uniform or equipment, or allowances in lieu of uniform or equipment, or
(b) so far as special treatment is accorded to women in connection with pregnancy or childbirth, or
(c) in relation to pensions to or in respect of special constables or police cadets.

(3) Nothing in this Part renders unlawful any discrimination between male and female constables as to matters such as are mentioned in subsection (2)(a).

(4) There shall be paid out of the police fund–

(a) any compensation, costs or expenses awarded against a chief officer of police in any proceedings brought against him under this Act, and any costs or expenses incurred by him in any such proceedings so far as not recovered by him in the proceedings; and
(b) any sum required by a chief officer of police for the settlement of any claim made against him under this Act if the settlement is approved by the police authority.

Section 17(4)
This section makes provision for the payment of damages and costs awarded in discrimination claims from public funds, i.e. the police budget.

(5) Any proceedings under this Act which, by virtue of subsection (1), would lie against a chief officer of police shall be brought against the chief officer of police for the time being or, in the case of a vacancy in that office, against the person for the time being performing the functions of that office; and references in subsection (4) to the chief officer of police shall be construed accordingly.

Section 17(5)
Claims brought by police officers in connection with their duties as officers are to be brought against the Chief Constable, or the person acting in that capacity for the time being and not the Constabulary or the Police Authority.

(6) Subsections (1) and (3) apply to a police cadet and appointment as a police cadet as they apply to a constable and the office of constable.

(7) In this section–

"chief officer of police"–

(a) in relation to a person appointed, or an appointment falling to be made, under a specified Act, has the same meaning as in the Police Act 1996.
(b) in relation to any other person or appointment means the officer who has the direction and control of the body of constables or cadets in question;

"police authority"–

(a) in relation to a person appointed, or an appointment falling to be made, under a specified Act, has the same meaning as in the Police Act 1996.
(b) in relation to any other person or appointment, means the authority by whom the person in question is or on appointment would be paid;

"police cadet" means any person appointed to undergo training with a view to becoming a constable;

"police fund" in relation to a chief officer of police within paragraph (a) of the above definition of that term has the same meaning as in the Police Act 1996, and in any other case means money provided by the police authority;

"specified Act" means the Metropolitan Police Act 1829, the City of London Police Act 1839 or the Police Act 1996.

(8) In the application of this section to Scotland, in subsection (7) for any reference to the Police Act 1996 there shall be substituted a reference to the Police (Scotland) Act 1967, and for the reference to sections 50, 51 and 52 of the former Act in subsection (2) there shall be substituted a reference to sections 26 and 27 of the latter Act.

Section 17(8)
With the exception of subsections (2) and (3) this section mirrors section 16 of the RRA.

Prison officers.

18.–(1) Nothing in this Part renders unlawful any discrimination between male and female prison officers as to requirements relating to height.

Section 18(1)
The differential height requirements as between male and female prison officers is rendered lawful by this section.

(2) ... *Amends the Prison Act 1952, s.7*

Ministers of religion etc.

19.–(1) Nothing in this Part applies to employment for purposes of an organised religion where the employment is limited to one sex so as to comply with the doctrines of the religion or avoid offending the religious susceptibilities of a significant number of its followers.

(2) Nothing in section 13 applies to an authorisation or qualification (as defined in that section) for purposes of an organised religion where the authorisation or qualification is limited to one sex so as to comply with the doctrines of the religion or avoid offending the religious susceptibilities of a significant number of its followers.

Section 19(2)
The exclusion does not appear to be confined to appointments as ministers of the religion concerned. If the doctrines of a particular religion discriminate as between men and women, this section allows members of that religious group to discriminate on those grounds when making appointments.

The exclusion also applies in relation to the authorisation of the bestowing of qualifications.

(3) In relation to discrimination falling within section 2A this Part does not apply to employment for purposes of an organised religion where the employment is limited to persons who are not undergoing and have not undergone gender reassignment, if the limitation is imposed to comply with the doctrines of the religion or avoid offending the religious susceptibilities of a significant number of its followers.

(4) In relation to discrimination falling within section 2A, section 13 does not apply to an authorisation or qualification (as defined in that section) for purposes of an organised religion where the authorisation or qualification is limited to persons who are not undergoing and have not undergone gender reassignment, if the limitation is imposed to comply with the doctrines of the religion or avoid offending the religious susceptibilities of a significant number of its followers.

Section 19(4)
It is not surprising that, if a religious organisation can discriminate against a person on grounds of his or her sex, it will not be unlawful for such organisations to discriminate against a person on the grounds that they are undergoing or have undergone gender reassignment.

Midwives.

20.–(1) Until 1st September 1983 section 6(1) does not apply to employment as a midwife.

(2) Until 1st September 1983 section 6(2)(a) does not apply to promotion, transfer or training as a midwife.

(3) Until 1st September 1983 section 14 does not apply to training as a midwife.

(4), (5) *...repealed*

21. *Repealed*

PART III DISCRIMINATION IN OTHER FIELDS

EDUCATION

Discrimination by bodies in charge of educational establishments.

22. It is unlawful in relation to an educational establishment falling within column 1 of the following table, for a person indicated in relation to the establishment in column 2 (the "responsible body") to discriminate against a woman–

(a) in the terms on which it offers to admit her to the establishment as a pupil, or

(b) by refusing or deliberately omitting to accept an application for her admission to the establishment as a pupil, or

(c) where she is a pupil of the establishment–

(i) in the way it affords her access to any benefits, facilities or services, or by refusing or deliberately omitting to afford her access to them, or

(ii) by excluding her from the establishment or subjecting her to any other detriment.

TABLE

ENGLAND AND WALES

Establishment	***Responsible Body***
1. Educational establishment maintained by a local education authority.	Local education authority or governing body, according to which of them has the function in question.
2. Independent school not being a special school.	Proprietor.
3. Special school not maintained by a local education authority.	Proprietor.
3B Institution within the further education sector (within the meaning of section 91(3) of the Further and Higher Education Act 1992	Governing body.
4. University.	Governing body.
4A. Institution other than a university, within the higher education sector (within the meaning of section 91(5) of the Further and Higher Education Act 1992)	Governing body.
5. Establishment (not falling within paragraphs 1 to 4A) providing full-time or part-time education, being an establishment designated under section 24(1).	Governing body.

Section 22

It is unlawful for any educational establishment to discriminate against a woman in the terms of admission, the training or education offered or the way in which she is treated whilst she is on a course of education.

If a complaint arises it must be brought against the responsible body identified in the table. Discrimination is unlawful even if it is for a positive motive. An admissions policy which sought to ensure that there were equal numbers of male and female pupils on a course would discriminate unlawfully if women with the same level of qualification were excluded while less qualified males were admitted because of the quota system.

The discrimination must be assessed in relation to that establishment alone. It is not open to a complainant to draw a comparison with another educational establishment in order to establish discrimination.

Indirect discrimination is also unlawful although the defence of justification is available. The difficulty with this defence in relation to education is that educational provision is subject to changing views and attitudes. A distinction which might once have been held to be reasonable may, at some time in the future, be considered unreasonable and an establishment slow to adopt the new orthodoxy might find itself liable under this section.

Meaning of Pupil in Section 22

22A. For the purposes of section 22, 'pupil' includes, in England and Wales, any person who receives education at a school or institution to which that section applies.

Other discrimination by local education authorities

23.–(1) It is unlawful for a local education authority, in carrying out such of its functions under the Education Acts as do not fall under section 22, to do any act which constitutes sex discrimination.

(2) It is unlawful for an education authority, in carrying out such of its functions under the Education (Scotland) Acts as do not fall under section 22, to do any act which constitutes sex discrimination.

Section 23

Any act of discrimination not covered by section 22 above may give rise to a liability on the part of the local education authority. Their duties are defined under sections 13 to 15 of the Education Act 1996 and those duties must be carried out without discrimination

Subsection (1) does not apply in Scotland; subsection (2) applies only in Scotland

Because there is an exception under section 26 for single sex educational establishments, a local authority may nevertheless discriminate on grounds of sex if, overall, it makes less provision for single sex establishments for girls than it does for boys or vice versa.

This obligation covers all the schools in the area covered by the local authority, even those which are grant maintained and not therefore under the control of the local education authority.

This obligation is binding on the authority all of the time. So even if a temporary difficulty prevents the authority from providing equal provision, for example, a fire at a boys only school, an immediate obligation arises to secure alternative facilities and it is liable for damages to anyone disadvantaged by the lack of provision until the alternative is secured.

Discrimination by Further Education and Higher Education Funding Councils

23A. It is unlawful for the Further Education Funding Council for England, the Further Education Funding Council for Wales, the Higher Education Funding Council for England or the Higher Education Funding Council for Wales in carrying out their functions under the Education Acts, to do any act which constitutes sex discrimination.

> **Section 23C**
> *This section was repealed by the School Standards and Framework Act 1998 as from 1 September 1999.*

Discrimination by Teacher Training Agency

23D. It is unlawful for the Teacher Training Agency in carrying out their functions under part I of the Education Act 1994 to do any act which constitutes sex discrimination.

> **Section 23A–D**
> *In carrying out their functions all the bodies named in these sections must ensure that they carry out their functions free of any discrimination.*

Designated establishments.

24.–(1) The Secretary of State may by order designate for the purposes of paragraph 5 of the table in section 22 such establishments of the description mentioned in that paragraph as he thinks fit.

(2) An establishment shall not be designated under subsection (1) unless–

- (a) *...repealed*
- (b) it is an establishment in respect of which grants are payable out of money provided by Parliament, or
- (c) it is assisted by a local education authority for the purposes of the Education Act 1996, or
- (d) it provides full-time education for persons who have attained the upper limit of compulsory school age construed in accordance with section 8 of the Education Act 1996 but not the age of nineteen.

(3) A designation under subsection (1) shall remain in force until revoked notwithstanding that the establishment ceases to be within subsection (2).

> **Section 24**
> *The Secretary of State has power, under this section, to bring specific educational establishments within the provisions of the Act, provided that they meet any of the conditions in subsections (b) to (d).*

General duty in public sector of education.

25.–(1) Without prejudice to its obligation to comply with any other provision of this Act, a body to which this subsection applies shall be under a general duty to secure that facilities for education provided by it, and any ancillary benefits or services, are provided without sex discrimination.

(2) The following provisions of the Education Act 1996, namely–

(a) section 496 (power of Secretary of State to require duties under that Act to be exercised reasonably), and

(b) section 497 (powers of Secretary of State where local education authorities etc. are in default),

shall apply to the performance by a body to which subsection (1) applies of the duties imposed by sections 22, 23, 23A, and 23D and shall also apply to the performance of the general duty imposed by subsection (1), as they apply to the performance by a local education authority of a duty imposed by that Act.

Section 25(3)
The corresponding principle applicable in Scotland

(4) The sanctions in subsections (2) and (3) shall be the only sanctions for breach of the general duty in subsection (1), but without prejudice to the enforcement of sections 22, 23, 23A, and 23D under section 66 or otherwise (where the breach is also a contravention of any of those sections).

(5) The Secretary of State shall have the power to cause a local inquiry to be held into any matter arising from subsection (3) under section 68 of the Education (Scotland) Act 1962.

Section 25(5)
Applicable in Scotland only

(6) Subsection (1) applies to–

(a) local education authorities in England and Wales;

(b) education authorities in Scotland;

(c) any other body which is a responsible body in relation to–

(i) an establishment falling within paragraph 1, 3, 3B of the table in section 22;

(ii) an establishment designated under section 24(1) as falling within paragraph (c) or section 24(2);

(iii) an establishment designated under section 24(1) as falling within paragraph (b) of section 24(2) where the grants in question are payable under section 485 of the Education Act 1996.

(d) the Further Education Funding Council for England and the Further Education Funding Council for Wales.

(e) the Funding Agency for Schools and the Schools Funding Council for Wales.
(f) The Teacher Training Agency.

Section 25(6)
Discrimination is rendered unlawful by other provisions of the Act. This section is intended to place a positive duty on education authorities to take action to ensure the elimination of discrimination. This section is only enforceable by action of the Secretary of State.

For the procedural requirements for bringing a claim against a public sector education or body see section 66 below.

The scope of sections 22 to 25 is covered by sections 17 to 19 of the RRA

Exception for single-sex establishments.

26.–(1) Sections 22(a) and (b) and 25 do not apply to the admission of pupils to any establishment (a "single-sex establishment") which admits pupils of one sex only, or which would be taken to admit pupils of one sex only if there were disregarded pupils of the opposite sex–

(a) whose admission is exceptional, or
(b) whose numbers are comparatively small and whose admission is confined to particular courses of instruction or teaching classes.

(2) Where a school which is not a single-sex establishment has some pupils as boarders and others as non-boarders, and admits as boarders pupils of one sex only (or would be taken to admit as boarders pupils of one sex only if there were disregarded boarders of the opposite sex whose numbers are comparatively small), sections 22(a) and (b) and 25 do not apply to the admission of boarders and sections 22(c)(i) and 25 do not apply to boarding facilities.

(3) Where an establishment is a single-sex establishment by reason of its inclusion in subsection (1)(b), the fact that pupils of one sex are confined to particular courses of instruction or teaching classes shall not be taken to contravene section 22(c)(i) or the duty in section 25.

Exception for single-sex establishments turning co-educational.

27.–(1) Where at any time–

(a) the responsible body for single-sex establishment falling within column 1 of the table in section 22 determines to alter its admissions arrangements so that the establishment will cease to be a single-sex establishment, or
(b) section 26(2) applies to the admission of boarders to a school falling within column 1 of that table but the responsible body determines to alter its admissions arrangements so that section 26(2) will cease so to apply,

the responsible body may apply in accordance with Schedule 2 for an order (a "transitional exemption order") authorising discriminatory admissions during the transitional period specified in the order.

(1A) Without prejudice to sub-section (1), a transitional exemption order may be made in accordance with paragraph 21 or 22 of Schedule 6 or paragraph 16 or 17 of Schedule 7 to the School Standards and Framework Act 1998 (transitional exemption orders for the purposes of the Sex Discrimination Act 1975: England and Wales).

(2) Where during the transitional period specified in a transitional exemption order applying to an establishment the responsible body refuses or deliberately omits to accept an application for the admission of a person to the establishment as a pupil the refusal or omission shall not be taken to contravene any provision of this Act.

(3) Subsection (2) does not apply if the refusal or omission contravenes any condition of the transitional exemption order.

(4) Except as mentioned in subsection (2), a transitional exemption order shall not afford any exemption from liability under this Act.

(5) Where, during the period between the making of an application for a transitional exemption order in relation to an establishment and the determination of the application, the responsible body refuses or deliberately omits to accept an application for the admission of a person to the establishment as a pupil the refusal or omission shall not be taken to contravene any provision of this Act.

(6) In this section, as it applies to an establishment in England and Wales, 'pupil' includes any person who receives education at that establishment.

Section 26 and 27

These provide general exemptions for single-sex establishments and those in the process of ceasing to be single-sex establishments.

EXCEPTION FOR PHYSICAL TRAINING.

28. Sections 22, 23 and 25 do not apply to any course in physical education which is a further education course or, in England and Wales, a higher education course within the meaning of the Education Reform Act 1988.

Goods, facilities, services and premises

Discrimination in provision of goods, facilities or services.

29.–(1) It is unlawful for any person concerned with the provision (for payment or not) of goods, facilities or services to the public or a section of the public to discriminate against a woman who seeks to obtain or use those goods, facilities or services–

(a) by refusing or deliberately omitting to provide her with any of them, or

(b) by refusing or deliberately omitting to provide her with goods, facilities or services of the like quality, in the like manner and on the like terms as are normal in his case in relation to male members of the public or (where she belongs to a section of the public) to male members of that section.

(2) The following are examples of the facilities and services mentioned in subsection (1)–

(a) access to and use of any place which members of the public or a section of the public are permitted to enter;
(b) accommodation in a hotel, boarding house or other similar establishment;
(c) facilities by way of banking or insurance or for grants, loans, credit or finance;
(d) facilities for education;
(e) facilities for entertainment, recreation or refreshment;
(f) facilities for transport or travel;
(g) the services of any profession or trade, or any local or other public authority.

Section 29(1) and (2)
As can be seen from subsection 2, the Act provides examples of what is meant by facilities and services but there is otherwise no definition as to what is meant. There is however a definition of the words "profession" and "trade" in section 82(1).

There is a special exception in section 45 which relates to the provision of insurance services. This is a similar exception to that allowed by pension schemes in using different figures for life expectancy for men and women as a result of which there may be some variation in the insurance premium charged.

(3) For the avoidance of doubt it is hereby declared that where a particular skill is commonly exercised in a different way for men and for women it does not contravene subsection (1) for a person who does not normally exercise it for women to insist on exercising it for a woman only in accordance with his normal practice or, if he reasonably considers it impracticable to do that in her case, to refuse or deliberately omit to exercise it.

Section 29(3)
This provision is to cover single-sex hairdressers or tailors, for example.

(4) In its application in relation to vocational training to discrimination falling within section 2A, subsection (1)(b) shall have effect as if references to male members of the public, or of a section of the public, where references to members of the public, or of a section of the public, who do not intend to undergo, are not undergoing and have not undergone gender reassignment.

Section 29(4)
This is merely an extension of the general provision in order to cover gender reassignment.

It may be useful to give some examples of those things which have, in the past, been held to be facilities or services. These include assistance by a police officer, tax advice from a tax officer, the ability to stand for election to a governing body of a friendly society, a hire purchase credit scheme, the provision of surgical treatment and the availability of advertising space.

A distinction has been drawn between the provision of a facility and permission to use such a facility. It is difficult to understand such a distinction if section 50 (section 40 RRA), which deals with indirect access to benefits, is considered. It is perhaps unlikely that such a distinction would be drawn today.

The goods facilities or services must be on offer to the public or to a section of the public in order to be caught by this provision. For membership of a club, for example if candidates were required to comply with formal conditions or criteria the facilities offered by the club were open to the public at large. If, however, membership of the club was dependent on the personal acceptability of the candidate to other members of the club, it would not be open to members of the public. But if such clubs admitted members of the public on payment of a fee they could not discriminate on grounds of sex as to whether or not to admit someone who was prepared to pay that fee.

In perhaps one of the best known cases under the Sex Discrimination Act a man complained that the refusal by a local authority to allow him to use a swimming pool at concessionary rates until he reached a pensionable age of 65 was discriminatory because his wife was allowed to use the same facilities at a reduced fee from the age of 60. This provision was held to be discriminatory.

There is an important distinction between facilities and services provided by public authorities, as in the example above, concerning access to a local authority swimming pool, and the implementation of policies adopted by the local authority or the carrying out of their statutory functions. A good example would be the Inland Revenue. When a tax officer is offering advice to a tax-payer this must be done in a way which doesn't discriminate on grounds of sex. However, the collection of tax is a public duty and is not therefore covered by Section 29. Although not covered by this Act any exercise of a statutory function is subject to judicial review in the normal way so that, if a discretion is exercised in a discriminatory way, judicial review may be sought on those grounds because it would not be a reasonable exercise of the discretion.

The corresponding provisions are to be found in section 20 of the RRA.

Discrimination in disposal or management of premises.

30.–(1) It is unlawful for a person, in relation to premises in Great Britain of which he has power to dispose, to discriminate against a woman–

(a) in the terms on which he offers her those premises, or
(b) by refusing her application for those premises, or
(c) in his treatment of her in relation to any list of persons in need of premises of that description.

(2) It is unlawful for a person, in relation to premises managed by him, to discriminate against a woman occupying the premises–

(a) in the way he affords her access to any benefits or facilities, or by refusing or deliberately omitting to afford her access to them, or
(b) by evicting her, or subjecting her to any other detriment.

(3) Subsection (1) does not apply to a person who owns an estate or interest in the premises and wholly occupies them unless he uses the services of an estate agent for the purposes of the disposal of the premises, or publishes or causes to be published an advertisement in connection with the disposal.

Section 30(3)
An owner occupier is exempt from the provisions of this section unless he uses the services of an estate agent or advertises the premises for disposal. Discriminatory advertisements are covered by section 38.

See section 21 RRA

Discrimination: consent for assignment or sub-letting.

31.–(1) Where the licence or consent of the landlord or of any other person is required for the disposal to any person of premises in Great Britain comprised in a tenancy, it is unlawful for the landlord or other person to discriminate against a woman by withholding the licence or consent for disposal of the premises to her.

(2) Subsection (1) does not apply if–

(a) the person withholding a licence or consent, or a near relative of his ("the relevant occupier") resides, and intends to continue to reside, on the premises, and
(b) there is on the premises, in addition to the accommodation occupied by the relevant occupier, accommodation (not being storage accommodation or means of access) shared by the relevant occupier with other persons residing on the premises who are not members of his household, and
(c) the premises are small premises as defined in section 32(2).

(3) In this section

"tenancy" means a tenancy created by a lease or sub-lease, by an agreement for a lease or sub-lease or by a tenancy agreement or in pursuance of any enactment; and

"disposal", in relation to premises comprised in a tenancy, includes assignment or assignation of the tenancy and sub-letting or parting with possession of the premises or any part of the premises.

(4) This section applies to tenancies created before the passing of this Act, as well as to others.

Section 30 and 31

Prohibits sex discrimination in the buying, renting or allocation of premises. This includes land, houses, flats and business premises, but hotel accommodation is dealt with in section 29.

A person letting premises includes a local authority or a company as well as an individual.

See section 24 RRA

Exception for small dwellings.

32.–(1) Sections 29(1) and 30 do not apply to the provision by a person of accommodation in any premises, or the disposal of premises by him, if–

(a) that person or a near relative of his ("the relevant occupier") resides, and intends to continue to reside, on the premises, and

(b) there is on the premises, in addition to the accommodation occupied by the relevant occupier, accommodation (not being storage accommodation or means of access) shared by the relevant occupier with other persons residing on the premises who are not members of his household, and

(c) the premises are small premises.

Section 32(1)

Premises where the owner or a near relative is living are exempt from the provisions of sections 30 and 31 but only if those premises amount to a small dwelling as defined in this section.

(2) Premises shall be treated for the purposes of subsection (1) as small premises if–

(a) in the case of premises comprising residential accommodation for one or more households (under separate letting or similar agreements) in addition to the accommodation occupied by the relevant occupier, there is not normally residential accommodation for more than two such households and only the relevant occupier and any member of his household reside in the accommodation occupied by him;

(b) in the case of premises not falling within paragraph (a), there is not normally residential accommodation on the premises for more than six persons in addition to the relevant occupier and any members of his household.

Section 32(2)(b)

Where the accommodation does not consist of separate households the exemption only applies if the accommodation is provided for not more than six people in addition to the owner-occupier. This would include bed and breakfast accommodation and guest houses.

See section 22 RRA

Exception for political parties.

33.–(1) This section applies to a political party if–

(a) it has as its main object, or one of its main objects, the promotion of parliamentary candidatures for the Parliament of the United Kingdom, or

(b) it is an affiliate of, or has as an affiliate, or has similar formal links with, a political party within paragraph (a).

(2) Nothing in section 29(1) shall be construed as affecting any special provision for persons of one sex only in the constitution, organisation or administration of the political party.

(3) Nothing in section 29(1) shall render unlawful an act done in order to give effect to such a special provision.

Section 33

This exception only covers the provision of goods facilities or services. It does not include the selection of candidates for local authorities or for parliament.

Exception for voluntary bodies.

34.–(1) This section applies to a body–

(a) the activities of which are carried on otherwise than for profit, and

(b) which was not set up by any enactment.

(2) Sections 29(1) and 30 shall not be construed as rendering unlawful–

(a) the restriction of membership of any such body to persons of one sex (disregarding any minor exceptions), or

(b) the provision of benefits, facilities or services to members of any such body where the membership is so restricted,

even though membership of the body is open to the public, or to a section of the public.

(3) Nothing in section 29 or 30 shall–

(a) be construed as affecting a provision to which this subsection applies, or

(b) render unlawful an act which is done in order to give effect to such a provision.

(4) Subsection (3) applies to a provision for conferring benefits on persons of one sex only (disregarding any benefits to persons of the opposite sex which are exceptional or are relatively insignificant), being a provision which constitutes the main object of a body within subsection (1).

Section 34

Although 'enactment' is not defined, this refers to bodies set up by act of parliament

Further exceptions from ss. 29(1) and 30.

35.–(1) A person who provides at any place facilities or services restricted to men does not for that reason contravene section 29(1) if–

(a) the place is, or is part of, a hospital, resettlement unit provided under Schedule 5 to the Supplementary Benefits Act 1976 or other establishment for persons requiring special care, supervision or attention, or

(b) the place is (permanently or for the time being) occupied or used for the purposes of an organised religion, and the facilities or services are restricted to men so as to comply with the doctrines of that religion or avoid offending the religious susceptibilities of a significant number of its followers, or

(c) the facilities or services are provided for, or are likely to be used by, two or more persons at the same time, and

(i) the facilities or services are such, or those persons are such, that male users are likely to suffer serious embarrassment at the presence of a woman, or

(ii) the facilities or services are such that a user is likely to be in a state of undress and a male user might reasonably object to the presence of a female user.

(2) A person who provides facilities or services restricted to men does not for that reason contravene section 29(1) if the services or facilities are such that physical contact between the user and any other person is likely, and that other person might reasonably object if the user were a woman.

(3) Sections 29(1) and 30 do not apply–

(a) to discrimination which is rendered unlawful by any provision in column 1 of the table below, or

(b) to discrimination which would be so unlawful but for any provision in column 2 of that table, or

(c) to discrimination which contravenes a term modified or included by virtue of an equality clause.

TABLE

Provision creating illegality	*Exception*
Part II	Section 6(3), 7(1)(b), 15(4). 19 and 20 Schedule 4 paragraphs 1 and 2.
Section 22 or 23	Sections 26, 27 and 28 Schedule 4 paragraph 4

Section 35

Places which provide special care, supervision or attention are generally exempt.

This section also provides general exemptions where the presence of members of the other sex is likely to cause 'serious embarrassment' either because users of the facilities might be in physical contact with each other or they may be in a state of undress.

Discrimination by, or in relation to barristers

35A.–(1) It is unlawful for a barrister or a barrister's clerk, in relation to any offer of a pupillage or tenancy, to discriminate against a woman–

(a) in the arrangements which are made for the purpose of determining to whom it should be offered;
(b) in respect of any terms on which it is offered; or
(c) by refusing, or deliberately omitting, to offer it to her.

(2) It is unlawful for a barrister or a barrister's clerk, in relation to a woman who is a pupil or tenant in the chambers in question, to discriminate against her–

(a) in respect of any terms applicable to her as a pupil or tenant;
(b) in the opportunities for training, or gaining experience, which are afforded or denied to her;
(c) in the benefits, facilities or services which are afforded or denied to her; or
(d) by terminating her pupillage or by subjecting her to any pressure to leave the chambers or other detriment.

(3) It is unlawful for any person, in relation to the giving, withholding or acceptance of instructions to a barrister, to discriminate against a woman.

(4) In this section–

'barrister's clerk' includes any person carrying out any of the functions of a barrister's clerk; and

'pupil', 'pupillage', 'tenancy' and 'tenant' have the meanings commonly associated with their use in the context of a set of barristers' chambers.

(5) Section 3 applies for the purposes of this section as it applies for the purposes of any provision of part II.

(6) This section does not apply to Scotland.

Section 35A

Barristers and pupils are not employees but self-employed practitioners. For this reason, the provisions of this act in relation to employment do not apply.

These provisions, introduced by the Courts and Legal Services Act 1990, outlaw discrimination in relation to barristers or pupils.

It not only means that the chambers or the chambers' clerk cannot discriminate but, by sub-section (3) solicitors and/or their clients cannot discriminate by refusing to instruct a barrister on the grounds of his or her sex.

Discrimination by, or in relation to advocates

35B.–(1) It is unlawful for an advocate, in relation to taking any person as his pupil, to discriminate against a woman–

(a) in the arrangements which are made for the purpose of determining to whom he will take as his pupil;
(b) in respect of any terms on which he offers to take her as his pupil; or
(c) by refusing, or deliberately omitting, to take her as his pupil.

(2) It is unlawful for an advocate, in relation to a woman who is a pupil, to discriminate against her–

(a) in respect of any terms applicable to her as a pupil;
(b) in the opportunities for training, or gaining experience, which are afforded or denied to her;
(c) in the benefits, facilities or services which are afforded or denied to her; or
(d) by terminating the relationship or by subjecting her to any pressure to terminate the relationship or other detriment.

(3) It is unlawful for any person, in relation to the giving, withholding or acceptance of instructions to an advocate, to discriminate against a woman.

(4) In this section–

"advocate" means a member of the Faculty of Advocates practising as such; and

"pupil" has the meaning commonly associated with its use in the context of a person training to be an advocate.

(5) Section 3 applies for the purposes of this section as it applies for the purposes of any provision of part II.

(6) This section does not apply to England and Wales.

Section 35B
See the note to 35A above.

Section 35B, while expressed in almost identical terms to 35A, is necessary because of the different system of court advocacy in Scotland.

See sections 26A and 26B RRA

Extent

Extent of Part III.

36.–(1) Section 29(1)–

(a) does not apply to goods, facilities or services outside Great Britain except as provided in subsections (2) and (3), and

(b) does not apply to facilities by way of banking or insurance or for grants, loans, credit or finance, where the facilities are for a purpose to be carried out, or in connection with risks wholly or mainly arising, outside Great Britain.

Section 36(1)(a)+(b)
The protection from discrimination in relation to the provision of goods facilities or services extends only to those which are offered or provided within Great Britain

Banking, insurance and finance are international industries. Even if the services are provided by a person or company based in Great Britain, the protection will not be available if the services or facilities are to be provided wholly or mainly outside Great Britain

(2) Section 29(1) applies to the provision of facilities for travel outside Great Britain where the refusal or omission occurs in Great Britain or on a ship, aircraft or hovercraft within subsection (3).

Section 36(2)
By contrast, where a travel agent offers facilities or services from a base in Great Britain the protection is afforded even if those facilities or services are to be enjoyed outside Great Britain on a ship, aircraft or hovercraft in the same circumstances as employment is protected under section 10 (see sub-section (3) below).

(3) Section 29(1) applies on and in relation to–

(a) any ship registered at a port of registry in Great Britain, and
(b) any aircraft or hovercraft registered in the United Kingdom and operated by a person who has his principal place of business, or is ordinarily resident, in Great Britain,
(c) any ship, aircraft or hovercraft belonging to or possessed by Her Majesty in right of the Government of the United Kingdom,

even if the ship, aircraft or hovercraft is outside Great Britain.

(4) This section shall not render unlawful an act done in or over a country outside the United Kingdom, or in or over that country's territorial waters, for the purpose of complying with the laws of that country.

Section 36(4)
Even if the protection is afforded under sub-sections (2) and (3) above, it is excluded if the act is done over a country's air space and/or territorial waters and the act is necessary to comply with the laws of that country.

(5) Sections 22, 23 and 25 do not apply to benefits, facilities or services outside Great Britain except–

(a) travel on a ship registered at a port of registry in Great Britain, and
(b) benefits, facilities or services provided on a ship so registered.

Section 36(5)
This sub-section corresponds to sub-section (1) of section 27 RRA and deals with education provided by local authorities. It is not easy to understand its purpose.

See generally section 27 RRA

PART IV OTHER UNLAWFUL ACTS

Discriminatory practices.

37.–(1) In this section

"discriminatory practice" means the application of a requirement or condition which results in an act of discrimination which is unlawful by virtue of any provision of Part II or III taken with section 1(1)(b) or 3(1)(b) or which would be likely to result in such an act of discrimination if the persons to whom it is applied were not all of one sex.

(2) A person acts in contravention of this section if and so long as–

(a) he applies a discriminatory practice, or
(b) he operates practices or other arrangements which in any circumstances would call for the application by him of a discriminatory practice.

(3) Proceedings in respect of a contravention of this section shall be brought only by the Commission in accordance with sections 67 to 71.

Section 37
It may be the case that individuals who are adversely affected by discriminatory practices are not willing to complain. This provision allows the Equal Opportunities Commission to take action against any person or body even if no individual is willing to complain.

This section also deals with a situation where discrimination is so deeply ingrained that no victims of discrimination are ever produced. For example, a company may be so well known for its opposition to employing men that men never make applications for positions with that company.

Only the EOC can take action under this section.

See section 28 RRA

Discriminatory advertisements.

38.–(1) It is unlawful to publish or cause to be published an advertisement which indicates, or might reasonably be understood as indicating, an intention by a person to do any act which is or might be unlawful by virtue of Part II or III.

Section 38(1)

A definition of the word advertisement appears in the section 82 and is very wide. Although this section corresponds to section 29 of the RRA it is more narrowly defined and covers only those acts which are or might be unlawful. However, sub-section (2) of section 29 RRA contains exceptions which, when read in conjunction with sub-section (1) have the same effect as this section.

(2) Subsection (1) does not apply to an advertisement if the intended act would not in fact be unlawful.

(3) For the purposes of subsection (1), use of a job description with a sexual connotation (such as "waiter", "salesgirl", "postman" or "stewardess") shall be taken to indicate an intention to discriminate, unless the advertisement contains an indication to the contrary.

Section 38(3)

In an advertisement for a job an employer might be tempted to use the excuse that the job title is one in common usage and carries no sexual connotation. This section gives examples of the kind of job titles which are no longer acceptable unless the advertisement also carries a positive assertion that members of both sex are free to apply and will be considered.

(4) The publisher of an advertisement made unlawful by subsection (1) shall not be subject to any liability under that subsection in respect of the publication of the advertisement if he proves–

(a) that the advertisement was published in reliance on a statement made to him by the person who caused it to be published to the effect that, by reason of the operation of subsection (2), the publication would not be unlawful, and

(b) that it was reasonable for him to rely on the statement.

Section 38(4)
Although the publication of a discriminatory advertisement will be unlawful, the publisher of the advertisement will not be made liable if he reasonably relied on a statement by the person placing the advertisement that it didn't contravene the provisions of the Act. This sub-section will not allow a publisher to escape liability unless it was reasonable to rely on the statement of the person publishing the advertisement. In other words, if it was obvious that the advertisement would contravene the provisions of the Act the publisher as well as the person placing the advertisement will be liable.

(5) A person who knowingly or recklessly makes a statement such as is referred to in subsection (4) which in a material respect is false or misleading commits an offence, and shall be liable on summary conviction to a fine not exceeding level 5 on the standard scale.

Section 38(5)
This provision, in relation to the making of misleading statements, is the same as in sub-section (6) of section 15 relating to employment agencies. A person who makes a misleading statement either knowing that it's misleading or not caring whether it would be misleading commits an offence and is liable to a fine on a scale which is subject to regular change.

See section 29 RRA

Instructions to discriminate.

39. It is unlawful for a person–

(a) who has authority over another person, or
(b) in accordance with whose wishes that other person is accustomed to act,

to instruct him to do any act which is unlawful by virtue of Part II or III, or procure or attempt to procure the doing by him of any such act.

Section 39
See section 30 RRA

Pressure to discriminate.

40.–(1) It is unlawful to induce, or attempt to induce, a person to do any act which contravenes Part II or III by–

(a) providing or offering to provide him with any benefit, or
(b) subjecting or threatening to subject him to any detriment.

(2) An offer or threat is not prevented from falling within subsection (1) because it is not made directly to the person in question, if it is made in such a way that he is likely to hear of it.

Section 39 & 40

These sections apply whether or not the unlawful act actually takes place. Their intention is to prevent either instructions or pressure being applied in order to make someone else carry out a discriminatory act.

Under the parallel provisions of the RRA (sections 30 and 31) the words 'whose wishes that other person is accustomed to act' in section 39(b) (section 30(b) RRA) have been held to mean that there has to be some relationship between the person giving the instruction and the person required to act on it. A request was made by a prospective employer to a local school to send along for interview people who might be employed as a filing clerk. The person at the school was asked not to send along any coloured applicants because that person would feel out of place since there were no other coloured employees. Because there was no evidence that that prospective employer had made a request either to the school or to the very person at the school who had taken a call she was not a person "in accordance with whose wishes" she was accustomed to act. The EAT went on to say that if there was evidence that that employer had made requests to the school before then the employer would be caught by sub-section (b). However, by giving a wide interpretation to the word induce or attempting to induce, the EAT found the prospective employer had contravened section 31 of the RRA (section 40 of the SDA).

See section 31 RRA

Liability of employers and principals.

41.–(1) Anything done by a person in the course of his employment shall be treated for the purposes of this Act as done by his employer as well as by him, whether or not it was done with the employer's knowledge or approval.

Section 41(1)

Whether or not the employer knew of the act, if an employee commits a discriminatory act against another during the course of his employment, the employer is liable for that act.

(2) Anything done by a person as agent for another person with the authority (whether express or implied, and whether precedent or subsequent) of that other person shall be treated for the purposes of this Act as done by that other person as well as by him.

Section 41(2)

Under this sub-section both the principal and the person committing the act are made liable.

(3) In proceedings brought under this Act against any person in respect of an act alleged to have been done by an employee of his it shall be a defence for that person to prove that he took such steps as were reasonably practicable to prevent the employee from doing that act, or from doing in the course of his employment acts of that description.

Section 41(3)

Providing the employer took such steps as were reasonably practicable to prevent the discriminatory act taking place he will escape liability. Ways in which this sub-section may be satisfied include showing that policies were in place to make clear that such acts were unacceptable and, for example, if proved would result in disciplinary action taking place against the offender. It can also include the provision of training to ensure that such policies are brought to the attention of managers and employees.

It would therefore be possible in proceedings brought against the employer and the individual employee, for the employer to escape liability under sub-section (3) but for the individual employee still to be held liable because he had aided the employer's unlawful act under section 42 below.

See section 32 RRA

Aiding unlawful acts.

42.–(1) A person who knowingly aids another person to do an act made unlawful by this Act shall be treated for the purposes of this Act as himself doing an unlawful act of the like description.

Section 42(1)

Whether or not an act by an employee is 'in the course of his employment' must be looked at quite liberally. It is not interpreted in the same way in which that phrase is used in an action in tort. So, even if the act by the employees would never have been authorised by the employer if the employer had known about them, it may still be 'in the course of employment' if there is a sufficient connection between those acts and the employment in question. This may even extent to works' functions after normal hours and off the employer's premises.

Two police cases might serve to draw a distinction between what is and what is not 'in the course of employment'. In the first case, a probationary constable met a male officer off duty and went back to the section house in which she was living during her probationary period and in which she was sexually harassed by that other officer. The Court of Appeal held that this could not be said to be in the course of employment.

In the second case, the police constable had been sexually harrassed in two locations. The first was in a local public bar where a group of officers had gone after the end of their shifts; the second was at a leaving celebration for a colleague. In this case the EAT decided that each incident had occurred during what were, in reality, 'extensions of the workplace'.

Even if the act is committed by somebody not under the employer's control, the employer might still be liable.

In another case under the RRA the hotel employing two black waitresses was found to be liable when it sent them back in to provide service at a function at which the comedian Bernard Manning was speaking. He had already made racist remarks about the women earlier in the function and, by sending them back in after that abuse, the employer was held to have subjected them to a detriment under section 4(2)(c) RRA (section 6(2)(b) SDA).

(2) For the purposes of subsection (1) an employee or agent for whose act the employer or principal is liable under section 41 (or would be so liable but for section 41(3)) shall be deemed to aid the doing of the act by the employer or principal.

Section 42(2)
Even if the employer has a defence under section 41(3) above the employee who commits the unlawful act is made liable by this sub-section.

(3) A person does not under this section knowingly aid another to do an unlawful act if–

(a) he acts in reliance on a statement made to him by that other person that, by reason of any provision of this Act, the act which he aids would not be unlawful, and
(b) it is reasonable for him to rely on the statement.

(4) A person who knowingly or recklessly makes a statement such as is referred to in subsection (3)(a) which in a material respect is false or misleading commits an offence, and shall be liable on summary conviction to a fine not exceeding level 5 on the standard scale.

Section 42 (3) & (4)
Provides for the same defence and penalty as in relation to discriminatory advertisements under section 38 and employment agencies under section 15.

The same provisions appear at section 33 RRA.

Part V General Exceptions from Parts II to IV

Charities.

43.–(1) Nothing in Parts II to IV shall–

(a) be construed as affecting a provision to which this subsection applies, or
(b) render unlawful an act which is done in order to give effect to such a provision.

(2) Subsection (1) applies to a provision for conferring benefits on persons of one sex only (disregarding any benefits to persons of the opposite sex which are exceptional or are relatively insignificant), being a provision which is contained in a charitable instrument.

(3) In this section 'charitable instrument' means an enactment or other instrument so far as it relates to charitable purposes, and in Scotland includes the governing instrument of an endowment or of an educational endowment as those expressions are defined in section 135(1) of the Education (Scotland) Act 1962.

In the application of this section to England and Wales, "charitable purposes" means purposes which are exclusively charitable according to the law of England and Wales.

Section 43

Charities may discriminate on grounds of sex in their treatment of beneficiaries if the trust establishing the charity permits it but they may not, of course, discriminate against their employees on those grounds.

Similar provisions appear in the RRA at section 34.

Sport etc.

44. Nothing in Parts II to IV shall, in relation to any sport, game or other activity of a competitive nature where the physical strength, stamina or physique of the average woman puts her at a disadvantage to the average man, render unlawful any act related to the participation of a person as a competitor in events involving that activity which are confined to competitors of one sex.

Section 44

This section is self explanatory and deals with sporting events. Sport in relation to education is dealt with at section 28.

Certain exceptions apply in relation to sport under the RRA at section 39.

Insurance etc.

45. Nothing in Parts II to IV shall render unlawful the treatment of a person in relation to an annuity, life assurance policy, accident insurance policy, or similar matter involving the assessment of risk, where the treatment–

(a) was effected by reference to actuarial or other data from a source on which it was reasonable to rely, and

(b) was reasonable having regard to the data and any other relevant factors.

> **Section 45**
> *Because statistical evidence still shows that men and women have different life expectancies, such statistical evidence can be used to justify different terms for life insurance, annuities and accident insurance being offered to men and women.*

Communal accommodation.

46.–(1) In this section "communal accommodation" means residential accommodation which includes dormitories or other shared sleeping accommodation which for reasons of privacy or decency should be used by men only, or by women only (but which may include some shared sleeping accommodation for men, and some for women, or some ordinary sleeping accommodation).

> **Section 46(1)**
> *It is only commonsense to allow discrimination where people are required to use communal facilities. Even where this is the case, sub-section (3) still requires the fair and equitable treatment of men and women so that, while not required to admit persons of one sex, to communal facilities used by another, it may be necessary to provide alternative facilities on an equitable basis.*

(2) In this section "communal accommodation" also includes residential accommodation all or part of which should be used by men only, or by women only, because of the nature of the sanitary facilities serving the accommodation.

(3) Nothing in Part II or III shall render unlawful sex discrimination in the admission of persons to communal accommodation if the accommodation is managed in a way which, given the exigencies of the situation, comes as near as may be to fair and equitable treatment of men and women.

(4) In applying subsection (3) account shall be taken of–

(a) whether and how far it is reasonable to expect that the accommodation should be altered or extended, or that further alternative accommodation should be provided; and

(b) the frequency of the demand or need for use of the accommodation by men as compared with women.

(5) Nothing in Part II or III shall render unlawful sex discrimination against a woman, or against a man, as respects the provision of any benefit, facility or service if–

(a) the benefit, facility or service cannot properly and effectively be provided except for those using communal accommodation, and

(b) in the relevant circumstances the woman or, as the case may be, the man could lawfully be refused the use of the accommodation by virtue of subsection (3).

(6) Neither subsection (3) nor subsection (5) is a defence to an act of sex discrimination under Part II unless such arrangements as are reasonably practicable are made to compensate for the detriment caused by the discrimination; but in considering under subsection (5)(b) whether the use of communal accommodation could lawfully be refused (in a case based on Part II), it shall be assumed that the requirements of this subsection have been complied with as respects subsection (3).

(7) Section 25 shall not apply to sex discrimination within subsection (3) or (5).

Section 46(7)
Section 25 is the section that deals with education in the public sector.

(8) This section is without prejudice to the generality of section 35(1)(c).

Section 46(8)
Section 35(1)(c) deals with more general exceptions where there is a risk of serious embarrassment or the users of facilities or services are likely to be in a state of undress.

Discriminatory training by certain bodies.

47.–(1) Nothing in Parts II to IV shall render unlawful any act done in relation to particular work by any person in, or in connection with–

(a) affording women only, or men only, access to facilities for training which would help to fit them for that work, or

(b) encouraging women only, or men only, to take advantage of opportunities for doing that work,

where it reasonably appears to that person that at any time within the 12 months immediately preceding the doing of the act there were no persons of the sex in question doing that work in Great Britain, or the number of persons of that sex doing the work in Great Britain was comparatively small.

Section 47(1)
Without this provision, occupations previously undertaken mainly or exclusively by members of one sex could end up with that imbalance almost permanently embedded this provision allows for what is, in effect, positive discrimination, by allowing training to be offered in order to equip the under-represented sex with the skills or abilities to undertake that work. Whether or not members of one sex are under-represented must be looked at in the period twelve months immediately before the training is offered.

(2) Where in relation to particular work it reasonably appears to any person that although the condition for the operation of subsection (1) is not met for the whole of Great Britain it is met for an area within Great Britain, nothing in Parts II to IV shall render unlawful any act done by that person in, or in connection with–

(a) affording persons who are of the sex in question, and who appear likely to take up that work in that area, access to facilities for training which would help to fit them for that work, or

(b) encouraging persons of that sex to take advantage of opportunities in the area for doing that work.

Section 47(2)
If women (or men) are under-represented in a particular area of the country, this provision allows a positive discrimination in a provision of those facilities in that particular area.

(3) Nothing in Parts II to IV shall render unlawful any act done by any person in, or in connection with, affording persons access to facilities for training which would help to fit them for employment, where it reasonably appears to that person that those persons are in special need of training by reason of the period for which they have been discharging domestic or family responsibilities to the exclusion of regular full time employment.

The discrimination in relation to which this subsection applies may result from confining the training to persons who have been discharging domestic or family responsibilities, or from the way persons are selected for training, or both.

Section 47(3)
Facilities for training can be offered specifically to women who have been out of the employment market for a significant period because of family responsibilities. In an era of fast moving technological development such people could be almost permanently excluded from the employment market without special training being offered to them.

(4) The preceding provisions of this section shall not apply in relation to any discrimination which is rendered unlawful by section 6.

Section 47(4)
While special facilities for training may be offered to people covered by this section, this sub-section makes it clear that positive discrimination for the purposes of deciding who should be employed is not allowed.

See the similar provisions in relation to race in section 37 RRA

Other discriminatory training etc.

48.–(1) Nothing in Parts II to IV shall render unlawful any act done by an employer in relation to particular work in his employment, being an act done in, or in connection with,–

(a) affording his female employees only, or his male employees only, access to facilities for training which would help to fit them for that work, or
(b) encouraging women only, or men only, to take advantage of opportunities for doing that work,

where at any time within the twelve months immediately preceding the doing of the act there were no persons of the sex in question among those doing that work or the number of persons of that sex doing the work was comparatively small.

Section 48(1)
This section allows employers to take positive action to redress historical imbalances in the workforce, in the same way that national or regional under representation can be tackled under section 47.

(2) Nothing in section 12 shall render unlawful any act done by an organisation to which that section applies in, or in connection with,–

(a) affording female members of the organisation only, or male members of the organisation only, access to facilities for training which would help to fit them for holding a post of any kind in the organisation, or
(b) encouraging female members only, or male members only, to take advantage of opportunities for holding such posts in the organisation,

where at any time within the twelve months immediately preceding the doing of the act there were no persons of the sex in question among persons holding such posts in the organisation or the number of persons of that sex holding such posts was comparatively small.

Section 48(2)
Trade unions and employers organisations can take limited positive action in the same way that employers may under sub-section (1) above.

(3) Nothing in Parts II to IV shall render unlawful any act done by an organisation to which section 12 applies in, or in connection with, encouraging women only, or men only, to become members of the organisation where at any time within the twelve months immediately preceding the doing of the act there were no persons of the sex in question among those members or the number of persons of that sex among the members was comparatively small.

Section 48(3)
Limited positive discrimination is permitted by this sub-section in order to allow members of an under-represented sex to become members of trade unions or employers' organisations.

The provisions of sections 47 and 48 appear in a slightly different form in sections 37 and 38 RRA.

Trade unions etc.: elective bodies.

49.–(1) If an organisation to which section 12 applies comprises a body the membership of which is wholly or mainly elected, nothing in section 12 shall render unlawful provision which ensures that a minimum number of persons of one sex are members of the body–

(a) by reserving seats on the body for persons of that sex, or
(b) by making extra seats on the body available (by election or co-option or otherwise) for persons of that sex on occasions when the number of persons of that sex in the other seats is below the minimum,

where in the opinion of the organisation the provision is in the circumstances needed to secure a reasonable lower limit to the number of members of that sex serving on the body; and nothing in Parts II to IV shall render unlawful any act done in order to give effect to such a provision.

Section 49(1)
Another provision which allows for historical under-representation to be addressed. In this section provision is made for special seats to be reserved on elective bodies in order to ensure that a minimum number of members of a particular sex are represented on that body.

(2) This section shall not be taken as making lawful–

(a) discrimination in the arrangements for determining the persons entitled to vote in an election of members of the body, or otherwise to choose the persons to serve on the body, or
(b) discrimination in any arrangements concerning membership of the organisation itself.

Section 49(2)
This does not allow discrimination in voting arrangements for the purposes of deciding who should serve on the body referred to in sub-section (1) above or in determining arrangements for who should be admitted to membership.

Indirect access to benefits etc.

50.–(1) References in this Act to the affording by any person of access to benefits, facilities or services are not limited to benefits, facilities or services provided by that person himself, but include any means by which it is in that person's power to facilitate access to benefits, facilities or services provided by any other person (the "actual provider").

> **Section 50(1)**
> *Section 29 deals with the direct provision of goods, facilities or services. This section deals with the provision of such services facilities or goods indirectly. If, for example, an employer makes available membership of a sports and leisure club the employer will not escape liability by relying on the discriminatory admissions practice of the club itself.*

(2) Where by any provision of this Act the affording by any person of access to benefits, facilities or services in a discriminatory way is in certain circumstances prevented from being unlawful, the effect of the provision shall extend also to the liability under this Act of any actual provider.

> **Section 50(2)**
> *If the employer can lawfully discriminate under any other provision of this Act, the person or body providing direct access to facilities or services will not be made liable under this sub-section.*
>
> *See also section 40 RRA.*

Acts done for purposes of protection of women

51.–(1) Nothing in the following provisions, namely–

(a) Part II,
(b) Part III so far as it applies to vocational training, or
(c) Part IV so far as it has effect in relation to the provisions mentioned in paragraphs (a) and (b), shall render unlawful any act done by a person in relation to a woman if–
(i) it was necessary for that person to do it in order to comply with a requirement of an existing statutory provision concerning the protection of women, or
(ii) it was necessary for that person to do it in order to comply with a requirement of a relevant statutory provision (within the meaning of part I of the Health and Safety at Work etc Act 1974) and it was done by that person for the purpose of the protection of the woman in question(or of any class of women that included that woman).

Section 51(1)
This avoids conflict between this Act and any other Act placing particular obligations on an employer to take action in order to protect women, for example, during pregnancy (see subsection (2) below).

(2) In subsection (1)–

(a) the reference in paragraph (i) of that subsection to an existing statutory provision concerning the protection of women is a reference to any such provision having effect for the purpose of protecting women as regards–

(i) pregnancy or maternity, or

(ii) other circumstances giving rise to risks specifically affecting women,

whether the provision relates only to such protection or to the protection of any other class of persons as well; and

(b) the reference in paragraph (ii) of that subsection to the protection of a particular woman or class of women is a reference to the protection of that woman or those women as regards any circumstances falling within paragraph (a)(i) or (ii) above.

(3) In this section "existing statutory provision" means (subject to subsection (4)) any provision of–

(a) an Act passed before this Act, or

(b) an instrument approved or made by or under such an Act (including one approved or made after the passing of this Act).

Section 51(3)
It would normally only be possible to exclude from the ambit of this Act other statutory provisions or instruments which were already in existence at the time of the passing of this Act. This sub-section allows the exemption to extend to any instrument under an existing Act which was made after the passing of the SDA.

(4) Where an Act passed after this Act re-enacts (with or without modification) a provision of an Act passed before this Act, that provision as re-enacted shall be treated for the purposes of subsection (3) as if it continued to be contained in an Act passed before this Act.

Section 51(4)
Where provisions that are now in an Act passed since 1975 were originally contained in an Act already in force at the time of the passing of the SDA this sub-section allows those provisions to be treated as if they were made before the passing of the SDA.

Acts done under statutory authority to be exempt from certain provisions of Part III

51A.–(1) Nothing in–

(a) the relevant provisions of Part III, or

(b) Part IV so far as it has effect in relation to those provisions,

shall render unlawful any act done by a person if it was necessary for that person to do it in order to comply with a requirement of an existing statutory provision within the meaning of section 51.

> **Section 51A(1)**
> *This is the same saving provision as in section 51 above but without limit to those provisions which are particularly for the protection of women. Unlike section 51, this section does not apply to instruments under enactments, only the statutes themselves.*

(2) In subsection (1)"the relevant provisions of Part III" means the provisions of that Part except so far as they apply to vocational training.

> **Section 51A(2)**
> *This sub-section prevents overlap with section 51(1)(b).*
> *Similar, though more extensive provisions, are contained in section 41 RRA.*

Acts safeguarding national security.

52.–(1) Nothing in Parts II to IV shall render unlawful an act done for the purpose of safeguarding national security.

(2) A certificate purporting to be signed by or on behalf of a Minister of the Crown and certifying that an act specified in the certificate was done for the purpose of safeguarding national security shall be conclusive evidence that it was done for that purpose.

(3) A document purporting to be a certificate such as is mentioned in subsection (2) shall be received in evidence and, unless the contrary is proved, shall be deemed to be such a certificate.

> **Section 52**
> *Any act done for the purposes of safeguarding national security is exempted from the provisions of this act.*
> *By the Sex Discrimination (Amendment) Order 1988, SI 1988/249, this part no longer has effect in relation to vocational training.*
> *The same general exemption for acts safeguarding national security appear in sections 42 and 69(2) RRA.*

52A. Construction of references to vocational training

In the following provisions, namely–

(a) sections 51 and 51A, and
(b) the provisions of any Order in Council modifying the effect of section 52, "vocational training" includes advanced vocational training and retraining; and any reference to vocational training in those provisions shall be construed as including a reference to vocational guidance.

Section 52A

This merely explains the meaning of vocational training.

(b) applies that meaning to the Sex Discrimination (Amendment) Order 1988 referred to in the note to section 52 above.

PART VI EQUAL OPPORTUNITIES COMMISSION

Establishment and duties of Commission.

53.–(1) There shall be a body of Commissioners named the Equal Opportunities Commission, consisting of at least eight but not more than fifteen individuals each appointed by the Secretary of State on a full-time or part-time basis, which shall have the following duties–

(a) to work towards the elimination of discrimination,
(b) to promote equality of opportunity between men and women generally, and
(ba) to promote equality of opportunity, in the field of employment and of vocational training, for persons who intend to undergo, are undergoing or have undergone gender reassignment, and
(c) to keep under review the working of this Act and the Equal Pay Act 1970 and, when they are so required by the Secretary of State or otherwise think it necessary, draw up and submit to the Secretary of State proposals for amending them.

Section 53(1)

Originally, the Commission had three main duties which are set out under paragraphs (a) – (c) above. Sub-section (ba) was inserted by the Gender Reassignment Regulations as from 1 May 1999.

In relation to the exercise of functions under sub-section (1), in relation to Wales, these are exercisable by the Secretary of State only with the agreement of the Welsh Assembly.

(1A) One of the Commissioners shall be a person who appears to the Secretary of State to have special knowledge of Scotland.

Section 53(1A)
With the establishing of the Scottish Parliament one of the Commission's members must now have special knowledge of Scotland.

(2) The Secretary of State shall appoint–

(a) one of the Commissioners to be chairman of the Commission, and

(b) either one or two of the Commissioners (as the Secretary of State thinks fit) to be deputy chairman or deputy chairmen of the Commission.

(3) The Secretary of State may by order amend subsection (1) so far as it regulates the number of Commissioners.

(4) Schedule 3 shall have effect with respect to the Commission.

Section 53(4)
Section 43 RRA deals with the establishment of the Commission for Racial Equality.

Research and education.

54.–(1) The Commission may undertake or assist (financially or otherwise) the undertaking by other persons of any research, and any educational activities, which appear to the Commission necessary or expedient for the purposes of section 53(1).

(2) The Commission may make charges for educational or other facilities or services made available by them.

Section 54
Although the SDA predates the RRA, these provisions were inserted by amendment after the RRA was enacted and copy the provisions of sections 43 and 45 RRA.

Review of discriminatory provisions in health and safety legislation.

55.–(1) Without prejudice to the generality of section 53(1), the Commission, in pursuance of the duties imposed by paragraphs (a) and (b) of that subsection–

(a) shall keep under review the relevant statutory provisions in so far as they require men and women to be treated differently, and

(b) if so required by the Secretary of State, make to him a report on any matter specified by him which is connected with those duties and concerns the relevant statutory provisions.

Any such report shall be made within the time specified by the Secretary of State, and the Secretary of State shall cause the report to be published.

(2) Whenever the Commission think it necessary, they shall draw up and submit to the Secretary of State proposals for amending the relevant statutory provisions.

(3) The Commission shall carry out their duties in relation to the relevant statutory provisions in consultation with the Health and Safety Commission.

(4) In this section

"the relevant statutory provisions" has the meaning given by section 53 of the Health and Safety at Work etc. Act 1974.

Section 55

Because the Act, in general, does not apply where a person or employer is required either to do or not to do something in order to comply with health and safety legislation, this section requires the EOC to keep that legislation under review in order to ensure that any exemptions are still relevant and justified.

Annual Reports

56.–(1) As soon as practicable after the end of each calendar year the Commission shall make to the Secretary of State a report on their activities during the year (an "annual report").

(2) Each annual report shall include a general survey of developments, during the period to which it relates, in respect of matters falling within the scope of the Commission's duties.

(3) The Secretary of State shall lay a copy of every annual report before each House of Parliament, and shall cause the report to be published.

Section 56

See section 46 RRA.

The EOC mirrors, both in its formation and its functions, the Commission for Racial Equality under section 43 of the RRA.

Codes of practice

56A–(1) The Commission may issue codes of practice containing such practical guidance as the Commission think fit for one or more of the following purposes, namely–

(a) the elimination of discrimination in the field of employment;
(b) the promotion of equality of opportunity in that field between men and women;
(ba) the promotion of equality of opportunity in that field for persons who intend to undergo, are undergoing or have undergone gender reassignment.

(2) When the Commission propose to issue a code of practice, they shall prepare and publish a draft of that code, shall consider any representations made to them about the draft and may modify the draft accordingly.

(3) In the course of preparing any draft code of practice for eventual publication under subsection (2) the Commission shall consult with–

(a) such organisations or associations of organisations representative of employers or of workers; and
(b) such other organisations, or bodies,

as appear to the Commission to be appropriate.

(4) If the Commission determine to proceed with the draft, they shall transmit the draft to the Secretary of State who shall–

(a) if he approves of it, lay it before both Houses of Parliament; and
(b) if he does not approve of it, publish details of his reasons for withholding approval.

(5) If, within the period of forty days beginning with the day on which a copy of a draft code of practice is laid before each House of Parliament, or, if such copies are laid on different days, with the later of the two days, either House so resolves, no further proceedings shall be taken thereon, but without prejudice to the laying before Parliament of a new draft.

(6) In reckoning the period of forty days referred to in subsection (5), no account shall be taken of any period during which Parliament is dissolved or prorogued or during which both Houses are adjourned for more than four days.

(7) If no such resolution is passed as is referred to in subsection (5), the Commission shall issue the code in the form of the draft and the code shall come into effect on such day as the Secretary of State may by order appoint.

(8) Without prejudice to section 81(4), an order under subsection (7) may contain such transitional provisions or savings as appear to the Secretary of State to be necessary or expedient in connection with the code of practice thereby brought into operation.

(9) The Commission may from time to time revise the whole or any part of a code of practice issued under this section and issue that revised code, and subsections (2) to (8) shall apply (with appropriate modifications) to such a revised code as they apply to the first issue of a code.

(10) A failure on the part of any person to observe any provision of a code of practice shall not of itself render him liable to any proceedings; but in any proceedings under this Act or the Equal Pay Act 1970 before an employment tribunal any code of practice issued under this section shall be admissible in evidence, and if any provision of such a code appears to the tribunal to be relevant to any question arising in the proceedings it shall be taken into account in determining that question.

Section 56A(10)
A breach of the Code is not an offence in itself but a failure to observe one or more of its provisions may be evidence that a person has committed a breach.

(11) Without prejudice to subsection (1), a code of practice issued under this section may include such practical guidance as the Commission think fit as to what steps it is reasonably practicable for employers to take for the purpose of preventing their employees from doing in the course of their employment acts made unlawful by this Act.

Section 56A(11)
See also section 47 RRA.

INVESTIGATIONS

Power to conduct formal investigations.

57.–(1) Without prejudice to their general power to do anything requisite for the performance of their duties under section 53(1), the Commission may if they think fit, and shall if required by the Secretary of State, conduct a formal investigation for any purpose connected with the carrying out of those duties.

(2) The Commission may, with the approval of the Secretary of State, appoint, on a full-time or part-time basis, one or more individuals as additional Commissioners for the purposes of a formal investigation.

(3) The Commission may nominate one or more Commissioners, with or without one or more additional Commissioners, to conduct a formal investigation on their behalf, and may delegate any of their functions in relation to the investigation to the persons so nominated.

Section 57
Section 37 dealt with discriminatory practices. The note to that section made reference to situations where it may be difficult, or even impossible, to identify victims of such practices. This section gives the EOC the power to conduct investigations where it believes such discriminatory practices exist, whether or not anyone complains, although in practice such investigations may well arise from reports from aggrieved persons who are not willing to pursue a claim on their own behalf.

See section 48 RRA.

Terms of reference.

58.–(1) The Commission shall not embark on a formal investigation unless the requirements of this section have been complied with.

(2) Terms of reference for the investigation shall be drawn up by the Commission or, if the Commission were required by the Secretary of State to conduct the investigation, by the Secretary of State after consulting the Commission.

(3) It shall be the duty of the Commission to give general notice of the holding of the investigation unless the terms of reference confine it to activities of persons named in them, but in such a case the Commission shall in the prescribed manner give those persons notice of the holding of the investigation.

(3A) Where the terms of reference of the investigation confine it to activities of persons named in them and the Commission in the course of it propose to investigate any act made unlawful by this Act which they believe that a person so named may have done, the Commission shall–

(a) inform that person of their belief and of their proposal to investigate the act in question; and

(b) offer him an opportunity of making oral or written representations with regard to it (or both oral and written representations if he thinks fit);

and a person so named who avails himself of an opportunity under this subsection of making oral representations may be represented–

(i) by counsel or a solicitor; or

(ii) by some other person of his choice, not being a person to whom the Commission object on the ground that he is unsuitable.

(4) The Commission or, if the Commission were required by the Secretary of State to conduct the investigation, the Secretary of State after consulting the Commission may from time to time revise the terms of reference; and subsections (1), (3) and (3A) shall apply to the revised investigation and terms of reference as they applied to the original.

Section 58

See section 49 RRA.

Power to obtain information.

59.–(1) For the purposes of a formal investigation the Commission, by a notice in the prescribed form served on him in the prescribed manner,–

(a) may require any person to furnish such written information as may be described in the notice, and may specify the time at which, and the manner and form in which, the information is to be furnished;

(b) may require any person to attend at such time and place as is specified in the notice and give oral information about, and produce all documents in his possession or control relating to, any matter specified in the notice.

(2) Except as provided by section 69, a notice shall be served under subsection (1) only where–

(a) service of the notice was authorised by an order made by or on behalf of the Secretary of State, or

(b) the terms of reference of the investigation state that the Commission believe that a person named in them may have done or may be doing acts of all or any of the following descriptions–

(i) unlawful discriminatory acts,

(ii) contraventions of section 37,

(iii) contraventions of sections 38, 39 or 40, and

(iv) acts in breach of a term modified or included by virtue of an equality clause, and confine the investigation to those acts.

Section 59(2)

ii operating a discriminatory practice.

iii discriminatory advertisements, instructions or pressure to discriminate.

(3) A notice under subsection (1) shall not require a person–

(a) to give information, or produce any documents, which he could not be compelled to give in evidence, or produce, in civil proceedings before the High Court or the Court of Session, or

Section 59(3)

this would include documents covered by legal or professional privilege such as letters between a person and his/her lawyer for the purposes of giving or receiving legal advice.

(b) to attend at any place unless the necessary expenses of his journey to and from that place are paid or tendered to him.

(4) If a person fails to comply with a notice served on him under subsection (1) or the Commission has reasonable cause to believe that he intends not to comply with it, the Commission may apply to a county court for an order requiring him to comply with it or with such directions for the like purpose as may be contained in the order; and section 84 (penalty for neglecting witness summons) of the County Courts Act 1959 shall apply to failure without reasonable excuse to comply with any such order as it applies in the cases there provided.

(5) In the application of subsection (4) to Scotland–

(a) for the reference to a county court there shall be substituted a reference to a sheriff court, and

(b) for the words after "order; and" to the end of the subsection there shall be substituted the words "paragraph 73 of the First Schedule to the Sheriff Courts (Scotland) Act 1907 (power of sheriff to grant second diligence for compelling the attendances of witnesses or havers) shall apply to any such order as it applies in proceedings in the sheriff court".

Section 59(5)
In other words, the Commission conducting an investigation has the same powers to compel witness to attend and/or to produce documents as the courts have…

(6) A person commits an offence if he–

(a) wilfully alters, suppresses, conceals or destroys a document which he has been required by a notice or order under this section to produce, or

(b) in complying with such a notice or order, knowingly or recklessly makes any statement which is false in a material particular,

and shall be liable on summary conviction to a fine not exceeding level 5 on the standard scale.

Section 59(6)
…and a failure to comply is punishable.

(7) Proceedings for an offence under subsection (6) may (without prejudice to any jurisdiction exercisable apart from this subsection) be instituted–

(a) against any person at any place at which he has an office or other place of business;

(b) against an individual at any place where he resides, or at which he is for the time being.

Section 59(7)
See section 50 RRA.

Recommendations and reports on formal investigations.

60.–(1) If in the light of any of their findings in a formal investigation it appears to the Commission necessary or expedient, whether during the course of the investigation or after its conclusion,–

(a) to make to any persons, with a view to promoting equality of opportunity between men and women who are affected by any of their activities, recommendations for changes in their policies or procedures, or as to any other matters, or

(b) to make to the Secretary of State any recommendations, whether for changes in the law or otherwise, the Commission shall make those recommendations accordingly.

(2) The Commission shall prepare a report of their findings in any formal investigation conducted by them.

(3) If the formal investigation is one required by the Secretary of State–

(a) the Commission shall deliver the report to the Secretary of State, and

(b) the Secretary of State shall cause the report to be published, and unless required by the Secretary of State the Commission shall not publish the report.

(4) If the formal investigation is not one required by the Secretary of State, the Commission shall either publish the report, or make it available for inspection in accordance with subsection (5).

(5) Where under subsection (4) a report is to be made available for inspection, any person shall be entitled, on payment of such fee (if any) as may be determined by the Commission–

(a) to inspect the report during ordinary office hours and take copies of all or any part of the report, or

(b) to obtain from the Commission a copy, certified by the Commission to be correct, of the report.

(6) The Commission may if they think fit determine that the right conferred by subsection (5)(a) shall be exercisable in relation to a copy of the report instead of, or in addition to, the original.

(7) The Commission shall give general notice of the place or places where, and the times when, reports may be inspected under subsection (5).

Section 60

Reports of investigations are thus available to the public (on payment of a reasonable fee) unless the Secretary of State orders otherwise.

See section 51 RRA.

Restriction on disclosure of information.

61.–(1) No information given to the Commission by any person ("the informant") in connection with a formal investigation shall be disclosed by the Commission, or by any person who is or has been a Commissioner, additional Commissioner or employee of the Commission, except–

(a) on the order of any court, or

(b) with the informant's consent, or

(c) in the form of a summary or other general statement published by the Commission which does not identify the informant or any other person to whom the information relates, or

(d) in a report of the investigation published by the Commission or made available for inspection under section 60(5), or

(e) to the Commissioners, additional Commissioners or employees of the Commission, or, so far as may be necessary for the proper performance of the functions of the Commission, to other persons, or

(f) or the purpose of any civil proceedings under this Act to which the Commission are a party, or any criminal proceedings.

(2) Any person who discloses information in contravention of subsection (1) commits an offence and shall be liable on summary conviction to a fine not exceeding level 5 on the standard scale.

(3) In preparing any report for publication or for inspection the Commission shall exclude, so far as is consistent with their duties and the object of the report, any matter which relates to the private affairs of any individual or business interests of any person where the publication of that matter might, in the opinion of the Commission, prejudicially affect that individual or person.

Section 58-61

These sections govern the conditions under which formal investigations under section 57 are conducted.

The restrictions on disclosure in section 61 are designed to encourage people to give evidence freely without fear that anything they may say will be published (unless, of course, they consent).

See section 52 RRA.

PART VII ENFORCEMENT

GENERAL

Restriction of proceedings for breach of Act

62.–(1) Except as provided by this Act no proceedings, whether civil or criminal, shall lie against any person in respect of an act by reason that the act is unlawful by virtue of a provision of this Act.

Section 62(1)

This ensures that a person or body does not face double liability under this Act and under other provisions.

(2) Subsection (1) does not preclude the making of an order of certiorari, mandamus or prohibition.

> **Section 62(2)**
> *Preserves the powers of the Courts to issue injunctions or compelling orders to prevent unlawful acts.*

(3) In Scotland, subsection (1) does not preclude the exercise of the jurisdiction of the Court of Session to entertain an application for reduction or suspension of any order or determination, or otherwise to consider the validity of any order or determination, or to require reasons for any order or determination to be stated.

> **Section 62(3)**
> *Preserves the same powers for the Scottish courts to make equivalent orders to those referred to in subsection (2) above.*
>
> *The same limitations appear in section 53 RRA.*

ENFORCEMENT IN EMPLOYMENT FIELD

Jurisdiction of employment tribunals

63.–(1) A complaint by any person ("the complainant") that another person ("the respondent")–

(a) has committed an act of discrimination against the complainant which is unlawful by virtue of Part II, or

(b) is by virtue of section 41 or 42 to be treated as having committed such an act of discrimination against the complainant,

may be presented to an employment tribunal.

> **Section 63(1)**
> *Time limits within which such applications are to be made are set out in section 76 (section 68 RRA).*
>
> *At the present time, the burden of proof in a sex discrimination case is generally on the complainant following the general legal principle that the person who alleges must prove. However, a European Directive of 15 December 1997 requires member states to take action to ensure that the burden of proof should shift to the Respondent where the court or tribunal has sufficient evidence to form a presumption that there has been direct or indirect discrimination.*
>
> *Once prima facie case has been made out the court or tribunal should presume that the less favourable treatment was on the grounds of the applicant's sex unless the respondent can prove that it was attributable to some other factor.*

No measures have yet been taken or announced by the UK government to transpose this Directive into UK law but, by article 7 of that directive, such measures must be adopted in the UK by 22nd July 2001.

Where the allegation is one of indirect discrimination and the Respondent seeks to show that the requirement or condition was justifiable under section 1(1)(b)(ii), the burden is then on the respondent to prove that it is justifiable.

Similarly where an employment agency seeks to show that they were acting in reliance on a statement made by the principal employer (section 15) or a publisher seeks to rely on the same defence in relation to a discriminatory advertisement (under section 38), it is for that person to prove that they relied on the statement and that it was reasonable for them to rely on the statement.

In deciding whether discrimination is proved a court or tribunal is entitled to draw inferences from the evidence where it is appropriate to do so. If the employer cannot or will not provide a credible explanation for the treatment or their replies, either in evidence or stated in the questionnaire, are misleading or evasive adverse inferences might be justifiably drawn.

It should be remembered that discrimination on the grounds of her sex is less favourable treatment than the treatment that employer would have meted out to a person of the other sex. It is irrelevant whether or not the employer acted reasonably. A wholly unreasonable employer may have treated everyone just as badly. If that is the case then a claim that a woman was discriminated against on the grounds of her sex will fail. She will only succeed if a man would have been treated differently.

It is also important to note that there does not have to be a conscious intention to discriminate. One of the intentions of anti-discrimination legislation is to try to stop people making decisions on assumptions which have no basis in fact. An employer who decides not to give a particular job to a woman because the stress is inherent in the job would be too much for a woman with primary responsibility for the care of two school aged children would be discriminating against her on the grounds of her sex even if he thought he was doing so for the best of reasons.

The tribunal's powers to conduct the proceedings are regulated in the same way as claims for unfair dismissal under the Employment Tribunals Act 1996 and the Employment Tribunals (Constitution and Rules of Procedure) Regulations 1993 [SI 1993/2687]. The Constitution deals with the appointment of tribunal members and Chairmen.

There is a whole body of case law dealing with tribunal procedure which is too extensive to review in a work of this kind. Apart from the differences in legal terminology, the regulations which govern tribunals in Scotland are the same (see the Employment Tribunals (Constitution and Rules of Procedure)(Scotland) Regulations 1993 [SI 1993/2688].

Brief reference will be made to those procedural matters which are more commonly, or sometimes exclusively, associated with discrimination claims:–

Direct evidence of discrimination is often difficult to find. The Respondent will try to explain apparent differences in treatment as being attributable to other factors. In order to clarify the basis of the employer's defence, a complainant may submit a questionnaire in a prescribed form and the Respondent will given time in which to reply. Further reference will be made to this under section 74 below (section 65 RRA).

Unlike in other court proceedings, there is no requirement for the parties to produce lists of all documents they have or had. The parties are free to produce those documents which help their case but they must not be unfairly selective in doing so. If part of a document is produced the other party is entitled to see the whole of it.

If a party knows of the existence of one or more documents the tribunal may be asked for an order compelling the other party to produce it. Before making such an order the tribunal will want to be satisfied that the document is relevant to the proceedings and that it is reasonable for them to make the order. It may be unreasonable if, for example, the documents have been destroyed or they have been archived and retrieval would be expensive or burdensome. However, the more important the document the greater the inconvenience and expense of producing it will be justified.

In cases which involve allegations of sexual misconduct, or a case under the Disability Discrimination Act 1995 in which evidence of a personal nature is to be given, the tribunal has power to make an order that the parties are not identified. The power, under rule 14, only extends to the promulgation of the tribunal's decision but such an order does afford a degree of anonymity while evidence is being given.

(2) Subsection (1) does not apply to a complaint under section 13(1) of an act in respect of which an appeal, or proceedings in the nature of an appeal, may be brought under any enactment.

Section 63(2)
This deals with qualification or authorisation for entry to a profession. If a statutory right of appeal exists against a refusal to confer the authorisation or qualification, that right is to be used rather than a complaint to a tribunal.

See section 54 RRA.

Conciliation in employment cases.

Section 64
The provisions set out below were originally in this section but were repealed and re-enacted in section 18(2),(3), (6) and (7) of the Employment Tribunals Act 1996:–

"Where a complaint has been presented to an industrial tribunal under section 63, or under section 2(1) of the Equal Pay Act 1970, and a copy of the complaint has been sent to a conciliation officer, it shall be the duty of the conciliation officer–

(a) if he is requested to do so both by the complainant and the respondent, or
(b) if, in the absence of requests by the complainant and the respondent, he considers that he could act under this subsection with a reasonable prospect of success,

to endeavour to promote a settlement of the complaint without its being determined by an industrial tribunal."

Remedies on complaint under section 63.

65.–(1) Where an industrial tribunal finds that a complaint presented to it under section 63 is well-founded the tribunal shall make such of the following as it considers just and equitable–

(a) an order declaring the rights of the complainant and the respondent in relation to the act to which the complaint relates;
(b) an order requiring the respondent to pay to the complainant compensation of an amount corresponding to any damages he could have been ordered by a county court or by a sheriff court to pay to the complainant if the complaint had fallen to be dealt with under section 66;
(c) a recommendation that the respondent take within a specified period action appearing to the tribunal to be practicable for the purpose of obviating or reducing the adverse effect on the complainant of any act of discrimination to which the complaint relates.

Section 65(1)(a)–(c)

(a) A declaration may be appropriate before an act of discrimination has occurred. For example, a mobility clause in a contract of employment may have a disproportionate effect on women because of their child-care responsibilities. A tribunal would be entitled to declare that, if the employer were to rely on that clause and require a female employee to move, it would be indirectly discriminatory.

(b) Compensation is usually ordered to be paid where a tribunal finds that a person has been discriminated against. That compensation can include loss of earnings, which may result from a dismissal or from a failure to appoint somebody to a more highly paid post; it may include compensation for the loss of the opportunity to be appointed to a more senior post where a person was prevented from applying and will almost always include a sum for injury to feelings.

It is not possible to give guidance on the level of damages which might be awarded under this head because of the enormous variety of individual circumstances. It should be noted, however, that a tribunal does have power to award aggravated damages where an employer's conduct is held to be particularly blameworthy or the conduct complained of particularly serious. Such an award may also be appropriate where, even though the original conduct complained of is not so serious, the employer's conduct of the proceedings themselves, for example, raising spurious allegations of misconduct or incompetence, merits such an award.

There will be cases where the victim of discrimination actually suffers stress or possibly even psychiatric injury as a result of the treatment she receives. In such cases the tribunal also has the power to award damages for personal injury. Where such injury has occurred, it is important that the claim is included in the tribunal proceedings. Medical evidence will almost certainly be required as to the nature of the injury and a tribunal will probably give directions as to how and when such medical evidence should be produced.

A separate claim for personal injury pursued in the ordinary courts will not be permitted once the tribunal case has concluded because of the general rule that all matters which could have been raised in a particular set of proceedings should have been raised. A failure to raise them at the appropriate time and an attempt to raise them in separate proceedings later will be regarded as an abuse of the process of the Court.

Exemplary damages, which are intended to punish the offender rather than compensate the victim, are not permitted.

As in other cases involving claims for damages, a complainant is required to take reasonable steps to mitigate any loss suffered. A tribunal must also consider whether to award interest on any damages. This is so whether or not the parties claim interest.

Interest is awarded under different heads of damage at different rates and for different periods. In a work of this kind it is not possible to set out all of the provisions for interest and detailed advice should be taken.

(c) The purpose of a recommendation is to remove the adverse consequences of the employer's action. This does not extend to a recommendation to increase the pay of a complainant. That must be covered by an order for compensation under subsection (b).

A recommendation could include the removal of conditions for appointment to a particular post, where those conditions are held to be discriminatory. It may also include the provision of training so that the complainant is not disadvantaged in future.

It does not include the power to recommend that the complainant be appointed to the next available post.

A failure to comply with a recommendation is dealt with under subsection (3) below.

(1A) In applying section 66 for the purposes of subsection (1)(b), no account shall be taken of subsection (3) of that section.

Section 65(1A)
Whether or not the employer intended to discriminate against the complainant on the ground of his or her sex, compensation is payable.

Appeals against decisions of employment tribunals may be made to the Employment Appeal Tribunal but only where the employment tribunal made an error of law. The detailed requirements for appeals and the procedural rules to be followed are outside of the scope of this work and specialist advice should be sought.

(1B) As respects an unlawful act of discrimination falling within section 1(1)(b) or section 3(1)(b), if the respondent proves that the requirement or condition in question was not applied with the intention of treating the complainant unfavourably on the ground of his sex or marital status as the case may be, an order may be made under subsection (1)(b) only if the employment tribunal–

(a) makes such order under subsection (1)(a) and such recommendation under subsection (1)(c) (if any) as it would have made if it had no power to make an order under subsection (1)(b); and

(b) (where it makes an order under subsection (1)(a) or a recommendation under subsection (1)(c) or both) considers that it is just and equitable to make an order under subsection (1)(b) as well.

(2) ...

Section 65(2)
There was a limit on the amount that could be awarded but that limit was removed in response to a decision of the European Court of Justice that the limit failed to provide an effective remedy for persons who had been discriminated against.

(3) If without reasonable justification the respondent to a complaint fails to comply with a recommendation made by an employment tribunal under subsection (1)(c), then, if they think it just and equitable to do so–

(a) the tribunal may increase the amount of compensation required to be paid to the complainant in respect of the complaint by an order made under subsection (1)(b), or

(b) if an order under subsection (1)(b) was not made, the tribunal may make such an order.

Section 65(3)
See section 56 RRA.

ENFORCEMENT OF PART III

Claims under Part III.

66.–(1) A claim by any person ("the claimant") that another person ("the respondent")–

(a) has committed an act of discrimination against the claimant which is unlawful by virtue of Part III, or

(b) is by virtue of section 41 or 42 to be treated as having committed such an act of discrimination against the claimant,

may be made the subject of civil proceedings in like manner as any other claim in tort or (in Scotland) in reparation for breach of statutory duty.

(2) Proceedings under subsection (1)–

(a) shall be brought in England and Wales only in a county court, and

(b) shall be brought in Scotland only in a sheriff court,

but all such remedies shall be obtainable in such proceedings as, apart from this subsection and section 62(1), would be obtainable in the High Court or the Court of Session, as the case may be.

Section 66(2)

All claims other than employment claims must be made in a county court (or a sheriff court in Scotland) regardless of their potential value. The normal financial limits for starting proceedings in the High Court do not apply to discrimination claims.

Under the Civil Procedure Rules ("CPR") (Schedule 2 CCR Order 49) a person bringing such a complaint must give notice of the proceedings to the EOC and file with the court a copy of that notice. A failure to do so may result in the action being struck out.

(3) As respects an unlawful act of discrimination falling within section 1(1)(b) no award of damages shall be made if the respondent proves that the requirement or condition in question was not applied with the intention of treating the claimant unfavourably on the ground of his sex.

Section 66(3)

Courts are not slow to find such intention where a requirement condition was applied with full knowledge of its discriminatory effect.

(4) For the avoidance of doubt it is hereby declared that damages in respect of an unlawful act of discrimination may include compensation for injury to feelings whether or not they include compensation under any other head.

Section 66(4)

See the note to section 65(1)(b) above in relation to claims for personal injury arising out of acts of discrimination.

(5) Civil proceedings in respect of a claim by any person that he has been discriminated against in contravention of section 22 or 23 by a body to which section 25(1) applies shall not be instituted unless the claimant has given notice of the claim to the Secretary of State and either the Secretary of State has by notice informed the claimant that the Secretary of State does not require further time to consider the matter, or the period of two months has elapsed since the claimant gave notice to the Secretary of State; but nothing in this subsection applies to a counterclaim.

Section 66(5)

This sub-section relates to education and corresponds to section 57(5) SDA. It gives the Secretary of State the right to pursue the complaint since any act of discrimination in respect of the provision of education is likely to have much wider application than the individual case and it would be reasonable for the Secretary of State to take on that burden rather than leaving it to an individual.

(5A) In Scotland, when any proceedings are brought under this section, in addition to the service on the defender of a copy of the summons or initial writ initiating the action a copy thereof shall be sent as soon as practicable to the Commission in a manner to be prescribed by Act of Sederunt.

(6) For the purposes of proceedings under subsection (1)–

(a) section 63(1) (assessors) of the County Courts Act 1984 shall apply with the omission of the words "on the application of any party", and

(b) the remuneration of assessors appointed under the said section 63(1) shall be at such rate as may be determined by the Lord Chancellor with the approval of the Minister for the Civil Service.

(7) For the purpose of proceedings before the sheriff, provision may be made by Act of Sederunt for the appointment of assessors by him, and the remuneration of any assessors so appointed shall be at such rate as the Lord President of the Court of Session with the approval of the Minister for the Civil Service may determine.

(8) A county court or sheriff court shall have jurisdiction to entertain proceedings under subsection (1) with respect to an act done on a ship, aircraft or hovercraft outside its district, including such an act done outside Great Britain.

Section 65(8)
The remedies available in courts are the same and compensation is calculated in exactly the same way as in employment tribunals so the reader is referred to the note to section 65 above.

While all employment tribunals are capable of hearing discrimination claims, certain county courts have been designated by the Lord Chancellor to have jurisdiction over discrimination claims. A list of such courts can be found in the County Court Directory. The court's procedure is governed by the Civil Procedure Rules 1998 under which any person bringing a claim of discrimination under this section must notify the EOC that the proceedings have been commenced.

A Judge hearing a claim must sit with two assessors unless each party consents to the Judge hearing the case alone.

The names and qualifications of the assessors must be notified to the parties in advance and either party can object to the appointment of a particular assessor.

The assessor's role is to advise the Judge but it is only the Judge who will make the decision in the case.

Except in relation to sub-section (8) (which appears at section 67(3) RRA) see also section 57 RRA.

NON-DISCRIMINATION NOTICES

Issue of non-discrimination notice.

67.–(1) This section applies to–

(a) an unlawful discriminatory act, and

(b) a contravention of section 37, and

(c) a contravention of section 38, 39 or 40, and

(d) an act in breach of a term modified or included by virtue of an equality clause, and so applies whether or not proceedings have been brought in respect of the act.

Section 67(1)(b) – (d)
(b) operating a discriminatory practice

(c) discriminatory advertisements, instructions or pressure to discriminate

(d) This gives the EOC power to act even if no individual is willing to bring a claim.

(2) If in the course of a formal investigation the Commission become satisfied that a person is committing, or has committed, any such acts, the Commission may in the prescribed manner serve on him a notice in the prescribed form ("a non-discrimination notice") requiring him–

(a) not to commit any such acts, and
(b) where compliance with paragraph (a) involves changes in any of his practices or other arrangements–
  (i) to inform the Commission that he has effected those changes and what those changes are, and
  (ii) to take such steps as may be reasonably required by the notice for the purpose of affording that information to other persons concerned.

(3) A non-discrimination notice may also require the person on whom it is served to furnish the Commission with such other information as may be reasonably required by the notice in order to verify that the notice has been complied with.

(4) The notice may specify the time at which, and the manner and form in which, any information is to be furnished to the Commission, but the time at which any information is to be furnished in compliance with the notice shall not be later than five years after the notice has become final.

Section 67 (2) – (4)
The non-discrimination notice may require the person receiving it to provide the commission with information. This is so that the Commission may be able to ascertain whether or not the discrimination has been eliminated. The person concerned can be required to furnish that information up to five years after the notice is issued and to convey that information to others, for example, those who may have been affected by the discriminatory practices which gave rise to the issue of the notice. However, there are requirements which must be complied with before the notice can be issued. See subsection (5) below.

(5) The Commission shall not serve a non-discrimination notice in respect of any person unless they have first–

(a) given him notice that they are minded to issue a non-discrimination notice in his case, specifying the grounds on which they contemplate doing so, and
(b) offered him an opportunity of making oral or written representations in the matter (or both oral and written representations if he thinks fit) within a period of not less than 28 days specified in the notice, and
(c) taken account of any representations so made by him.

(6) Subsection (2) does not apply to any acts in respect of which the Secretary of State could exercise the powers conferred on him by section 25(2) and (3); but if the Commission become aware of any such acts they shall give notice of them to the Secretary of State.

Section 67(6)
The EOC cannot issue a non-discrimination notice against an education authority in the public sector since that power is reserved to the Secretary of State. If, during the course of an investigation, the EOC comes across evidence that such discrimination is taking place it must notify the Secretary of State.

(7) Section 59(4) shall apply to requirements under subsection (2)(b), (3) and (4) contained in a non-discrimination notice which has become final as it applies to requirements in a notice served under section 59(1).

Section 67(7)
This refers to the EOCs ability to apply to the court for an order that the person shall comply with an order to provide information.

See section 58 RRA.

Appeal against non-discrimination notice.

68.–(1) Not later than six weeks after a non–discrimination notice is served on any person he may appeal against any requirement of the notice–

(a) to an employment tribunal, so far as the requirement relates to acts which are within the jurisdiction of the tribunal;

(b) to a county court or to a sheriff court so far as the requirement relates to acts which are within the jurisdiction of the court and are not within the jurisdiction of an employment tribunal.

(2) Where the court or tribunal considers a requirement in respect of which an appeal is brought under subsection (1) to be unreasonable because it is based on an incorrect finding of fact or for any other reason, the court or tribunal shall quash the requirement.

(3) On quashing a requirement under subsection (2) the court or tribunal may direct that the non-discrimination notice shall be treated as if, in place of the requirement quashed, it had contained a requirement in terms specified in the direction.

Section 68(3)
If the appeal against the non-discrimination notice is upheld the court or tribunal may substitute its own terms.

(4) Subsection (1) does not apply to a requirement treated as included in a non-discrimination notice by virtue of a direction under subsection (3).

Section 68(4)
There is no appeal against the non-discrimination notice as substituted during the process of appeal.

The appeal must specify each of the findings of fact set out in non-discrimination notice which are appealed against and to set out the positive case which the person appealing intends to prove at the appeal.

The non-discrimination notice becomes final either when the time for lodging an appeal has passed without an appeal being lodged or on the disposal of the appeal if the court or tribunal substitutes different requirements in that notice.

See section 59 RRA.

Investigation as to compliance with non-discrimination notice.

69.–(1) If–

(a) the terms of reference of a formal investigation state that its purpose is to determine whether any requirements of a non-discrimination notice are being or have been carried out, but section 59(2)(b) does not apply, and

(b) section 58(3) is complied with in relation to the investigation on a date ("the commencement date") not later than the expiration of the period of five years beginning when the non–discrimination notice became final,

the Commission may within the period referred to in subsection (2) serve notices under section 59(1) for the purposes of the investigation without needing to obtain the consent of the Secretary of State.

Section 69(1)(a) – (b)
i.e. there is a belief stated in the terms of reference for the investigation that a named person is doing the act made unlawful by the SDA.

Such an investigation must begin within five years of the non-discrimination notice becoming final.

(2) The said period begins on the commencement date and ends on the later of the following dates–

(a) the date on which the period of five years mentioned in subsection (1)(b) expires;

(b) the date two years after the commencement date.

Section 69(2)
This means that the investigation must be completed within two years of its commencement or within five years of the date the non-discrimination notice became final.

See section 60 RRA.

Register of non-discrimination notices.

70.–(1) The Commission shall establish and maintain a register ("the register") of non-discrimination notices which have become final.

(2) Any person shall be entitled, on payment of such fee (if any) as may be determined by the Commission,–

(a) to inspect the register during ordinary office hours and take copies of any entry, or

(b) to obtain from the Commission a copy, certified by the Commission to be correct, of any entry in the register.

(3) The Commission may, if they think fit, determine that the right conferred by subsection (2)(a) shall be exercisable in relation to a copy of the register instead of, or in addition to, the original.

(4) The Commission shall give general notice of the place or places where, and the times when, the register or a copy of it may be inspected.

Section 70

All non-discrimination notices are accessible to members of the public on payment of a fee.

See section 61 RRA.

OTHER ENFORCEMENT BY COMMISSION

Persistent discrimination.

71.–(1) If, during the period of five years beginning on the date on which either of the following became final in the case of any person, namely,–

(a) a non-discrimination notice served on him,

(b) a finding by a court or tribunal under section 63 or 66, or section 2 of the Equal Pay Act 1970, that he has done an unlawful discriminatory act or an act in breach of a term modified or included by virtue of an equality clause,

it appears to the Commission that unless restrained he is likely to do one or more acts falling within paragraph (b), or contravening section 37, the Commission may apply to a county court for an injunction, or to the sheriff court for an order, restraining him from doing so; and the court, if satisfied that the application is well-founded, may grant the injunction or order in the terms applied for or in more limited terms.

(2) In proceedings under this section the Commission shall not allege that the person to whom the proceedings relate has done an act which is within the jurisdiction of an employment tribunal unless a finding by an employment tribunal that he did that act has become final.

Section 71
It would be inappropriate to grant an injunction if the terms of the non-discrimination notice are being appealed

Where there is no individual complaint, damages will not be awarded and a person who is merely served with a non-discrimination notice might be inclined not to comply with any requirement in that notice. This provision allows an application for an injunction to be made, either to the county court or to the sheriff court. If the court is satisfied that the person is likely to continue to do discriminatory acts it may grant an order in specific terms prohibiting that person from doing that act or those acts. A breach of an injunction would be a contempt of Court and is punishable, possibly by imprisonment

See section 62 RRA.

Enforcement of ss. 38 to 40.

72.–(1) Proceedings in respect of a contravention of section 38, 39 or 40 shall be brought only by the Commission in accordance with the following provisions of this section.

Section 72(1)
38 deals with discriminatory advertisements, 39 with instructions to discriminate and 40 with pressure to discriminate.

(2) The proceedings shall be–
(a) an application for a decision whether the alleged contravention occurred, or
(b) an application under subsection (4) below, or both.

(3) An application under subsection (2)(a) shall be made–
(a) in a case based on any provision of Part II, to an employment tribunal, and
(b) in any other case to a county court or sheriff court.

(4) If it appears to the Commission–
(a) that a person has done an act which by virtue of section 38, 39 or 40 was unlawful, and
(b) that unless restrained he is likely to do further acts which by virtue of that section are unlawful,

the Commission may apply to a county court for an injunction, or to a sheriff court for an order, restraining him from doing such acts; and the court, if satisfied that the application is well-founded, may grant the injunction or order in the terms applied for or more limited terms.

Section 72(4)
See the note to section 71 above.

(5) In proceedings under subsection (4) the Commission shall not allege that the person to whom the proceedings relate has done an act which is unlawful under this Act and within the jurisdiction of an employment tribunal unless a finding by an employment tribunal that he did that act has become final.

Section 72(5)
See the note to section 71(2) above.

See section 63 RRA.

Preliminary action in employment cases.

73.–(1) With a view to making an application under section 71(1) or 72(4) in relation to a person the Commission may present to an employment tribunal a complaint that he has done an act within the jurisdiction of an employment tribunal, and if the tribunal considers that the complaint is well–founded they shall make a finding to that effect and, if they think it just and equitable to do so in the case of an act contravening any provision of Part II may also (as if the complaint had been presented by the person discriminated against) make an order such as is referred to in section 65(1)(a), or a recommendation such as is referred to in section 65(1)(c), or both.

Section 73(1)
The tribunal cannot, of course, make an award of compensation where there is no individual complainant.

(2) Subsection (1) is without prejudice to the jurisdiction conferred by section 72(2).

Section 73(2)
Exercising the right to make such an application to the tribunal does not prevent the Commission from seeking an injunction from the county court or from the sheriff court.

(3) Any finding of an employment tribunal under–

(a) this Act, or
(b) the Equal Pay Act 1970,

in respect of any act shall, if it has become final, be treated as conclusive–

(i) by the county court or sheriff court on an application under section 71(1) or 72(4) or in proceedings on an equality clause,
(ii) by an employment tribunal on a complaint made by the person affected by the act under section 63 or in relation to an equality clause.

Section 73(3)
In other words, no further evidence that the offender has committed the acts will be necessary and the offender will not be able to produce evidence intending to show that he has not committed those acts.

(4) In sections 71 and 72 and this section, the acts "within the jurisdiction of an employment tribunal" are those in respect of which such jurisdiction is conferred by sections 63 and 72 and by section 2 of the Equal Pay Act 1970.

Section 73(4)
With the exception of sub-section (3) (which appears as section 69 RRA), see section 64 RRA.

HELP FOR PERSONS SUFFERING DISCRIMINATION

Help for aggrieved persons in obtaining information etc.

74.–(1) With a view to helping a person ("the person aggrieved") who considers he may have been discriminated against in contravention of this Act to decide whether to institute proceedings and, if he does so, to formulate and present his case in the most effective manner, the Secretary of State shall by order prescribe–

(a) forms by which the person aggrieved may question the respondent on his reasons for doing any relevant act, or on any other matter which is or may be relevant;

(b) forms by which the respondent may if he so wishes reply to any questions.

Section 74(1)
These are the questionnaires, referred to in the note to Section 63(1) above, which a complainant may serve on a Respondent to a claim and the forms on which the Respondent may reply.

(2) Where the person aggrieved questions the respondent (whether in accordance with an order under subsection (1) or not)–

(a) the question, and any reply by the respondent (whether in accordance with such an order or not) shall, subject to the following provisions of this section, be admissible as evidence in the proceedings;

(b) if it appears to the court or tribunal that the respondent deliberately, and without reasonable excuse, omitted to reply within a reasonable period or that his reply is evasive or equivocal, the court or tribunal may draw any inference from that fact that it considers it just and equitable to draw, including an inference that he committed an unlawful act.

Section 74(2)
This is a way of 'encouraging' a respondent to a claim to treat the questionnaires seriously and to answer reasonably promptly. Note that the tribunal is not obliged to draw an adverse inference but the replies or lack of them are part of the picture the tribunal must consider when determining the case.

(3) The Secretary of State may by order–

(a) prescribe the period within which questions must be duly served in order to be admissible under subsection (2)(a), and
(b) prescribe the manner in which a question, and any reply by the respondent, may be duly served.

(4) Rules may enable the court entertaining a claim under section 66 to determine, before the date fixed for the hearing of the claim, whether a question or reply is admissible under this section or not.

(5) This section is without prejudice to any other enactment or rule of law regulating interlocutory and preliminary matters in proceedings before a county court, sheriff court or employment tribunal, and has effect subject to any enactment or rule of law regulating the admissibility of evidence in such proceedings.

Section 74 (4) & (5)
It may be that a respondent will consider the questions inappropriate or irrelevant. These subsections allow the court or tribunal to decide ahead of the hearing whether to order that the questions be answered or whether any reply will be admissible in the proceedings. The normal rules in court or tribunal proceedings regulating the production and admissibility of documents continue to apply.

(6) In this section "respondent" includes a prospective respondent and "rules"–

(a) in relation to county court proceedings, means county court rules;
(b) in relation to sheriff court proceedings, means sheriff court rules.

Section 74(6)
Because the questionnaires may be submitted before the claim is made this subsection applies the rules to those who may be the subject of a claim.

See the Sex Discrimination (Questions and Replies) Order 1975, SI 1975/2048.

See section 65 RRA.

Assistance by Commission.

75.–(1) Where, in relation to proceedings or prospective proceedings either under this Act or in respect of an equality clause, an individual who is an actual or prospective complainant or claimant applies to the Commission for assistance under this section, the Commission shall consider the application and may grant it if they think fit to do so on the ground that–

(a) the case raises a question of principle, or

(b) it is unreasonable, having regard to the complexity of the case or the applicant's position in relation to the respondent or another person involved or any other matter, to expect the applicant to deal with the case unaided,

or by reason of any other special consideration.

(2) Assistance by the Commission under this section may include–

(a) giving advice;

(b) procuring or attempting to procure the settlement of any matter in dispute;

(c) arranging for the giving of advice or assistance by a solicitor or counsel;

(d) arranging for representation by any person including all such assistance as is usually given by a solicitor or counsel in the steps preliminary or incidental to any proceedings, or in arriving at or giving effect to a compromise to avoid or bring to an end any proceedings,

(e) any other form of assistance which the Commission may consider appropriate,

but paragraph (d) shall not affect the law and practice regulating the descriptions of persons who may appear in, conduct, defend and address the court in, any proceedings.

Section 75 (1) & (2)

Under these sections, the Commission may give advice on pursuing a claim and help a complainant to seek a settlement or submit an application. It may go on to provide legal representation at the hearing in the case but other rules and practice govern who may appear in Court and the fact that the Commission has provided representation does not grant that person rights of audience in the courts.

Section 66 (1) and (2) RRA.

(3) In so far as expenses are incurred by the Commission in providing the applicant with assistance under this section the recovery of those expenses (as taxed or assessed in such manner as may be prescribed by rules or regulations) shall constitute a first charge for the benefit of the Commission–

(a) on any costs or expenses which (whether by virtue of a judgment or order of a court or tribunal or an agreement or otherwise) are payable to the applicant by any other person in respect of the matter in connection with which the assistance is given, and

(b) so far as relates to any costs or expenses, on his rights under any compromise or settlement arrived at in connection with that matter to avoid or bring to an end any proceedings.

Section 75(3)
If a person is assisted by the EOC and obtains an order at the end of the hearing that the respondent should pay her legal costs, the EOC can recover its costs from that award or from any settlement reached between the parties in order to avoid a hearing or the claim being filed with the court or tribunal. For this reason, subsection (5) below defines respondent as including prospective respondent.

Section 66(3) RRA.

(4) The charge conferred by subsection (3) is subject to any charge under the Legal Aid Act 1988 *[imposed by section 10(7) of the Access to Justice Act 1999]*, or any charge or obligation for payment in priority to other debts under the Legal Aid (Scotland) Act 1986, and is subject to any provision in, or made under, either of those Acts for payment of any sum to the Legal Aid Board *[Legal Services Commission]* or into the Scottish Legal Aid Fund.

Section 75(4)
The words underlined are to be replaced by those in italics in square brackets from a day to be appointed.

See section 66(6) RRA.

(5) In this section "respondent" includes a prospective respondent and "rules or regulations"–
(a) in relation to county court proceedings, means county court rules;
(b) in relation to sheriff court proceedings, means sheriff court rules;
(c) in relation to employment tribunal proceedings, means regulations made under Part I of the Employment Tribunals Act 1996.

Section 75(5)
See section 66(7) RRA.

PERIOD WITHIN WHICH PROCEEDINGS TO BE BROUGHT

Period within which proceedings to be brought.

76.–(1) An industrial tribunal shall not consider a complaint under section 63 unless it is presented to the tribunal before the end of–
(a) the period of three months beginning when the act complained of was done; or
(b) in a case to which section 85(9A) applies, the period of six months so beginning.

Section 76(1)
Relates to complaints by members of the armed forces.

(2) A county court or a sheriff court shall not consider a claim under section 66 unless proceedings in respect of the claim are instituted before the end of–
(a) the period of six months beginning when the act complained of was done; or
(b) in a case to which section 66(5) applies, the period of eight months so beginning.

Section 76(2)
Relates to discrimination in public sector education.

(3) An employment tribunal, county court or sheriff court shall not consider an application under section 72(2)(a) unless it is made before the end of the period of six months beginning when the act to which it relates was done; and a county court or sheriff court shall not consider an application under section 72(4) unless it is made before the end of the period of five years so beginning.

Section 76(3)
This relates to discriminatory advertisements and to instructions and pressure to discriminate.

(4) An employment tribunal shall not consider a complaint under section 73(1) unless it is presented to the tribunal before the end of the period of six months beginning when the act complained of was done.

Section 76(4)
Preliminary action before seeking an injunction.

(5) A court or tribunal may nevertheless consider any such complaint, claim or application which is out of time if, in all the circumstances of the case, it considers that it is just and equitable to do so.

Section 76(5)
This subsection allows quite a wide discretion to extend the time limits. The discretion is much wider than that for ordinary employment tribunal claims where, in order to extend the time, the tribunal must first find that it was' not reasonably practicable' for the claim to be brought in time (section 111(2)(b) Employment Rights Act 1996)

The claim must be received by the tribunal within the time limit so a complaint about an act which took place on the 14th of February, for example, must be received by the tribunal on or before 13th May.

(6) For the purposes of this section–

(a) where the inclusion of any term in a contract renders the making of the contract an unlawful act that act shall be treated as extending throughout the duration of the contract, and

(b) any act extending over a period shall be treated as done at the end of that period, and

(c) a deliberate omission shall be treated as done when the person in question decided upon it, and in the absence of evidence establishing the contrary a person shall be taken for the purposes of this section to decide upon an omission when he does an act inconsistent with doing the omitted act or, if he has done no such inconsistent act, when the period expires within which he might reasonably have been expected to do the omitted act if it was to be done.

Section 76(6) (a) – (c)

(a). The complaint may therefore be made at any time up to three months after the termination of the employment.

(b) & (c). It is important to distinguish between these two provisions. A policy or rule which was operated in a discriminatory manner would be a continuing act under sub-section (b). However, a refusal or an omission to provide a benefit would be dealt with under subsection (c). So if, by the operation of a rule or policy, a person was prevented from applying for promotion to a particular post by a discriminatory rule, that would be a continuing act. If the person was allowed to make the application but, for discriminatory reasons, was not appointed to the post, that would be a one off act or omission and would be dealt with under subsection (c).

Difficulty may arise in cases of repeated refusal. It may be necessary to consider whether the subsequent refusals are merely the reiteration of an earlier decision or result from reconsideration of circumstances. The repeated refusal based on an earlier decision would result in time running from the date the first decision was made. The refusal based on a reconsideration of the circumstances would mean that time ran from the date of the subsequent decision.

Where a claim is being made under a provision of European law, the time limits are usually those laid down in national law for similar claims so the above paragraphs would apply. However, if the claim is brought by an employee in the public sector or is being brought by an employee against the state for a failure to implement the provisions of European directive, the time limit cannot begin to run until the member state has complied with its obligations under the directive. In other words, time only begins to run once the provisions of national law comply fully with the requirements of European law. In these circumstances, a claim can be made some considerable time after the act complained of has taken place.

If the claim is being brought against the state for a failure to implement the terms of a European Directive, the claim must be made in the High Court or County Court. An employment tribunal has no jurisdiction to hear such claims.

With the exception of provisions relating to European law see section 68 RRA.

PART VIII

SUPPLEMENTAL

Validity and revision of contracts.

77.–(1) A term of a contract is void where–

(a) its inclusion renders the making of the contract unlawful by virtue of this Act, or
(b) it is included in furtherance of an act rendered unlawful by this Act, or
(c) it provides for the doing of an act which would be rendered unlawful by this Act.

Section 77(1)
It is not possible to include a term in a contract which permits unlawful discrimination. This section renders such a term void so as to preserve the rest of the contract.

(2) Subsection (1) does not apply to a term the inclusion of which constitutes, or is in furtherance of, or provides for, unlawful discrimination against a party to the contract, but the term shall be unenforceable against that party.

Section 77(2)
If the whole of the term were to be void, any benefit conferred on a party to a contract as part of an unlawful clause would also be rendered void. This subsection allows the party who would benefit under that clause to retain the benefit while rendering the discriminatory provisions of that clause unenforceable against him or her.

(3) A term in a contract which purports to exclude or limit any provision of this Act or the Equal Pay Act 1970 is unenforceable by any person in whose favour the term would operate apart from this subsection.

Section 77(3)
It is not possible under the act to prevent a person from bringing a claim in a Court or tribunal under this act unless subsection (4) applies.

(4) Subsection (3) does not apply–

(a) to a contract settling a complaint to which section 63(1) of this Act or section 2 of the Equal Pay Act 1970 applies where the contract is made with the assistance of a conciliation officer;

(aa) to a contract settling a complaint to which section 63(l) of this Act or section 2 of the Equal Pay Act 1970 applies if the conditions regulating compromise contracts under this Act are satisfied in relation to the contract;

(b) to a contract settling a claim to which section 66 applies.

Section 77(4) (a) – (b)

(a). If a conciliation officer employed by the Advisory Conciliation and Arbitration Service (ACAS) is involved in discussions between the parties for the purpose of settling a claim brought under this Act or under the Equal Pay Act, any agreement reached as a consequence will be recorded on a form which ACAS produced for this purpose (called a "COT3"). The agreement recorded on that form is effective to prevent the person from bringing or pursuing their claim in the employment tribunal.

(aa) & (b). It is possible in the normal way to draw up a contract which settles a claim brought under section 66. Subsection (3) above prevents a term in the original contract from operating so as to bar the assertion of the right not to be discriminated against. This subsection allows the claim, once asserted, to be settled in the normal way.

(4A) The conditions regulating compromise contracts under this Act are that–

(a) the contract must be in writing;

(b) the contract must relate to the particular complaint;

(c) the complainant must have received advice from a relevant independent adviser as to the terms and effect of the proposed contract and in particular its effect on his ability to pursue his complaint before an employment tribunal;

(d) there must be in force, when the adviser gives the advice, a contract of insurance, or an indemnity provided for members of a profession or professional body, covering the risk of a claim by the complainant in respect of loss arising in consequence of the advice;

(e) the contract must identify the adviser; and

(f) the contract must state that the conditions regulating compromise contracts under this Act are satisfied.

Section 77(4) (c) – (f)
(c),(d) & (e). The combined effects of these provisions are that, if a person compromises a claim on the basis of advice from a suitable person and that advice is wrong, the complainant may then pursue a claim against the adviser.

(f). These provisions are strictly enforced so a failure to comply with any one of them will result in the claim still being permitted to proceed. Where money has been paid under such an agreement, the tribunal may take account of such payment and award nothing in addition or only such further sum as it considers just and equitable under section 65 above.

When the SDA was originally enacted it was only possible to settle a complaint through ACAS with the assistance of a conciliation officer. Subsequent amendments have permitted the settling of complaints in a variety of circumstances. Even the expanded provisions narrowly confine the circumstances in which a complaint can be settled in order to protect the rights of the complainant.

(4B) A person is a relevant independent adviser for the purposes of subsection (4A)(c)–

(a) if he is a qualified lawyer,

(b) if he is an officer, official, employee or member of an independent trade union who has been certified in writing by the trade union as competent to give advice and as authorised to do so on behalf of the trade union,

(c) if he works at an advice centre (whether as an employee or a volunteer) and has been certified in writing by the centre as competent to give advice and as authorised to do so on behalf of the centre, or

(d) if he is a person of a description specified in an order made by the Secretary of State.

Section 77(4B)
Identifies the kinds of persons who can be relevant independent advisers for the purposes of this section. To date no other advisers have been specified under subsection (d).

(4BA) But a person is not a relevant independent adviser for the purposes of subsection (4A)(c) in relation to the complainant–

(a) if he is, is employed by or is acting in the matter for the other party or a person who is connected with the other party,

(b) in the case of a person within subsection (4B)(b) or (c), if the trade union or advice centre is the other party or a person who is connected with the other party,

(c) in the case of a person within subsection (4B)(c), if the complainant makes a payment for the advice received from him, or

(d) in the case of a person of a description specified in an order under subsection (4B)(d), if any condition specified in the order in relation to the giving of advice by persons of that description is not satisfied.

> **Section 77 (4BA)**
> *This is to ensure that the adviser is properly independent, has no connection with the other party and is not the other party to the complaint.*

(4BB) In subsection (4B)(a) "qualified lawyer" means–

(a) as respects England and Wales, a barrister (whether in practice as such or employed to give legal advice), a solicitor who holds a practising certificate, or a person other than a barrister or solicitor who is an authorised advocate or authorised litigator (within the meaning of the Courts and Legal Services Act 1990), and

> **Section 77 (4BB)**
> *This includes, for example, Legal Executives who are members of the Institute of Legal Executives. This is designed to ensure that anyone who gives advice is properly qualified to do so. It does not include people who style themselves 'Employment Law Consultants' unless they are otherwise qualified under this subsection.*

(b) as respects Scotland, an advocate (whether in practice as such or employed to give legal advice), or a solicitor who holds a practising certificate.

(4BC) In subsection (4B)(b)"independent trade union" has the same meaning as in the Trade Union and Labour Relations (Consolidation) Act 1992.

> **Section 77 (4BC)**
> *Whether or not a trade union is "independent" can only be determined by the Certification Officer under that Act.*

(4C) For the purposes of subsection (4BA) any two persons are to be treated as connected–

(a) if one is a company of which the other (directly or indirectly) has control, or

(b) if both are companies of which a third person (directly or indirectly) has control.

(4D) An agreement under which the parties agree to submit a dispute to arbitration–

(a) shall be regarded for the purposes of subsection (4)(a) and (aa) as being a contract settling a complaint if–

(i) the dispute is covered by a scheme having effect by virtue of an order under section 21(2A) of the Trade Union and Labour Relations (Consolidation) Act 1992, and

(ii) the agreement is to submit it to arbitration in accordance with the scheme, but

(b) shall be regarded for those purposes as neither being nor including such a contract in any other case.

> **Section 77 (4D)**
> *The only arbitration permitted under this subsection is that provided for in section 21(2A) of the Trade Union and Labour Relations (Consolidation) Act 1992. This provision was inserted by the Employment Rights (Dispute Resolution) Act 1998 and is effective for arbitration agreements entered into on or after 1 August 1998.*

(5) On the application of any person interested in a contract to which subsection (2) applies, a county court or sheriff court may make such order as it thinks just for removing or modifying any term made unenforceable by that subsection; but such an order shall not be made unless all persons affected have been given notice of the application (except where under rules of court notice may be dispensed with) and have been afforded an opportunity to make representations to the court.

> **Section 77 (5)**
> *Where a discriminatory provision has been included in a term of a contract, this subsection allows the courts to modify the terms or to remove them provided all interested parties have been given an opportunity to make representations to the court.*

(6) An order under subsection (5) may include provision as respects any period before the making of the order.

> **Section 77 (6)**
> *This allows the order of the court to have retrospective effect*
>
> *See section 72 RRA..*

Educational charities in England and Wales.

78.–(1) This section applies to any trust deed or other instrument–

(a) which concerns property applicable for or in connection with the provision of education in any establishment in paragraphs 1 to 5 of the Table in section 22, and

(b) which in any way restricts the benefits available under the instrument to persons of one sex.

(2) If on the application of the trustees, or of the responsible body (as defined in section 22), the Secretary of State is satisfied that the removal or modification of the restriction would conduce to the advancement of education without sex discrimination, he may by order make such modifications of the instrument as appear to him expedient for removing or modifying the restrictions, and for any supplemental or incidental purposes.

Section 78 (2)
This allows a single sex educational establishment to apply to the Secretary of State for permission to modify the trust deed or other instrument so as to enable it to become co-educational.

(3) If the trust was created by gift or bequest, no order shall be made until 25 years after the date on which the gift or bequest took effect, unless the donor or his personal representatives, or the personal representatives of the testator, have consented in writing to the making of the application for the order.

Section 78 (3)
If the donor or the testator, or their personal representatives, do not consent to the making of the application the Secretary of State cannot make the order until 25 years has elapsed

(4) The Secretary of State shall require the applicant to publish notice–

(a) containing particulars of the proposed order, and
(b) stating that representations may be made to the Secretary of State within a period specified in the notice.

(5) The period specified in the notice shall not be less than one month from the date of the notice.

(6) The applicants shall publish the notice in such manner as may be specified by the Secretary of State, and the cost of any publication of the notice may be defrayed out of the property of the trust.

(7) Before making the order the Secretary of State shall take into account any representations duly made in accordance with the notice.

Section 78 (7)
The Secretary of State must publish details of a proposal to allow such an establishment to become co-educational and must allow a minimum specified period for consultations with interested parties. The Secretary of State must then take account of any representations made to him or her before making the final order.

(8) This section does not apply in Scotland.

Educational endowments etc. to which Part VI of the Education (Scotland) Act 1962 applies.

79.–(1) This section applies to any educational endowment to which Part VI of the Education (Scotland) Act 1962 applies and which in any way restricts the benefit of the endowment to persons of one sex, and any reference to an educational endowment in this section includes a reference to–

(a) a scheme made or approved for that endowment under that Part of the Education (Scotland) Act 1962;
(b) any endowment which is, by virtue of section 121(1) of that Act, dealt with as if it were an educational endowment; and
(c) a university endowment, the Carnegie Trust, a theological endowment and a new endowment.

(2) If, on the application of the governing body of an educational endowment, the Secretary of State is satisfied that the removal or modification of the provision which restricts the benefit of the endowment to persons of one sex would conduce to the advancement of education without sex discrimination, he may, by order, make such modifications to the endowment as appear to him expedient for removing or modifying the restriction and for any supplemental or incidental purposes.

(3) Where the Secretary of State proposes to make an order under this section, he shall publish a notice, in such manner as he thinks sufficient for giving information to persons whom he considers may be interested in the endowment–

(a) containing particulars of the proposed order; and
(b) stating that representations may be made with respect thereto within such period as may be specified in the notice, not being less than one month from the date of publication of the notice,

and the cost of publication of any such notice shall be paid out of the funds of the endowment to which the notice relates.

(4) Before making any order under this section, the Secretary of State shall consider any representations duly made in accordance with the said notice and he may cause a local inquiry to be held into such representations under section 68 of the Education (Scotland) Act 1962.

(5) Without prejudice to section 81(5) of this Act, any order made under this section may be varied or revoked in a scheme made or approved under Part VI of the Education (Scotland) Act 1962.

(6) DELETED MATTER

(7) This section shall be construed as one with Part VI of the Education (Scotland) Act 1962.

Section 79
This mirrors the provisions of section 78 in relation to Scotland.

Power to amend certain provisions of Act.

80.–(1) The Secretary of State may by an order the draft of which has been approved by each House of Parliament–

(a) amend any of the following provisions, namely, sections 6(3), 7, 19, 20(1), (2) and (3), 31(2), 32, 34, 35 and 43 to 48 (including any such provision as amended by a previous order under this subsection);

(b) amend or repeal any of the following provisions, namely, sections 11(4), 12(4), 33 and 49 (including any such provision as amended by a previous order under this subsection);

(c) amend Part II, III or IV so as to render lawful an act which, apart from the amendment, would be unlawful by reason of section 6(1) or (2), 29(1), 30 or 31;

(d) amend section 11(1) so as to alter the number of partners specified in that provision.

Section 80(1)(a) - (c)

(a) *The reference to section 6(3) is wrong since that section was repealed by the Sex Discrimination Act 1986. This reference presumably remains as a result of a failure to make an appropriate tidying up amendment. The other sections referred to deal with the provisions listed below;*

7 - Genuine occupational qualification.

19 - Ministers of religion.

20 - Midwives.

31 - The sharing of residential premises.

34 - Exception for voluntary bodies.

35 - Other exceptions dealing with hospitals, organised religions and facilities or services restricted to the members of one sex.

43-48 - General exceptions relating to charities, sports facilities, the provision of insurance, communal accommodation and discriminatory training where members of one sex and under represented.

(b) *11 - Partnerships.*

12 - Trade unions.

33 - Political parties.

49 - Reserved seats on elective bodies.

(c) *6 - Discrimination in employment.*

29 - Discrimination in the provision of goods facilities and services.

30 - Discrimination in disposal or management of premises.

31 - Discrimination in the consent for assignment or sub-letting of residential premises.

Provided the EOC has been consulted in advance and the amendments are approved by both Houses of Parliament, this section allows the Secretary of State to amend the provisions of the Act referred to without the measures having to go through or the usual parliamentary stages

(2) The Secretary of State shall not lay before Parliament the draft of an order under subsection (1) unless he has consulted the Commission about the contents of the draft.

> **Section 80(2)**
> *Similar provisions appear in section 73 RRA.*

(3) An order under subsection (1)(c) may make such amendments to the list of provisions given in subsection (1)(a) as in the opinion of the Secretary of State are expedient having regard to the contents of the order.

Orders.

81.–(1) Any power of the Secretary of State to make orders under the provisions of this Act (except sections 27 and 59(2)) shall be exercisable by statutory instrument.

(2) An order made by the Secretary of State under the preceding provisions of this Act (except sections 27, 59(2) and 80(1)) shall be subject to annulment in pursuance of a resolution of either House of Parliament.

> **Section 81(2)**
> *27 - Single-sex establishments turning co-educational;*
>
> *59 - The power of the EOC to require persons to furnish information;*
>
> *80(1) – amendments once approved by both Houses of Parliament.*

(3) Subsections (1) and (2) do not apply to an order under section 78 or 79, but–

(a) an order under section 78 which modifies an enactment, and

(b) any order under section 79 other than one which relates to an endowment to which section 128 of the Education (Scotland) Act 1962 (small endowments) applies,

shall be made by statutory instrument subject to annulment in pursuance of a resolution of either House of Parliament.

> **Section 81(3)**
> *Educational charities in England and Wales (78) and Scotland (79).*
>
> *The approval of both Houses of Parliament is not required for this section but either house may annul.*

(4) An order under this Act may make different provision in relation to different cases or classes of case, may exclude certain cases or classes of case, and may contain transitional provisions and savings.

(5) Any power conferred by this Act to make orders includes power (exercisable in the like manner and subject to the like conditions) to vary or revoke any order so made.

Section 81(4) & (5)
Provides that the power to amend is wide ranging and includes the power to vary or revoke earlier amendments made under this section.

Similar provisions appear in section 74 RRA.

General interpretation provisions.

82.–(1) In this Act, unless the context otherwise requires–

"access" shall be construed in accordance with section 50;

"act" includes a deliberate omission;

"advertisement" includes every form of advertisement, whether to the public or not, and whether in a newspaper or other publication, by television or radio, by display of notices, signs, labels, showcards or goods, by distribution of samples, circulars, catalogues, price lists or other material, by exhibition of pictures, models or films, or in any other way, and references to the publishing of advertisements shall be construed accordingly;

"associated employer" shall be construed in accordance with subsection (2);

"the Commission" means the Equal Opportunities Commission;

"Commissioner" means a member of the Commission;

"designate" shall be construed in accordance with subsection (3);

"discrimination" and related terms shall be construed in accordance with section 5(1);

"dispose", in relation to premises, includes granting a right to occupy the premises, and any reference to acquiring premises shall be construed accordingly;

"education" includes any form of training or instruction;

"the Education Acts" has the same meaning given by section 578 of the Education Act 1996;

"education authority" and "educational establishment" in relation to Scotland have the same meaning as they have respectively in section 135(1) of the Education (Scotland) Act 1980;

"employment" means employment under a contract of service or of apprenticeship or a contract personally to execute any work or labour, and related expressions shall be construed accordingly;

"employment agency" means a person who, for profit or not, provides services for the purpose of finding employment for workers or supplying employers with workers;

"equality clause" has the meaning given in section 1(2) of the Equal Pay Act 1970 (as set out in section 8(1) of this Act);

"estate agent" means a person who, by way of profession or trade, provides services for the purpose of finding premises for persons seeking to acquire them or assisting in the disposal of premises;

"final" shall be construed in accordance with subsection (4);

"firm" has the meaning given by section 4 of the Partnership Act 1890;

"formal investigation" means an investigation under section 57;

"further education" has the meaning given by section 2 of the Education Act 1996 and in Scotland has the meaning given by section 135(1) of the Education (Scotland) Act 1980;

"gender reassignment" means a process which is undertaken under medical supervision for the purpose of reassigning a person's sex by changing physiological or other characteristics of sex, and includes any part of such a process;

"general notice", in relation to any person, means a notice published by him at a time and in a manner appearing to him suitable for securing that the notice is seen within a reasonable time by persons likely to be affected by it;

"genuine occupational qualification" shall be construed in accordance with section 7(2), except in the expression "supplementary genuine occupational qualification", which shall be construed in accordance with section 7B(2);

"Great Britain" includes such of the territorial waters of the United Kingdom as are adjacent to Great Britain;

"independent school" has the meaning given by section 463 of the Education Act 1996 and in Scotland has the meaning given by section 135(1) of the Education (Scotland) Act 1980;

"man" includes a male of any age;

"managers" has the same meaning for Scotland as in section 135(1) of the Education (Scotland) Act 1980;

"near relative" shall be construed in accordance with subsection (5);

"non-discrimination notice" means a notice under section 67;

"notice" means a notice in writing;

"prescribed" means prescribed by regulations made by the Secretary of State by statutory instrument;

"profession" includes any vocation or occupation;

"proprietor", in relation to any school, has the meaning given by section 579 of the Education Act 1996 and in Scotland has the meaning given by section 135(1) of the Education (Scotland) Act 1980;

"pupil" in Scotland includes a student of any age;

"retirement" includes retirement (whether voluntary or not) on grounds of age, length of service, or incapacity;

"school" has the meaning given by section 4 of the Education Act 1996, and in Scotland has the meaning given by section 135(1) of the Education (Scotland) Act 1980;

"school education" has the meaning given by section 135(1) of the Education (Scotland) Act 1980;

"self-governing school" has the same meaning as in the Education (Scotland) Act 1980

"trade" includes any business;

"training" includes any form of education or instruction;

"university" includes a university college and the college, school or hall of a university;

"woman" includes a female of any age.

Section 82
The interpretation provisions in the RRA are in section 78

82.–(1A) References in this Act to the dismissal of a person from employment or to the expulsion of a person from a position as a partner include references–

(a) to the termination of that person's employment or partnership by the expiration of any period (including a period expiring by reference to an event or circumstance) not being a termination immediately after which the employment or partnership is renewed on the same terms; and

(b) to the termination of that person's employment or partnership by any act of his (including the giving of notice) in circumstances such that he is entitled to terminate it without notice by reason of the conduct of the employer or, as the case may be, the conduct of the other parties.

Section 82(1A)(a) - (b)

(a) The contract may terminate without the employment terminating. This subsection prevents claims being made where the termination is merely technical but the employment or partnership continues on the same terms.

(b) Usually referred to as constructive dismissal.

(2) For the purposes of this Act two employers are to be treated as associated if one is a company of which the other (directly or indirectly) has control or if both are companies of which a third person (directly or indirectly) has control.

(3) Any power conferred by this Act to designate establishments or persons may be exercised either by naming them or by identifying them by reference to a class or other description.

Section 82(1A)(3)
This gives the Secretary of State the power to designate establishments either individually or by reference to a class or description. See also section 78(3) RRA.

(4) For the purposes of this Act a non-discrimination notice or a finding by a court or tribunal becomes final when an appeal against the notice or finding is dismissed, withdrawn or abandoned or when the time for appealing expires without an appeal having been brought; and for this purpose an appeal against a non-discrimination notice shall be taken to be dismissed if, notwithstanding that a requirement of the notice is quashed on appeal, a direction is given in respect of it under section 68(3).

Section 82(1A)(4)
The finality of a non-discrimination notice is important for determining the time during which the EOC can take action under section 69 to 72 inclusive.

See section 78(4) RRA.

(5) For the purposes of this Act a person is a near relative of another if that person is the wife or husband, a parent or child, a grandparent or grandchild, or a brother or sister of the other (whether of full blood or half-blood or by affinity), and "child" includes an illegitimate child and the wife or husband of an illegitimate child.

Section 82(1A)(5)
Section 78(5) RRA.

(6) Except so far as the context otherwise requires, any reference in this Act to an enactment shall be construed as a reference to that enactment as amended by or under any other enactment, including this Act.

Section 82(1A)(6)
This preserves the applicability of the Act referred to even if it is amended after the passage of the SDA.

Section 78(6) RRA

(7) In this Act, except where otherwise indicated–

(a) a reference to a numbered Part, section of Schedule is a reference to the Part of or section of, or the Schedule to, this Act so numbered, and

(b) a reference in a section to a numbered subsection is a reference to the subsection of that section so numbered, and

(c) a reference in a section, subsection or Schedule to a numbered paragraph is a reference to the paragraph of that section, subsection or Schedule so numbered, and

(d) a reference to any provision of an Act (including this Act) includes a Schedule incorporated in the Act by that provision.

Section 82(1A)(7)
Section 78(7) RRA

Transitional and commencement provisions, amendments and repeals.

83.–(1) The provisions of Schedule 4 shall have effect for making transitional provision for the purposes of this Act.

(2) Parts II to VII shall come into operation on such day as the Secretary of State may by order appoint, and different days may be so appointed for different provisions and for different purposes.

(3) Subject to subsection (4)–

(a) the enactments specified in Schedule 5 shall have effect subject to the amendments specified in that Schedule (being minor amendments or amendments consequential on the preceding provisions of this Act), and

(b) the enactments specified in Schedule 6 are hereby repealed to the extent shown in column 3 of that Schedule.

(4) The Secretary of State shall by order provide for the coming into operation of the amendments contained in Schedule 5 and the repeals contained in Schedule 6, and those amendments and repeals shall have effect only as provided by an order so made.

(5) An order under this section may make such transitional provision as appears to the Secretary of State to be necessary or expedient in connection with the provisions thereby brought into operation, including such adaptations of those provisions, or of any provisions of this Act then in operation, as appear to the Secretary of State necessary or expedient in consequence of the partial operation of this Act.

Financial provisions.

84. There shall be defrayed out of money provided by Parliament–

(a) sums required by the Secretary of State for making payments under paragraph 5 or 14 of Schedule 3, and for defraying any other expenditure falling to be made by him under or by virtue of this Act;

(b) payments falling to be made under section 66(6)(b) or (7) in respect of the remuneration of assessors; and

(c) any increase attributable to the provisions of this Act in the sums payable out of money provided by Parliament under any other Act.

Section 84
This provides funds for the payment of salaries and expenses for members of the EOC.
Section 77 RRA in relation to the CRE

Application to Crown.

85.–(1) This Act applies–

(a) to an act done by or for purposes of a Minister of the Crown or government department, or

(b) to an act done on behalf of the Crown by a statutory body, or a person holding a statutory office,

as it applies to an act done by a private person.

Section 85(1)
Wherever a Minister of the Crown, a government department, a statutory body or a person holding a statutory office exercises a discretion in the performance of their duties they cannot do so on a discriminatory basis; any such decision would therefore be liable to judicial review since, by this section, there would be no jurisdiction to exercise the discretion in that manner.

(2) Parts II and IV apply to–

Section 85(2)
Part II - Discrimination in the employment field.
Part IV – other unlawful acts

(a) service for purposes of a Minister of the Crown or government department, other than service of a person holding a statutory office, or

(b) service on behalf of the Crown for purposes of a person holding a statutory office or purposes of a statutory body, as they apply to employment by a private person, and shall so apply as if references to a contract of employment included references to the terms of service.

Section 85(2)(a)-(b)
This provision may be now have to disapplied because it is inconsistent with Article 141 of the EU Treaty guaranteeing equal treatment. A decision to that effect in relation to the right of employment tribunal chairmen to claim equal pay has been made by the Northern Ireland Court of Appeal.

Until there is provision on race relations in European law this would not apply to section 75 RRA.

(3) Subsections (1) and (2) have effect subject to section 17.

Section 85(3)
Section 17 deals with the police.

(4) Nothing in this Act shall render unlawful an act done for the purpose of ensuring the combat effectiveness of the armed forces.

Section 85(4)
It is contrary to the Equal Treatment Directive to operate a blanket exclusion of women from armed units and this provision is subject to Community law. However, women can justifiably be excluded from the Royal Marines in order to maintain the principle of "inter operability". The Royal Marines require that, whatever the person's occupational speciality, all members must be capable of fighting as members of a commander unit. The exclusion of women is not disproportionate to the aim of maintaining inter operability and can therefore be justified under the Equal Treatment Directive by reason of the nature of the activities in question and the context in which they were carried out.

(5) Nothing in this Act shall render unlawful discrimination in admission to the Army Cadet Force, Air Training Corps, Sea Cadet Corps or Combined Cadet Force, or any other cadet training corps for the time being administered by the Ministry of Defence.

(6) ...repealed

(7) Subsection (2) of section 10 shall have effect in relation to any ship, aircraft or hovercraft belonging to or possessed by Her Majesty in right of the Government of the United Kingdom as it has effect in relation to a ship, aircraft or hovercraft mentioned in paragraph (a) or (b) of that subsection, and section 10(5) shall apply accordingly.

Section 85(7)
Applies section 10 to ships, aircraft and hovercraft belong to the Crown.

(8) The provisions of Parts II to IV of the Crown Proceedings Act 1947 shall apply to proceedings against the Crown under this Act as they apply to proceedings in England and Wales which by virtue of section 23 of that Act are treated for the purposes of Part II of that Act as civil proceedings by or against the Crown, except that in their application to proceedings under this Act section 20 of that Act (removal of proceedings from county court to High Court) shall not apply.

Section 85(8)
Proceedings against the Crown are normally transferred to the High Court. Under section 66 of this Act all proceedings are required to be commenced in a County Court in England and Wales and in a Sheriff Court in Scotland. This section and subsection (9) below remove the potential conflict.

(9) The provisions of Part V of the Crown Proceedings Act 1947 shall apply to proceedings against the Crown under this Act as they apply to proceedings in Scotland which by virtue of the said Part are treated as civil proceedings by or against the Crown, except that in their application to proceedings under this Act the proviso to section 44 of that Act (removal of proceedings from the sheriff court to the Court of Session) shall not apply.

(9A) This subsection applies to any complaint by a person (" " the complainant" ") that another person–

(a) has committed an act of discrimination against the complainant which is unlawful by virtue of section 6; or
(b) is by virtue of section 41 or 42 to be treated as having committed such an act of discrimination against the complainant, if at the time when the act complained of done the complainant was serving in the armed forces and the discrimination in question relates to his service in those forces.

(9B) No complaint to which subsection (9A) applies shall be presented to an employment tribunal under section 63 unless–

(a) the complainant has made a complaint to an officer under the service redress procedures applicable to him and has submitted that complaint to the Defence Counsel under those procedures; and
(b) the Defence Counsel have made a determination with respect to the complaint.

Section 85(9A) & (9B).
Allows members of the armed forces to present claims to employment tribunals provided they have used the internal service redress procedures first.

(9C) Regulations may make provision enabling a complainant to which subsection 9(A) applies to be presented to an employment tribunal under section 63 in such circumstances as may be specified by the regulations, notwithstanding that subsection (9B) would otherwise preclude the presentation of the complaint to an employment tribunal.

(9D) Where a complaint is presented to an employment tribunal under section 63 by virtue of regulations under subsection (9C) the service redress procedures may continue after the complaint is so presented.

Section 85(9C) & (9D)
The normal time limits for presenting claims to employment tribunals apply to members of the armed forces. So a person who waited for the internal service redress procedures to be completed before presenting a claim might well be out of time.

These sections allow a claim to be presented to an employment tribunal while the service redress procedures are underway.

(9E) Regulations under subsection (9C) shall be made by the Secretary of State by statutory instrument and shall be subject to annulment in pursuance of a resolution of either House of Parliament.

Section 85(9E)
See the Sex Discrimination (Complaints to Employment Tribunals) (Armed Forces) Regulations 1997, SI 1997/2163.

(10) In this section–

"armed forces" means any of the naval, military or air forces of the Crown;

"service for purposes of a Minister of the Crown or government department" does not include service in any office for the time being mentioned in Schedule 2 (Ministerial offices) to the House of Commons Disqualification Act 1975;

"the service redress procedures" means the procedures, excluding those which relate to the making of a report on a complaint to Her Majesty, referred to in section 180 of the Army Act 1955, section 180 of the Air Force Act 1955 and section 130 of the Naval Discipline Act 1957; and

"statutory body" means a body set up by or in pursuance of an enactment, and "statutory office" means an office so set up.

Section 85(10)
See section 75 RRA.

Application to House of Commons staff

85A.–(1) Parts II and IV apply to an act done by an employer of a relevant member of the House of Commons staff, and to service as such a member, as they apply to an act done by and to service for the purposes of a Minister of the Crown or government department, and accordingly apply as if references to a contract of employment included references to the terms of service of such a member.

(2) In this section "relevant member of the House of Commons staff" has the same meaning as in section 195 of the Employment Rights Act 1996; and subsections (6) to (12) of that section (person to be treated as employer of House of Commons staff) apply, with any necessary modifications, for the purposes of Parts II and IV as they apply by virtue of this section.

Section 85A

House of Commons' staff may be employed personally by the speaker, by the House of Commons' Commission or by some other person designated by the speaker or by the Commission.

This section applies the protection in relation to employment and in relation to discriminatory practices, advertisements, instructions to discriminate, pressure to discriminate, the liability of employers and aiding unlawful acts to such staff.

See section 75A RRA.

Application to House of Lords staff

85B.–(1) Parts II and IV apply in relation to employment as a relevant member of the House of Lords staff as they apply in relation to other employment.

(2) In this section "relevant member of the House of Lords staff" has the same meaning as in section 194 of the Employment Rights Act 1996; and subsection (7) of that section applies for the purposes of this section.

Section 85B

The corresponding provisions in relation to House of Lords' staff as in section 85A above.

See section 75B RRA.

Government appointments outside section 6.

86.–(1) This section applies to any appointment by a Minister of the Crown or government department to an office or post where section 6 does not apply in relation to the appointment.

(2) In making the appointment, and in making the arrangements for determining who should be offered the office or post, the Minister of the Crown or government department shall not do an act which would be unlawful under section 6 if the Crown were the employer for the purposes of this Act.

Section 86

This relates to appointments which are not in the nature of employment.

See section 76 RRA.

Short title and extent.

87.–(1) This Act may be cited as the Sex Discrimination Act 1975.

(2) This Act (except paragraph 16 of Schedule 3) does not extend to Northern Ireland.

SCHEDULES

SCHEDULE 1

DELETED SCHEDULE

SCHEDULE 2

Schedule 2
Deals with transitional arrangements in education.

SCHEDULE 3

(Deals with the establishment of the EOC)

Schedule 3
(Schedule 1 RRA deals with the establishment of the Commission for Racial Equality)

RACE DISCRIMINATION

The scheme of the Race Relations Act 1976 ('RRA') the main statutory provision dealing with race relations, is very similar so that of the Sex Discrimination Act 1975 and in many cases the wording of particular sections is identical. For this reason, principles which are decided under the provisions of one Act are usually applied to the corresponding provisions of the other Act. The essential difference between sex discrimination and race discrimination in the United Kingdom is that there is currently no provision in European law dealing with race discrimination. There is a general prohibition on discrimination on the ground of nationality only between the citizens of EU member states but this affords no rights as between citizens of the same member state and no rights for those citizens of non-member states.

This is soon to be changed since article 13 of the Treaty of Amsterdam contains a general anti-discrimination provision. This confers on the European Union the competence to deal with race-related matters. It is likely that under this new jurisdiction two new directives will be introduced. Those directives are likely to cover race discrimination in employment and in the provision of goods, facilities and services. Since these will be the first measures of their kind in European law it is possible that the provisions of the directives will be more than adequately provided for in existing in UK law, especially since the European Parliament has decided to follow the UK model in drawing up its own measures.

Other provisions dealing with race relations can also be found in the Public Order Act 1986, the Protection from Harassment Act 1997, and the Crime and Disorder Act 1998 and the Local Government Act 1988. These provisions will be dealt with at the end of this section.

The Race Relations (Amendment) Bill, currently before Parliament, will make changes to the RRA. These changes arise from recommendations made it in the Macpherson report which was published at the conclusion of the Stephen Lawrence inquiry. The effect of these amendments will be to extend the RRA to apply fully to the police and immigration services and will, in future, cover all aspects of government and public bodies.

Under the Human Rights Act 1998, the European Convention on Human Rights will be incorporated into UK law by October 2000. Article 14 of the Convention contains a general prohibition on discrimination which is wider than the provisions of the RRA and may therefore encompass kinds of discrimination which are not covered under this Act.

Race Relations Act 1976

PART I DISCRIMINATION TO WHICH ACT APPLIES

Racial discrimination

1.–(1) A person discriminates against another in any circumstances relevant for the purposes of any provision of this Act if-

(a) on racial grounds he treats that other less favourably than he treats or would treat other persons; or

Section 1(1)

To be on racial grounds (defined in section 3 below) it is not necessary to show that the treatment was aimed at the complainant or even that the motive was discriminatory as long as the difference is on racial grounds. This applies even if the motive is a worthy one, for example to redress existing imbalance, unless it is covered by one of the exceptions in Part VI of the Act.

For discrimination to occur the person must be treated less favourably so if the discriminator can show that it was not intended that the victim should, or was likely to, become aware he will not have been less favourably treated. In a case where the claimant was referred to in racially derogatory terms but not to her face or within her hearing – and she only became aware of it later – she would not have been less favourably treated . This may seem a curious result since the treatment still has an effect on the way the person is or will be treated whether the alleged victim was likely to become aware of it or not.

Less favourable treatment may include a failure to provide a person with a choice or an opportunity such as, for example, allowing applications to be made for a particular post or a place at a particular school. Treating someone in a particular way because of stereotypical assumptions would amount to less favourable treatment.

In a very recent tribunal case, it was held to be less favourable treatment where a security guard said it to an Afro Caribbean employee 'The trouble with you lot is that you think you can get away with anything'. The employee was a Rastafarian and it was unclear whether those remarks were a reference to his being a Rastafarian or being of West Indian origin. The tribunal inferred from the evidence that this was a reference to him being a West Indian and found that this amounted to less favourable treatment. If they had found that this was a reference to him being a Rastafarian it would not have amounted to race discrimination because of the way in which race is defined in section 3 below.

There is an important distinction between sex and race discrimination. A person who is refused employment because he/she is married to a black person would be discriminated against 'on racial grounds' even though it is not his or her race which is in issue. If a

person faced with an instruction to discriminate unlawfully on racial grounds against someone else refuses to do so, and is consequently dismissed, his dismissal is 'on racial grounds'. Unsurprisingly, this also extends to constructive dismissal where the employee instructed to discriminate resigns. This could result in a finding that there was discrimination against the person instructed but not, because of the decision referred to above, against the intended victim because it was never intended that he or she should become aware of it.

A single act, if sufficiently serious, can be enough.

This section uses the same terms as section 1 of the Sex Discrimination Act 1975 (the "SDA") and cases on the principles set out decided under one Act are applicable to the other.

(b) he applies to that other a requirement or condition which he applies or would apply equally to persons not of the same racial group as that other but-
  (i) which is such that the proportion of persons of the same racial group as that other who can comply with it is considerably smaller than the proportion of persons not of that racial group who can comply with it; and
  (ii) which he cannot show to be justifiable irrespective of the colour, race, nationality or ethnic or national origins of the person to whom it is applied; and
  (iii) which is to the detriment of that other because he cannot comply with it.

Section 1(b)
This is what is commonly known as indirect discrimination. The principles which apply are the same as those which apply to sex discrimination and cases decided under the provisions of one Act apply to the corresponding provisions of the other.

There is some doubt as to whether a 'requirement or condition' must operate as an absolute bar. Although this was the approach adopted in early cases decided under the Act, the words 'requirement or condition' do not appear in the EU Equal Treatment Directive in relation to sex discrimination. For this reason it is probable that the provisions ought now to be operated more flexibly. If this proves to be the case, it is likely to have an effect on the operation of the same provisions under this Act because of the identical wording of the sections.

In order to show indirect discrimination a complainant must demonstrate that the proportion of people within his/her racial group who can comply with that condition is considerably smaller than the proportion of those not in that group who can comply with it. In order to decide whether this is the case it is necessary to define a pool of workers for comparison. For a valid comparison, the relevant circumstances of the one group must be the same or not materially different to the other.

Care must be taken in choosing the relevant pool because, if the wrong one is chosen and the disparate impact is not established, even if another pool for comparison would show a disparate impact, the claim will fail. This is usually less of a problem in race discrimination than in discrimination on grounds of sex because of the nature of the treatment. For example, a condition that employees must wear a particular type of headgear may discriminate against a Sikh man who must wear a turban; a requirement to work on a Saturday may discriminate against an orthodox Jew for whom Saturday is the Sabbath.

Having identified the pool for comparison it is then necessary to go on to consider whether a considerably smaller proportion of the group to which the complainant belongs can comply with the requirement or the condition. This is usually calculated by calculating the proportion of people of the same racial group as the complainant who can comply with the requirement and then look at the proportion of people not of that same group who can comply and comparing the two.

This is not simply a requirement to compare the number of the group to which the complainant belongs who can comply with the number not of that group; it may be appropriate to be selective. It could, for example, be right to limit the pool for comparison to candidates for promotion or for redundancy. Any limit on the pool must not be operated on criteria which are themselves discriminatory, for example, limiting candidates for redundancy to those who will not work on Saturdays or for candidates for promotion only to those who speak fluent English, unless such requirements are justified on grounds which do not include race. This is a matter for the tribunal to determine on the evidence presented to it. The Tribunal's choice of the pool for comparison will not be disturbed on appeal unless such choice is perverse or is one which no reasonable tribunal would have made.

Compliance with the condition must be more than theoretically possible. A Sikh is physically able to remove a turban and so comply with a requirement to wear a particular type of headgear but it would require the person to be in breach of an important custom or rule of his/her ethnic group. A Romany gypsy traveller is capable of giving up the nomadic life and so avoid a ban on 'travellers' imposed by a shop-keeper or publican but not without giving up his cultural customs and traditions.

Whether the requirement or condition is justifiable depends on striking a balance between the discriminatory effect of the requirement or condition and the needs of the person or body which applies that condition. So if the discriminatory effect of the measure far outweighs the needs of an employer in imposing the condition it is not likely to be justified. It will not be justified if the same effect could be achieved by a non-discriminatory route, provided that the alternative route is not disproportionately expensive or administratively burdensome.

'Considerably smaller' may mean a difference of one or two where the pool for comparison is small; it may mean a difference of a few percentage points where the difference has been consistent over a long period of time but it may require greater statistical disparity where the difference is a recent phenomenon or has fluctuated over a period.

The complainant must then show that he/she has suffered a detriment in not being able to comply with the requirement or condition. It is sufficient for a detriment to be established that the person is merely denied an advantage rather than having to suffer a disadvantage.

(2) It is hereby declared that, for the purposes of this Act, segregating a person from other persons on racial grounds is treating him less favourably than they are treated.

Section 1(2)
This section prevents a discriminator from arguing that the treatment is 'different but equal'.

See also section 1 SDA.

Discrimination by way of victimisation.

2.–(1) A person ("the discriminator") discriminates against another person ("the person victimised") in any circumstances relevant for the purposes of any provision of this Act if he treats the person victimised less favourably than in those circumstances he treats or would treat other persons, and does so by reason that the person victimised has–

(a) brought proceedings against the discriminator or any other person under this Act; or
(b) given evidence or information in connection with proceedings brought by any person against the discriminator or any other person under this Act; or
(c) otherwise done anything under or by reference to this Act in relation to the discriminator or any other person; or
(d) alleged that the discriminator or any other person has committed an act which (whether or not the allegation so states) would amount to a contravention of this Act,

or by reason that the discriminator knows that the person victimised intends to do any of those things, or suspects that the person victimised has done, or intends to do, any of them.

(2) Subsection (1) does not apply to treatment of a person by reason of any allegation made by him if the allegation was false and not made in good faith.

Section 2
This section corresponds to section 4 of the SDA.

The section is designed to protect a person who makes a claim that he/she has suffered discrimination on racial grounds. The person is covered even if the claim is only made to the alleged discriminator and no claim has been lodged at a court or tribunal. It also protects potential witnesses in discrimination claims and the complainant is protected even if the alleged discriminator only suspects that the person has done something in connection with the Act or intends to do so.

In a case where an employer refuses to provide a reference to an employee because the employee made a complaint of discrimination and the employer was concerned that giving such a reference might prejudice his case before the employment tribunal, the refusal to provide such a reference amounts to victimisation.

The protection against victimisation only applies if the allegation that discrimination has occurred is made in good faith. Although section 2(2) refers only to an allegation and appears to be confined to section 2(1)(d) it is likely that the defence will also be available if somebody had brought a claim in the tribunal which was not brought in good faith or where the evidence was not given in good faith.

Great care needs to be taken when dealing with somebody who has brought a claim, made an allegation or given evidence in a discrimination claim because the victimisation does not have to be a conscious act on the part of the person victimising. If the person is treated differently because the complaint was brought, even if there was no conscious intention to discriminate against him/her, the claim that he/she has been victimised under this section may succeed.

Meaning of "racial grounds", "racial group" etc.

3.–(1) In this Act, unless the context otherwise requires-

"racial grounds" means any of the following grounds, namely colour, race, nationality or ethnic or national origins;

"racial group" means a group of persons defined by reference to colour, race, nationality or ethnic or national origins, and references to a person's racial group refer to any racial group into which he falls.

Section 3(1)
It may be thought that this section provides an all-encompassing definition of what is covered by the Act. It is to be noted that the word 'Religion' does not appear in this section. Nevertheless, a person's 'Ethnic origins' have been held to include certain religious groups such as, for example Sikhs.

Ethnic origins are to be construed in a broad historical and cultural context. People who share a common language, a common religion and a shared history and/ or cultural tradition could be included.

Jewish people, for example, are both an ethnic group and a religious one. If a Jew is treated less favourably, a tribunal, having established that fact, must go on to consider whether the difference in treatment is because of the complainant's ethnic origins or religious practices.

Muslims, however, do not constitute an ethnic group because their faith is widespread, covers many languages, colours and nationalities.

West Indians are a particular ethnic group but Rastafarians are not because of the absence of a shared history. An Englishman who suffers discrimination in Scotland would be treated less favourably on grounds of his national origin and therefore comes within the definition of 'Racial grounds' under this section. Because there is no common racial element in being Scottish such discrimination would not be on the grounds of the person's ethnic origins.

The fact that the treatment is wholly unreasonable does not mean that it amounts to discrimination. If the person would treat everyone unreasonably, regardless of their racial origin, it will not amount to unlawful discrimination.

(2) The fact that a racial group comprises two or more distinct racial groups does not prevent it from constituting a particular racial group for the purposes of this Act.

(3) In this Act-

(a) references to discrimination refer to any discrimination falling within section 1 or 2; and
(b) references to racial discrimination refer to any discrimination falling within section 1, and related expressions shall be construed accordingly.

(4) A comparison of the case of a person of a particular racial group with that of a person not of that group under section 1(1) must be such that the relevant circumstances in the one case are the same, or not materially different, in the other.

Section 3(4)
This section requires that the comparison must be on a 'like-for-like' basis but excluding any conditions which are themselves based on race. It would not, for example, excuse discrimination against an Indian national merely because all foreigners would be discriminated against.

Part II Discrimination in the Employment Field

Discrimination by employers

Discrimination against applicants and employees.

4.–(1) It is unlawful for a person, in relation to employment by him at an establishment in Great Britain, to discriminate against another–

(a) in the arrangements he makes for the purpose of determining who should be offered that employment; or

(b) in the terms on which he offers him that employment; or

This section applies to an offer of employment. Once the offer is accepted a complaint about discriminatory terms in the contract must be brought under section 4(2) below.

(c) by refusing or deliberately omitting to offer him that employment.

Section 4(1)

The importance of the training of those who are to be involved in the recruitment process cannot be overstated. The selection criteria used to select those who are to be offered employment will be subject to scrutiny in the event that a complaint is made by someone who was unsuccessful in obtaining employment. Objective criteria for selection should be adopted and carefully applied and any failure to justify those criteria or to show that they were applied fairly may result in a tribunal drawing an inference that the selection (or non-selection) was racially motivated.

The only work excluded from these provisions is work which is done wholly or mainly outside Great Britain (see section 8 – but note the limitation on section 8 under Article 8 of the European Treaty which provides for the free movement of workers between member states. The obligation under the Treaty overrides the provisions of national legislation so a citizen of a member state can obtain a remedy under the RRA even if the work is to be done wholly outside Great Britain but still within another member state but the same remedy would not be available to a citizen of a non-member state). The definition under the Race Relations Act (and the Sex Discrimination Act) is wider than under the Employment Rights Act where an employee is covered for the protection under that Act unless he 'ordinarily works outside Great Britain'.

The meaning of employment is also wider than that in the Employment Rights Act 1996. The definition is contained in section 78(1) and includes partners and the self- employed provided that the work is to be undertaken personally.

Provided that there is a legally binding contract to do the work, the wider definition may even include volunteers working for a charity, for example.

(2) It is unlawful for a person, in the case of a person employed by him at an establishment in Great Britain, to discriminate against that employee–

(a) in the terms of employment which he affords him; or
(b) in the way he affords him access to opportunities for promotion, transfer or training, or to any other benefits, facilities or services, or by refusing or deliberately omitting to afford him access to them; or
(c) by dismissing him, or subjecting him to any other detriment.

Section 4(2)

The whole of the employment relationship is governed by this section from recruitment through to dismissal.

Only the Commission for Racial Equality (or the Equal Opportunities Commission in a sex discrimination case) can make a complaint about an advertisement for a job. This is covered by sections 29 and 63 of the Act. An applicant may, however, complain that she has been disadvantaged, or has suffered a detriment, as a consequence of a discriminatory advertisement by reason that he/she has been excluded from those who may apply for the post.

Even if the advertisement is not discriminatory, other aspects of the selection procedure including the interview may give rise to a complaint that an interviewee has been discriminated against. For this reason care should be taken about the structure of an interview and questions which are likely to have a disproportionate effect on members of a particular racial group, such as dress codes (which cannot be objectively justified on grounds of health, safety or hygiene) or the requirement to work on Saturdays, for example, should be avoided. For the same reason questions which betrayed stereotypical assumptions should also be avoided. It would be wholly inappropriate to ask questions about how an applicant from a particular ethnic minority would fit in with the work force consisting largely of members of a different group.

A complaint will not fail by reason that the vacancy was not eventually filled. The detriment suffered by the complainant is the loss of the opportunity to be considered for the post.

It is also important to remember that indirect discrimination can arise in the recruitment process where no advertising precedes the appointment. In 1999 the Lord Chancellor appointed a special adviser without advertising a post and without carrying out a process of selection. He appointed someone well known to him. Two people complained that this amounted to the imposition of a requirement or condition that the successful applicant should be known to the Lord Chancellor. The evidence was that the Lord Chancellor in his close circle of friends had more men than women and it was held that this did amount to indirect sex discrimination.

One of the applicants succeeded in her claim that she had been discriminated against because she did have the necessary skills and experience to be considered for the post. The applicant who had claimed that she had been excluded by reason of her race did not succeed because she did not remotely have the necessary skills and experience and there was no chance that she would have been appointed. She, therefore, had suffered no detriment.

Although the words 'employed by him' appear to confine the protection to an act or omission during the currency of the employment, it has been held that this section also applies, in sex discrimination claims, after the employment has ended. The European Court of Justice held that this protection can extend beyond the ending of the employment. A woman complained that her previous employer had refused to provide a reference because, while she was still employed by them, she had brought a claim of sex discrimination against them. The European Court of Justice held that the Equal Treatment Directive did extend beyond the date on which the employment was terminated and therefore section 6(2) had to be interpreted in order to give effect to the directive. The complainant recovered substantial damages for the discrimination she had thus suffered.

Although the provisions of section 4 of the Race Relations Act 1976 are in precisely the same words, the extended definition does not, as yet, apply because there is no corresponding European Directive.

It is advisable for an employer setting out to recruit staff to consult the Commission for Racial Equality Code of Practice 'for the elimination of racial discrimination and the promotion of equality of opportunity in employment' which sets out a number of recommendations for good practice in recruitment and promotion. It is not legally enforceable but Tribunals will have regard to whether its provisions were followed or applied when considering a complaint of discrimination.

As in sex discrimination, there is no specific provision for 'harassment' but such complaints would generally be brought under sub-section (c).

A similar Code, published by the Equal Opportunities Commission, exists on sex discrimination in employment.

Although set out slightly differently the terms used are the same as those in section 6(1) and (2) of the SDA

(3) Except in relation to discrimination falling within section 2, subsections (1) and (2) do not apply to employment for the purposes of a private household.

(4) Subsection (2) does not apply to benefits, facilities or services of any description if the employer is concerned with the provision (for payment or not) of benefits, facilities or services of that description to the public, or to a section of the public comprising the employee in question, unless–

(a) that provision differs in a material respect from the provision of the benefits, facilities or services by the employer to his employees; or

(b) the provision of the benefits, facilities or services to the employee in question is regulated by his contract of employment; or
(c) the benefits, facilities or services relate to training.

Section 4(4)
These provisions draw a distinction between the services provided to the person as an employee and those provided to him/her, albeit by her employer, as a member of the public. If they are provided under the contract of employment, the complaint must be brought under sub-section (b) above; if it relates to those provided to members of the public generally, the complaint can only be brought in the county court under section 20.

See section 6(7) SDA.

Exceptions for genuine occupational qualifications.

5.–(1) In relation to racial discrimination–

(a) section 4(1)(a) or (c) does not apply to any employment where being of a particular racial group is a genuine occupational qualification for the job; and
(b) section 4(2)(b) does not apply to opportunities for promotion or transfer to, or training for, such employment.

(2) Being of a particular racial group is a genuine occupational qualification for a job only where–

(a) the job involves participation in a dramatic performance or other entertainment in a capacity for which a person of that racial group is required for reasons of authenticity; or
(b) the job involves participation as an artist's or photographic model in the production of a work of art, visual image or sequence of visual images for which a person of that racial group is required for reasons of authenticity; or
(c) the job involves working in a place where food or drink is (for payment or not) provided to and consumed by members of the public or a section of the public in a particular setting for which, in that job, a person of that racial group is required for reasons of authenticity; or
(d) the holder of the job provides persons of that racial group with personal services promoting their welfare, and those services can most effectively be provided by a person of that racial group.

Section 5(c)–(d)
(c) Note that this section states '...provided to and consumed by members of the public...'; it does not therefore apply to take-away services.
(d) This section has been applied in a case where a woman of Afro-Caribbean origin was appointed to a post in a child care centre in preference to a white applicant because the post required a personal awareness of Afro-Caribbean culture for the benefit of her charges. 'Personal services' connotes some degree of personal or face-to-face contact and the cultural knowledge must be directly relevant to the services provided. It is unlikely to be sufficient if the knowledge is purely theoretical and has no practical applicant.

(3) Subsection (2) applies where some only of the duties of the job fall within paragraph (a), (b), (c) or (d) as well as where all of them do.

(4) Paragraph (a), (b), (c) or (d) of subsection (2) does not apply in relation to the filling of a vacancy at a time when the employer already has employees of the racial group in question–
 (a) who are capable of carrying out the duties falling within that paragraph; and
 (b) whom it would be reasonable to employ on those duties; and
 (c) whose numbers are sufficient to meet the employer's likely requirements in respect of those duties without undue inconvenience.

Section 5(4)
An employer cannot therefore rely on this section if there are already employees, with the appropriate attributes, who can be called upon to perform those particular duties.
See also section 7 SDA, although such GOQs are different.

Exception for employment intended to provide training in skills to be exercised outside Great Britain.

6. Nothing in section 4 shall render unlawful any act done by an employer for the benefit of a person not ordinarily resident in Great Britain in or in connection with employing him at an establishment in Great Britain, where the purpose of that employment is to provide him with training in skills which he appears to the employer to intend to exercise wholly outside Great Britain.

Section 6
Further exceptions are contained in sections 35-38 below.

Discrimination against contract workers.

7.–(1) This section applies to any work for a person ("the principal") which is available for doing by individuals ("contract workers") who are employed not by the principal himself but by another person, who supplies them under a contract made with the principal.

(2) It is unlawful for the principal, in relation to work to which this section applies, to discriminate against a contract worker–

(a) in the terms on which he allows him to do that work; or
(b) by not allowing him to do it or continue to do it; or
(c) in the way he affords him access to any benefits, facilities or services or by refusing or deliberately omitting to afford him access to them; or
(d) by subjecting him to any other detriment.

Section 7(2)
In normal employment circumstances a worker supplied by an agency to a principal employer is regarded as an employee of the agency. This section prevents principal employers from discriminating on racial grounds against workers provided to them by agencies.

(3) The principal does not contravene subsection (2)(b) by doing any act in relation to a person not of a particular racial group at a time when, if the work were to be done by a person taken into the principal's employment, being of that racial group would be a genuine occupational qualification for the job.

Section 7(3)
The grounds on which discrimination is prohibited are the same as for direct employees and the "genuine occupational qualification" defence is also available.

See the corresponding provisions of the SDA, section 9.

(4) Nothing in this section shall render unlawful any act done by the principal for the benefit of a contract worker not ordinarily resident in Great Britain in or in connection with allowing him to do work to which this section applies, where the purpose of his being allowed to do that work is to provide him with training in skills which he appears to the principal to intend to exercise wholly outside Great Britain.

Section 7(4)
This is the same exclusion in relation to contract workers as applies to employees under section 6 above.

(5) Subsection (2)(c) does not apply to benefits, facilities or services of any description if the principal is concerned with the provision (for payment or not) of benefits, facilities or services of that description to the public, or to a section of the public to which the contract worker in question belongs, unless that provision differs in a material respect from the provision of the benefits, facilities or services by the principal to his contract workers.

Section 7(5)

As with section 4(4), this subsection draws a distinction between benefits facilities or services provided to the contract worker as part of the arrangements for the employment and those benefits facilities or services made available to them as an ordinary member of the public.

See also section 9(4) SDA.

Meaning of employment at establishment in Great Britain.

8.–(1) For the purposes of this Part ("the relevant purposes"), employment is to be regarded as being at an establishment in Great Britain unless the employee does his work wholly or mainly outside Great Britain.

(2) In relation to–

(a) employment on board a ship registered at a port of registry in Great Britain; or

(b) employment on an aircraft or hovercraft registered in the United Kingdom and operated by a person who has his principal place of business, or is ordinarily resident, in Great Britain, other than an aircraft or hovercraft while so operated in pursuance of a contract with a person who has his principal place of business, or is ordinarily resident, outside the United Kingdom,

subsection (1) shall have effect as if the words "or mainly" were omitted.

Section 8(2)

For some reason, this is one of the few sub-sections of the Act which is not worded identically to the corresponding provisions of the SDA even though its effect is broadly the same, i.e. in omitting the words "or mainly" (see section 10(2) SDA). Sub-section (b) additionally refers to aircraft and hovercraft operated under a contract with a person normally resident or whose principal place of business is outside the UK, which provision does not appear in section 10(2) SDA.

(3) In the case of employment on board a ship registered at a port of registry in Great Britain (except where the employee does his work wholly outside Great Britain) the ship shall for the relevant purposes be deemed to be the establishment.

(4) Where work is not done at an establishment it shall be treated for the relevant purposes as done at the establishment from which it is done or (where it is not done from any establishment) at the establishment with which it has the closest connection.

(5) In relation to employment concerned with exploration of the sea bed or subsoil or the exploitation of their natural resources, Her Majesty may by Order in Council provide that subsections (1) to (3) shall have effect as if in both subsection (1) and subsection (3) the last reference to Great Britain included any area for the time being designated under section 1(7) of the Continental Shelf Act 1964 [or specified

under section 10(8) of the Petroleum Act 1998] except an area or part of an area in which the law of Northern Ireland applies.

Section 8(5)
The words underlined above are to be replaced with the words 'any activity within section 11(2) of the Petroleum Act 1998' from a day to be appointed. The words 'or specified under section 10(8) of the Petroleum Act 1998' were inserted by section 50, Schedule 4, paragraph 11 of that Act but have not yet been brought into force.

(6) An Order in Council under subsection (5) may provide that, in relation to employment to which the Order applies, this Part is to have effect with such modifications as are specified in the Order.

(7) An Order in Council under subsection (5) shall be of no effect unless a draft of the Order has been laid before and approved by resolution of each House of Parliament.

Section 8(7)
The note to section 4(1) makes clear that the scope of protection for employees under the RRA (and the SDA) is wider than that afforded under the Employment Rights Act 1996 so that a person who has a complaint of unfair dismissal and a claim of race discrimination but who works only occasionally in the UK will be prevented from pursuing an unfair dismissal claim but will be allowed to proceed with the claim under the RRA.

This section corresponds to section 10 of the SDA.

Exception for seamen recruited abroad.

9.–(1) Nothing in section 4 shall render unlawful any act done by an employer in or in connection with employment by him on any ship in the case of a person who applied or was engaged for that employment outside Great Britain.

(2) Nothing in section 7 shall, as regards work to which that section applies, render unlawful any act done by the principal in or in connection with such work on any ship in the case of a contract worker who was engaged outside Great Britain by the person by whom he is supplied.

(3) Subsections (1) and (2) do not apply to employment or work concerned with exploration of the sea bed or subsoil or the exploitation of their natural resources in any area for the time being designated under section 1(7) of the Continental Shelf Act 1964 [or specified under section 10(8) of the Petroleum Act 1998], not being an area or part of an area in which the law of Northern Ireland applies.

Section 9(3)
The words underlined above are to be replaced with the words 'any activity within section 11(2) of the Petroleum Act 1998' from a day to be appointed. The words 'or specified under section 10(8) of the Petroleum Act 1998' were inserted by section 50, Schedule 4, paragraph 11 of that Act but have not yet been brought into force.

(4) For the purposes of subsection (1) a person brought to Great Britain with a view to his entering into an agreement in Great Britain to be employed on any ship shall be treated as having applied for the employment outside Great Britain.

DISCRIMINATION BY OTHER BODIES

Partnerships.

Section 10
This part is intended to govern relationships where, although not directly one of employer and employee, access to employment is affected or controlled.

10.–(1) It is unlawful for a firm consisting of six or more partners, in relation to a position as partner in the firm, to discriminate against a person–

(a) in the arrangements they make for the purpose of determining who should be offered that position; or

(b) in the terms on which they offer him that position; or

(c) by refusing or deliberately omitting to offer him that position; or

(d) in a case where the person already holds that position–

(i) in the way they afford him access to any benefits, facilities or services, or by refusing or deliberately omitting to afford him access to them; or

(ii) by expelling him from that position, or subjecting him to any other detriment.

(2) Subsection (1) shall apply in relation to persons proposing to form themselves into a partnership as it applies in relation to a firm.

Section 10(2)
Corresponding to section 11 SDA, the protection offered to employees and prospective employees is extended, by this section, to partners, applicants for partnership, those who wish to be considered in the formation of new partnerships. However, under the SDA there is no minimum requirement for six partners.

(3) Subsection (1)(a) and (c) do not apply to a position as partner where, if it were employment, being of a particular racial group would be a genuine occupational qualification for the job.

Section 10(3)
The "genuine occupational qualification" defence is also available.

(4) In the case of a limited partnership references in this section to a partner shall be construed as references to a general partner as defined in section 3 of the Limited Partnerships Act 1907.

Section 10(4)
See section 11 SDA

Trade unions etc.

Section 11
Despite its heading, this section applies both to organisations of employees and of employers. It also applies to professional and trade associations.

11.–(1) This section applies to an organisation of workers, an organisation of employers, or any other organisation whose members carry on a particular profession or trade for the purposes of which the organisation exists.

(2) It is unlawful for an organisation to which this section applies, in the case of a person who is not a member of the organisation, to discriminate against him–

(a) in the terms on which it is prepared to admit him to membership; or
(b) by refusing or deliberately omitting to accept, his application for membership.

(3) It is unlawful for an organisation to which this section applies, in the case of a person who is a member of the organisation, to discriminate against him–

(a) in the way it affords him access to any benefits, facilities or services, or by refusing or deliberately omitting to afford him access to them; or
(b) by depriving him of membership, or varying the terms on which he is a member; or
(c) by subjecting him to any other detriment.

Section 11(3)
Without this section protection from discrimination and access to employment might be rendered void if those seeking employment could otherwise be prevented from working by virtue of them being denied membership of an organisation which is a condition of employment.

For this reason the section also covers organisations of self-employed people.

This section is the same as section 12 of the SDA except that the latter makes provisions for death and retirement benefits.

Qualifying bodies.

12.–(1) It is unlawful for an authority or body which can confer an authorisation or qualification which is needed for, or facilitates, engagement in a particular profession or trade to discriminate against a person-

(a) in the terms on which it is prepared to confer on him that authorisation or qualification; or
(b) by refusing, or deliberately omitting to grant, his application for it; or
(c) by withdrawing it from him or varying the terms on which he holds it.

(2) In this section–

(a) "authorisation or qualification" includes recognition, registration, enrolment, approval and certification;
(b) "confer" includes renew or extend.

(3) Subsection (1) does not apply to discrimination which is rendered unlawful by section 17 or 18.

Section 12
Bodies which have the power to confer authorisation or qualification or some other form of certification which is necessary for a person to be able to work at a particular trade or profession are required not to discriminate on grounds of race. Such bodies include the BMA, the General Medical Council and the Licensing Justices. It also includes those bodies responsible for adopting Parliamentary candidates. Surprisingly it does not include the body which makes recommendations on the appointment of lay justices although the matter is now before the Court of Appeal.

Under section 13(2) SDA, a body may be entitled to withhold the qualification or certification if it considers that, in the past the person or organisation has engaged in discrimination. No similar provision appears here.

Subsection (3) avoids double liability arising under the other provisions mentioned.

For the corresponding provisions in relation to sex, see section 13 SDA.

Persons concerned with provision of vocational training.

13.–(1) It is unlawful, in the case of an individual seeking or undergoing training which would help fit him for any employment, for any person who provides, or makes arrangements for the provision of, facilities for such training to discriminate against him–

(a) in the terms on which that person affords him access to any training courses or other facilities; or
(b) by refusing or deliberately omitting to afford him such access; or
(c) by terminating his training; or
(d) by subjecting him to any detriment during the course of his training.

Section 13(1)
The lack of access to training may also limit a person's ability to take up a particular employment or profession. Although worded slightly differently, this section, like section 14 SDA, outlaws discrimination by those providing the training in relation to access to the training or training facilities and the terms on which training is provided.

> *There are certain limited circumstances in which positive discrimination in the provision of training is allowed - see section 38 below (and section 47 SDA).*

(2) Subsection (1) does not apply to–

(a) discrimination which is rendered unlawful by section 4(1) or (2) or section 17 or 18; or

(b) discrimination which would be rendered unlawful by any of those provisions but for the operation of any other provision of this Act.

> **Section 13(2)**
> *This avoids liability arising twice for the same act.*
> *See also section 14 SDA*

Employment agencies.

14.–(1) It is unlawful for an employment agency to discriminate against a person–

(a) in the terms on which the agency offers to provide any of its services; or

(b) by refusing or deliberately omitting to provide any of its services; or

(c) in the way it provides any of its services.

> **Section 14(1)**
> *Employment agencies are not allowed to refuse to take a person on or to provide services which are less favourable on racial grounds.*

(2) It is unlawful for a local education authority or education authority or any other person to do any acting providing services in pursuance of arrangements made, or a direction given, under section 10 of the Employment and Training Act 1973 which constitutes discrimination.

(3) References in subsection (1) to the services of an employment agency include guidance on careers and any other services related to employment.

(4) This section does not apply if the discrimination only concerns employment which the employer could lawfully refuse to offer the person in question.

> **Section 14(4)**
> *makes available the "genuine occupational qualification" defence.*

(5) An employment agency or local education authority, education authority or other person shall not be subject to any liability under this section if it proves-

(a) that it acted in reliance on a statement made to it by the employer to the effect that, by reason of the operation of subsection (4), its action would not be unlawful; and

(b) that it was reasonable for it to rely on the statement.

Section 14(5)
An agency will escape liability for acts of discrimination if it was misled by the employer. In such a case there may be criminal liability for the making of the misleading statement - see subsection (6) below.

(6) A person who knowingly or recklessly makes a statement such as is referred to in subsection (5)(a) which in a material respect is false or misleading commits an offence, and shall be liable on summary conviction to a fine not exceeding level 5 on the standard scale.

Section 14(6)
The scale of fine is subject to change and applies to a wide range of criminal offences.

See also section 15 SDA

Training Commission etc.

15.–(1) It is unlawful for the Secretary of State to discriminate in the provision of facilities or services under section 2 of the Employment and Training Act 1973

(1A) It is unlawful for Scottish Enterprise or Highlands and Islands Enterprise to discriminate in the provision of facilities or services under such arrangements as are mentioned in section 2(3) of the Enterprise and New Towns (Scotland) Act 1990 (arrangements analogous to arrangements in pursuance of section 2 of the said Act of 1973.

Section 15(1)–(1A)
This subsection applies only in Scotland

(2) This section does not apply in a case where–

(a) section 13 applies; or
(b) the Secretary of State is acting as an employment agency.

Section 15(2)
This section deals with the provision for training related to unemployment for the purposes of equipping somebody to return to work. Subsection (2) is designed to avoid double liability under sections 13 and 15 above.

Police

16.–(1) For the purposes of this Part, the holding of the office of constable shall be treated as employment-

(a) by the chief officer of police as respects any act done by him in relation to a constable or that office;

(b) by the police authority as respects any act done by them in relation to a constable or that office.

Section 16(1)

Police constables are not employees but office holders. Without this section police officers would be excluded from the protection of the Act. A person complaining of discrimination must bring their complaint against either the chief officer or the police authority, depending on who committed the unlawful act against the officer concerned.

It is important to note that this Part deals only with discrimination in employment. It permits officers or applicants who are victims of race discrimination to complain as if they were employees. Separate considerations apply in relation to the actions of police officers in the performance of their duties.

(2) There shall be paid out of the police fund–

(a) any compensation, costs or expenses awarded against a chief officer of police in any proceedings brought against him under this Act, and any costs or expenses incurred by him in any such proceedings so far as not recovered by him in the proceedings; and

(b) any sum required by a chief officer of police for the settlement of any claim made against him under this Act if the settlement is approved by the police authority.

Section 16(2)

This section makes provision for the payment of damages and costs awarded in discrimination claims from public funds, i.e. the police budget.

(3) Any proceedings under this Act which, by virtue of subsection (1), would lie against a chief officer of police shall be brought against the chief officer of police for the time being or, in the case of a vacancy in that office, against the person for the time being performing the functions of that office; and references in subsection (2) to the chief officer of police shall be construed accordingly.

Section 16(3)

Claims brought by police officers in connection with their duties as officers are to be brought against the Chief Constable, or the person acting in that capacity for the time being and not the Constabulary or the Police Authority.

(4) Subsection (1) applies to a police cadet and an appointment as a police cadet as it applies to a constable and the office of constable.

(5) In this section-

"chief officer of police"–

(a) in relation to a person appointed, or an appointment falling to be made, under a specified Act, has the same meaning as in the Police Act,
(b) in relation to any other person or appointment, means the officer who has the direction and control of the body of constables or cadets in question;

"the Police Act" means, for England and Wales, the Police Act 1996 or, for Scotland, the Police (Scotland) Act 1967;

"police authority"–

(a) in relation to a person appointed, or an appointment falling to be made, under a specified Act, has the same meaning as in the Police Act,
(b) in relation to any other person or appointment, means the authority by whom the person in question is or on appointment would be paid;

"police cadet" means any person appointed to undergo training with a view to becoming a constable;

"police fund" in relation to a chief officer of police within paragraph (a) of the above definition of that term has the same meaning as in the Police Act, and in any other case means money provided by the police authority;

"specified Act" means the Metropolitan Police Act 1829, the City of London Police Act 1839 or the Police Act.

Section 16(5)
See section 17 SDA (with the exception of subsections (2) and (3))

PART III DISCRIMINATION IN OTHER FIELDS

EDUCATION

Discrimination by bodies in charge of educational establishments.

17. It is unlawful, in relation to an educational establishment falling within column 1 of the following table, for a person indicated in relation to the establishment in column 2 (the "responsible body") to discriminate against a person–

(a) in the terms on which it offers to admit him to the establishment as a pupil; or
(b) by refusing or deliberately omitting to accept an application for his admission to the establishment as a pupil; or
(c) where he is a pupil of the establishment–
    (i) in the way it affords him access to any benefits, facilities or services, or by refusing or deliberately omitting to afford him access to them; or
    (ii) by excluding him from the establishment or subjecting him to any other detriment.

TABLE

ENGLAND AND WALES

Establishment	*Responsible Body*
1. Educational establishment maintained by a local education authority.	Local education authority or governing body, according to which of them has the function in question.
2. Independent school not being a special school.	Proprietor.
3. Special school not maintained by a local education authority.	Proprietor.
3B. Institution within the further education sector (within the meaning of section 91(3) of the Further and Higher Education Act 1992	Governing body.
4. University.	Governing body.
4A. Institution, other than a university, within the higher education sector (within the meaning of section 91(5) of the Further and Higher Education Act 1992)	Governing body.
5. Establishment (not falling within paragraphs 1 to 4A) providing full-time or part-time education, being an establishment designated under section 24(1) of the Sex Discrimination Act 1975 for the purposes of paragraph 5 of the corresponding table in section 22 of that Act.	Governing body.
Scotland	
6. Educational establishment managed by an education authority.	Education Authority.

Establishment	*Responsible Body*
7. Educational establishment in respect of which the managers are for the time being receiving grants under section 75(c) or (d) of the Education (Scotland) Act 1962.	Managers of the educational establishment
8. University	Governing body.
9. Independent school.	Proprietor.
10. Any other educational establishment (not falling within paragraphs 6, 7 and 9) providing full or part-time school education or futher education.	Managers of the educational establishment.

Meaning of pupil in section 17

17A. For the purposes of section 17, 'pupil' includes, in England and Wales, any person who receives education at a school or institution to which that section applies.

Section 17A

It is unlawful for any educational establishment to discriminate against a person on racial grounds in the terms of admission the training or education offered or the way in which he/she is treated whilst on a course of education. This includes the exclusion of pupils (section 17(c)(ii)) so statistical information showing a significantly higher incidence of exclusion of black pupils or a tendency to exclude black pupils for lesser offences would be evidence of direct discrimination.

If a complaint arises it must be brought against the responsible body identified in the table. Discrimination is unlawful even if it is for a positive motive. An admissions policy which sought to ensure that there were equal numbers of pupils from different racial or ethnic groups on a course would discriminate unlawfully if people with the same level of qualification were excluded while less qualified people from that racial or ethnic group were admitted because of the quota system.

The discrimination must be assessed in relation to that establishment alone. It is not open to a complainant to draw a comparison with another educational establishment in order to establish discrimination.

Indirect discrimination is also unlawful although the defence of justification is available.

See section 22 SDA

Other discrimination by local education authorities.

18.–(1) It is unlawful for a local education authority, in carrying out such of its functions under the Education Acts as do not fall under section 17, to do any act which constitutes racial discrimination.

(2) It is unlawful for an education authority, in carrying out such of its functions under the Education (Scotland) Acts as do not fall under section 17, to do any act which constitutes racial discrimination.

Discrimination by Further Education and Higher Education Funding Councils

18A. It is unlawful for the Further Education Funding Council for England, the Further Education Funding Council for Wales, the Higher Education Funding Council for England or the Higher Education Funding Council for Wales in carrying out their functions under the Education Acts, to do any act which constitutes sex discrimination.

Section 18C

This section was repealed by the School Standards and Framework Act 1998 as from 1 September 1999.

Discrimination by Teacher Training Agency

18D. It is unlawful for the Teacher Training Agency in carrying out their functions under part I of the Education Act 1994 to any act which constitutes sex discrimination.

Section 18A–D

In carrying out their functions all the bodies named in these sections must ensure that they carry out their functions free of any discrimination.

Any act of discrimination not covered by section 17 above may give rise to a liability on the part of the local education authority. This will include the provision of school meals, educational welfare services, transport, recreational facilities and the awarding of discretionary grants.

Subsection (1) does not apply in Scotland; subsection (2) applies only in Scotland.

The obligations under sections 17 and 18 cover all the schools in the area covered by the local authority, even those which are grant maintained and not therefore under the control of the local education authority.

They are binding on the authority all of the time. If the drawing up of catchment areas has the effect of excluding a disproportionate number of members of a particular ethnic minority, this could be unlawful. So even if a temporary difficulty prevents the authority from providing equal provision, for example, a fire at a particular school, an immediate obligation arises to secure alternative facilities and it may be liable for damages to anyone disadvantaged by the lack of provision until the alternative is secured.

See section 23 SDA.

General duty in public sector of education.

19.–(1) Without prejudice to its obligation to comply with any other provision of this Act, a body to which this subsection applies shall be under a general duty to secure that facilities for education provided by it, and any ancillary benefits or services, are provided without racial discrimination.

(2) The following provisions of the Education Act 1996, namely–

(a) section 496 (power of Secretary of State to require duties under that Act to be exercised reasonably); and
(b) section 497 (powers of Secretary of State where local education authorities etc. are in default), shall apply to the performance by a body to which subsection (1) applies of the duties imposed by sections 17, 18, 18A, and 18D, and shall also apply to the performance of the general duty imposed by subsection (1), as they apply to the performance by a local education authority of a duty imposed by that Act.

(3) Section 71 of the Education (Scotland) Act 1962 (power of the Secretary of State to require duties in that Act to be exercised) shall apply to the performance by a body to which subsection (1) applies of the duties imposed by sections 17, 18, 18A, and 18D, and shall also apply to the performance of the general duty imposed by subsection (1), as the said section 71 applies to the performance by an education authority of a duty imposed by that Act.

(4) The sanctions in subsections (2) and (3) shall be the only sanctions for breach of the general duty in subsection (1), but without prejudice to the enforcement of sections 17, 18, 18A, and 18D, under section 57 or otherwise (where the breach is also a contravention of either of those sections).

(5) The Secretary of State shall have the power to cause a local inquiry to be held under section 68 of the Education (Scotland) Act 1962 into any matter arising from subsection (3).

(6) Subsection (1) applies to–

(a) local education authorities in England and Wales;
(b) education authorities in Scotland;
(c) any other body which is a responsible body in relation to–
  (i) an establishment falling within paragraph 1, 3, 3A or 3B of the table in section 17;
  (ii) an establishment designated under section 24(1) of the Sex Discrimination Act 1975 as falling within paragraph (c) of section 24(2) of that Act;
  (iii) an establishment designated under the said section 24(1) as falling within paragraph (b) of the said section 24(2) where the grants in question are payable under section 485 of the Education Act 1996.
(d) the Further Education Funding Council for England and the Further Education Funding Council for Wales.
(e) the Funding Agency for Schools and the Schools Funding Council for Wales.
(f) the Teacher Training Agency.

Section 19

This section is intended to place a positive duty on education authorities to take action to ensure the elimination of discrimination. This section is only enforceable by action of the Secretary of State, except that, in relation to Wales, those functions have been transferred to the National Assembly for Wales.

For the procedural requirements for bringing a claim against a public sector education or body see section 57 below.

The scope of sections 17 to 19 is similar to that covered by section s22 to 25 of the SDA

Discrimination by planning authorities

19A.–(1) It is unlawful for a planning authority to discriminate against a person carrying out their planning functions.

(2) In this section 'planning authority' means–

(a) in England and Wales, a county, county borough, district or London borough council, the Broads Authority, a National Park authority or a joint planning board, and

(b) in Scotland, a planning authority or regional planning authority,

and includes an urban development corporation and a body having functions (whether as an enterprise zone authority or a body invited to prepare a scheme) under Schedule 32 to the Local Government, Planning and Land Act 1980.

(3) In this section 'planning function' means-

(a) in England and Wales, functions under the Town and Country Planning Act 1990, the Planning (Listed Buildings and Conservation Areas) Act 1990 and the Planning (Hazardous Substances) Act 1990, and such other functions as may be prescribed, and

(b) in Scotland, the functions under the Town and Country Planning (Scotland) Act 1997, the Planning (Listed Buildings and Conservation Areas) (Scotland) Act 1997 and the Planning (Hazardous Substances) (Scotland) Act 1997 or Part IX of the Local Government (Scotland) Act 1973, and such other functions as may be prescribed,

and includes, in relation to an urban development corporation, planning functions under Part XVI of the Local Government, Planning and Land Act 1980 and, in relation to an enterprise zone authority or a body invited to prepare an enterprise zone scheme, functions under Part XVIII of that Act.

Section 19A

This provides an alternative remedy to judicial review of an authority's decision and would prevent the authority from succumbing to political or local pressure in the granting or withholding of planning consent.

GOODS, FACILITIES, SERVICES AND PREMISES

Discrimination in provision of goods, facilities or services.

20.– (1) It is unlawful for any person concerned with the provision (for payment or not) of goods, facilities or services to the public or a section of the public to discriminate against a person who seeks to obtain or use those goods, facilities or services-

(a) by refusing or deliberately omitting to provide him with any of them; or

(b) by refusing or deliberately omitting to provide him with goods, facilities or services of the like quality, in the like manner and on the like terms as are normal in the first-mentioned person's case in relation to other members of the public or (where the person so seeking belongs to a section of the public) to other members of that section.

(2) The following are examples of the facilities and services mentioned in subsection (1)-

(a) access to and use of any place which members of the public are permitted to enter;
(b) accommodation in a hotel, boarding house or other similar establishment;
(c) facilities by way of banking or insurance or for grants, loans, credit or finance;
(d) facilities for education;
(e) facilities for entertainment, recreation or refreshment;
(f) facilities for transport or travel;
(g) the services of any profession or trade, or any local or other public authority.

Section 20(1) and (2)

As can be seen from subsection (2) the Act provides examples of what is meant by facilities and services but there is otherwise no definition as to what is meant. There is however a definition of the words "profession" and "trade" in section 78.

It may be useful to give some examples of those things which have, in the past, been held to be facilities or services. These include assistance by a police officer, tax advice from a tax officer, the ability to stand for election to a governing body of a friendly society, a hire purchase credit scheme, the provision of surgical treatment and the availability of advertising space.

It does not, at present, include the actions of an immigration officer in dealing with the admission of a person to the country but the Race Relations (Amendment) Bill will remedy this by making those exercising statutory authority liable under the Act. Similarly, the services of a public authority under sub-section (g) is defined as including those things which can be compared to those provided in the private sector but this too will change when the amendment is in force.

A distinction has been drawn between the provision of a facility and permission to use such a facility. It is difficult to understand such a distinction if section 40 (section 50 SDA), which deals with indirect access to benefits, is considered. It is perhaps unlikely that such a distinction would be drawn today.

The goods facilities or services must be on offer to the public or to a section of the public in order to be caught by this provision. For membership of a club, for example if candidates were required to comply with formal conditions or criteria the facilities offered by the club were open to the public at large. If, however, membership of the club was dependant on the personal acceptability of the candidate to other members of the club, it would not be open to members of the public. But if such clubs admitted members of the public on payment of a fee they could not discriminate on grounds of race as to whether or not to admit someone who was prepared to pay that fee.

In perhaps one of the best known cases under the Sex Discrimination Act a man complained that the refusal by a local authority to allow him to use a swimming pool at concessionary rates until he reached a pensionable age of 65 was discriminatory because his wife was allowed to use the same facilities at a reduced fee from the age of 60. This provision was held to be discriminatory.

There is an important distinction between facilities and services provided by public authorities, as in the example above, concerning access to a local authority swimming pool, and the implementation of policies adopted by an authority or the carrying out of their statutory functions. A good example would be the Inland Revenue. When a tax officer is offering advice to a tax-payer this must be done in a way which doesn't discriminate on grounds of race. However, the collection of tax is a public duty and is not therefore covered by Section 20. Although not covered by this Act, any exercise of a statutory function is subject to judicial review in the normal way so that, if a discretion is exercised in a discriminatory way, judicial review may be sought on those grounds because it would not be a reasonable exercise of the discretion.

See section 29 SDA

Discrimination in disposal or management of premises.

21.–(1) It is unlawful for a person, in relation to premises in Great Britain of which he has power to dispose, to discriminate against another–

(a) in the terms on which he offers him those premises; or
(b) by refusing his application for those premises; or
(c) in his treatment of him in relation to any list of persons in need of premises of that description.

(2) It is unlawful for a person, in relation to premises managed by him, to discriminate against a person occupying the premises–

(a) in the way he affords him access to any benefits or facilities, or by refusing or deliberately omitting to afford him access to them; or
(b) by evicting him, or subjecting him to any other detriment.

(3) Subsection (1) does not apply to a person who owns an estate or interest in the premises and wholly occupies them unless he uses the services of an estate agent for the purposes of the disposal of the premises, or publishes or causes to be published an advertisement in connection with the disposal.

Section 21(3)
An owner occupier is exempt from the provisions of this section unless he uses the services of an estate agent or advertises the premises for disposal. Discriminatory advertisements are covered by section 29.
See section 30 SDA

Exception from ss. 20(1) and 21: small dwellings.

22.–(1) Sections 20(1) and 21 do not apply to the provision by a person of accommodation in any premises, or the disposal of premises by him, if–

(a) that person or a near relative of his ("the relevant occupier") resides, and intends to continue to reside, on the premises; and
(b) there is on the premises, in addition to the accommodation occupied by the relevant occupier, accommodation (not being storage accommodation or means of access) shared by the relevant occupier with other persons residing on the premises who are not members of his household; and
(c) the premises are small premises.

Section 22(1)
Premises where the owner or a near relative is living are exempt from the provisions of sections 20 and 21 but only if those premises amount to a small dwelling as defined in this section.

(2) Premises shall be treated for the purposes of this section as small premises if–

(a) in the case of premises comprising residential accommodation for one or more households (under separate letting or similar agreements) in addition to the accommodation occupied by the relevant occupier, there is not normally residential accommodation for more than two such households and only the relevant occupier and any member of his household reside in the accommodation occupied by him;
(b) in the case of premises not falling within paragraph (a), there is not normally residential accommodation on the premises for more than six persons in addition to the relevant occupier and any members of his household.

Section 22
Where the accommodation does not consist of separate households the exemption only applies if the accommodation is provided for not more than six people in addition to the owner-occupier. This would include bed and breakfast accommodation and guest houses.
See section 32 SDA

Further exceptions from ss. 20(1) and 21.

23.–(1) Sections 20(1) and 21 do not apply–

(a) to discrimination which is rendered unlawful by any provision of Part II or section 17 or 18; or

(b) to discrimination which would be rendered unlawful by any provision of Part II but for any of the following provisions, namely sections 4(3), 5(1)(b), 6, 7(4), 9 and 14(4).

Section 23(1) (a)–(b)

(a) Thus avoiding double liability in respect of employment or education.

(b) 4(3) – employment in a private household;

5(1)(b) – the GOQ defence;

6 – the provision of skills to be exercised outside Great Britain;

7(4) – the section 6 defence in respect of contract workers;

9 – seamen recruited abroad;

14(4) – the employment agencies general defence.

(2) Section 20(1) does not apply to anything done by a person as a participant in arrangements under which he (for reward or not) takes into his home, and treats as if they were members of his family, children, elderly persons, or persons requiring a special degree of care and attention.

Discrimination: consent for assignment or sub-letting.

24.–(1) Where the licence or consent of the landlord or of any other person is required for the disposal to any person of premises in Great Britain comprised in a tenancy, it is unlawful for the landlord or other person to discriminate against a person by withholding the licence or consent for disposal of the premises to him.

(2) Subsection (1) does not apply if–

(a) the person withholding a licence of consent, or a near relative of his ("the relevant occupier") resides, and intends to continue to reside, on the premises; and

(b) there is on the premises, in addition to the accommodation occupied by the relevant occupier, accommodation (not being storage accommodation or means of access) shared by the relevant occupier with other persons residing on the premises who are not members of his household; and

(c) the premises are small premises.

(3) Section 22(2) (meaning of "small premises") shall apply for the purposes of this as well as of that section.

(4) In this section

"tenancy" means a tenancy created by a lease or sub-lease, by an agreement for a lease or sub-lease or by a tenancy agreement or in pursuance of any enactment; and

"disposal", in relation to premises comprised in a tenancy, includes assignment or assignation of the tenancy and sub-letting or parting with possession of the premises or any part of the premises.

(5) This section applies to tenancies created before the passing of this Act, as well as to others.

Sections 21 and 24
Prohibit discrimination in the buying, renting or allocation of premises. This includes land, houses, flats and business premises, but hotel accommodation is dealt with in section 20.

A person letting premises includes a local authority or a company as well as an individual.

Two Codes of Practice issued by the CRE provide guidance and examples of good practice on the provision of housing:

The Code of Practice in Rented Housing (SI 1991/227)

The Code of Practice in Non-Rented (Owner-Occupied) Housing (SI 1992/619)

See section 35 for the general exemptions.

See also section 31 SDA.

Discrimination: associations not within s. 11.

25.–(1) This section applies to any association of persons (however described, whether corporate or unincorporate, and whether or not its activities are carried on for profit) if–

(a) it has twenty-five or more members; and
(b) admission to membership is regulated by its constitution and is so conducted that the members do not constitute a section of the public within the meaning of section 20(1); and
(c) it is not an organisation to which section 11 applies.

Section 25(1)
i.e. trade unions and employers' associations.

(2) It is unlawful for an association to which this section applies, in the case of a person who is not a member of the association, to discriminate against him–

(a) in the terms on which it is prepared to admit him to membership; or
(b) by refusing or deliberately omitting to accept his application for membership.

(3) It is unlawful for an association to which this section applies, in the case of a person who is a member or associate of the association, to discriminate against him–

(a) in the way it affords him access to any benefits, facilities or services, or by refusing or deliberately omitting to afford him access to them; or
(b) in the case of a member, by depriving him of membership, or varying the terms on which he is a member; or
(c) in the case of an associate, by depriving him of his rights as an associate, or varying those rights; or
(d) in either case, by subjecting him to any other detriment.

(4) For the purposes of this section–

(a) a person is a member of an association if he belongs to it by virtue of his admission to any sort of membership provided for by its constitution (and is not merely a person with certain rights under its constitution by virtue of his membership of some other association), and references to membership of an association shall be construed accordingly;
(b) a person is an associate of an association to which this section applies if, not being a member of it, he has under its constitution some or all of the rights enjoyed by members (or would have apart from any provision in its constitution authorising the refusal of those rights in particular cases).

Section 25(4)
This section renders unlawful membership requirements for private clubs which discriminate on racial grounds but see the exemptions in section 26 below.

Exception from s. 25 for certain associations.

26.–(1) An association to which section 25 applies is within this subsection if the main object of the association is to enable the benefits of membership (whatever they may be) to be enjoyed by persons of a particular racial group defined otherwise than by reference to colour; and in determining whether that is the main object of an association regard shall be had to the essential character of the association and to all relevant circumstances including, in particular, the extent to which the affairs of the association are so conducted that the persons primarily enjoying the benefits of membership are of the racial group in question.

(2) In the case of an association within subsection (1), nothing in section 25 shall render unlawful any act not involving discrimination on the ground of colour.

Section 26

The exemption does not include any discrimination or membership requirement based on a person's colour but permits membership to be confined to particular national or ethnic groups, e.g. ex-patriates clubs.

26A. Discrimination by, or in relation to, barristers

(1) It is unlawful for a barrister or barrister's clerk, in relation to any offer of a pupillage or tenancy, to discriminate against a person–

(a) in the arrangements which are made for the purpose of determining to whom it should be offered;
(b) in respect of any terms on which it is offered; or
(c) by refusing, or deliberately omitting, to offer it to him.

(2) It is unlawful for a barrister or barrister's clerk, in relation to a pupil or tenant in the chambers in question, to discriminate against him–

(a) in respect of any terms applicable to him as a pupil or tenant;
(b) in the opportunities for training, or gaining experience which are afforded or denied to him;
(c) in the benefits, facilities or services which are afforded or denied to him; or
(d) by terminating his pupillage or by subjecting him to any pressure to leave the chambers or other detriment.

(3) It is unlawful for any person, in relation to the giving, withholding or acceptance of instructions to a barrister, to discriminate against any person.

(4) In this section—

"barrister's clerk" includes any person carrying out any of the functions of a barrister's clerk; and

"pupil", "pupillage", "tenancy" and "tenant" have the meanings commonly associated with their use in the context of a set of barristers' chambers.

(5) This section does not apply to Scotland.

Section 26A

Barristers and pupils are not employees but self-employed practitioners. For this reason, the provisions of this Act in relation to employment do not apply.

These provisions, introduced by the Courts and Legal Services Act 1990, outlaw discrimination in relation to barristers or pupils.

It not only means that the chambers or the chambers' clerk cannot discriminate but, by sub-section (3) solicitors and/or their clients cannot discriminate by refusing to instruct a barrister on racial grounds.

26B. Discrimination by, or in relation to, advocates

(1) It is unlawful for an advocate, in relation to taking any person as his pupil, to discriminate against a person—

(a) in the arrangements which he makes for the purpose of determining whom he will take as his pupil;
(b) in respect of any terms on which he offers to take a person as his pupil; or
(c) by refusing, or deliberately omitting, to take a person as his pupil.

(2) It is unlawful for an advocate, in relation to a person who is a pupil, to discriminate against him—

(a) in respect of any terms applicable to him as a pupil;
(b) in the opportunities for training, or gaining experience which are afforded or denied to him;
(c) in the benefits, facilities or services which are afforded or denied to him; or
(d) by terminating the relationship or by subjecting him to any pressure to terminate the relationship or other detriment.

(3) It is unlawful for any person, in relation to the giving, withholding or acceptance of instructions to an advocate, to discriminate against any person.

(4) In this section—

"advocate" means a member of the Faculty of Advocates practising as such; and

"pupil" has the meaning commonly associated with its use in the context of a person training to be an advocate.

(5) Section 3 applies for the purposes of this section as it applies for the purposes of any provision of Part II.

(6) This section does not apply to England and Wales.

Section 26B
See the note to 26A above.

Section 26B, while expressed in almost identical terms to 26A, is necessary because of the different system of court advocacy in Scotland.

See sections 35A and 35B SDA.

EXTENT

Extent of Part III.

27.–(1) Sections 17 to 19 do not apply to benefits, facilities or services outside Great Britain except–

(a) travel in a ship registered at a port of registry in Great Britain; and
(b) benefits, facilities or services provided on a ship so registered.

Section 27(1)
It is not easy to understand this section as sections 17 to 19 deal with education and planning. See section 36(5) SDA.

(2) Section 20(1)–

(a) does not apply to goods, facilities or services outside Great Britain except as provided in subsections (3) and (4); and

(b) does not apply to facilities by way of banking or insurance or for grants, loans, credit or finance, where the facilities are for a purpose to be carried out, or in connection with risks wholly or mainly arising, outside Great Britain.

Section 27(2)(a)–(b)
(a) The protection from discrimination in relation to the provision of goods facilities or services extends only to those which are offered or provided within Great Britain

(b) Banking, insurance and finance are international industries. Even if the services are provided by a person or company based in Great Britain, the protection will not be available if the services or facilities are to be provided wholly or mainly outside Great Britain.

(3) Section 20(1) applies to the provision of facilities for travel outside Great Britain where the refusal or omission occurs in Great Britain or on a ship, aircraft or hovercraft within subsection (4).

Section 27(3)
By contrast, where a travel agent offers facilities or services from a base in Great Britain the protection is afforded even if those facilities or services are to be enjoyed outside Great Britain on a ship, aircraft or hovercraft in the same circumstances as employment is protected under section 8 (see sub-section (4) below).

(4) Section 20(1) applies on and in relation to–

(a) any ship registered at a port of registry in Great Britain; and

(b) any aircraft or hovercraft registered in the United Kingdom and operated by a person who has his principal place of business, or is ordinarily resident, in Great Britain,

even if the ship, aircraft or hovercraft is outside Great Britain.

(5) This section shall not render unlawful an act done in or over a country outside the United Kingdom, or in or over that country's territorial waters, for the purpose of complying with the laws of that country.

> **Section 27(5)**
> *Even if the protection is afforded under sub-sections (3) and (4) above, it is excluded if the act is done over a country's air space and/or territorial waters and the act is necessary to comply with the laws of that country.*

Part IV Other Unlawful Acts

Discriminatory practices.

28.–(1) In this section "discriminatory practice" means the application of a requirement or condition which results in an act of discrimination which is unlawful by virtue of any provision of Part II or III taken with section 1(1)(b), or which would be likely to result in such an act of discrimination if the persons to whom it is applied included persons of any particular racial group as regards which there has been no occasion for applying it.

(2) A person acts in contravention of this section if and so long as–

(a) he applies a discriminatory practice; or

(b) he operates practices or other arrangements which in any circumstances would call for the application by him of a discriminatory practice.

(3) Proceedings in respect of a contravention of this section shall be brought only by the Commission in accordance with sections 58 to 62.

> **Section 28**
> *It may be the case that individuals who are adversely affected by discriminatory practices are not willing to complain. This provision allows the Commission for Racial Equality to take action against any person or body even if no individual is willing to complain.*
>
> *This section also deals with a situation where discrimination is so deeply ingrained that no victims of discrimination are ever produced. For example, a company may be so well known for its opposition to employing members of a particular racial or ethnic group that they never make applications for positions with that company.*
>
> *Only the CRE can take action under this section.*
>
> *See section 37 SDA*

Discriminatory advertisements.

29.–(1) It is unlawful to publish or to cause to be published an advertisement which indicates, or might reasonably be understood as indicating, an intention by a person to do an act of discrimination, whether the doing of that act by him would be lawful or, by virtue of Part II or III, unlawful.

Section 29(1)
A definition of the word advertisement appears in section 78 and is very wide. Although this section corresponds to section 38 of the SDA it is more widely defined and covers discriminatory acts whether or not they are or might be unlawful. However, sub-section (2) below goes on to exclude those circumstances where the discrimination would be lawful. When taken together, sub-sections (1) and (2) have the same effect as section 38(1) SDA.

(2) Subsection (1) does not apply to an advertisement–

(a) if the intended act would be lawful by virtue of any of sections 5, 6, 7(3) and (4), 10(3), 26, 34(2)(b), 35 to 39 and 41; or

(b) if the advertisement relates to the services of an employment agency (within the meaning of section 14(1)) and the intended act only concerns employment which the employer could by virtue of section 5, 6 or 7(3) or (4) lawfully refuse to offer to persons against whom the advertisement indicates an intention to discriminate.

Section 29(2)
(a) Section 5 – the GOQ defence;

section 6 – training in skills to be exercised outside Great Britain;

section 7(3) and (4) – contract workers;

section 10(3) – partnerships;

section 26 – certain private clubs and associations;

section 34(2)(b) – charities;

sections 35 to 39 – the general exceptions relating to education, welfare, training, sports and competitions;

section 41 – acts done under statutory authority.

(3) Subsection (1) does not apply to an advertisement which indicates that persons of any class defined otherwise than by reference to colour, race or ethnic or national origins are required for employment outside Great Britain.

(4) The publisher of an advertisement made unlawful by subsection (1) shall not be subject to any liability under that subsection in respect of the publication of the advertisement if he proves-

(a) that the advertisement was published in reliance on a statement made to him by the person who caused it to be published to the effect that, by reason of the operation of subsection (2) or (3), the publication would not be unlawful; and

(b) that it was reasonable for him to rely on the statement.

Section 29(4)
Although the publication of a discriminatory advertisement will be unlawful, the publisher of the advertisement will not be made liable if he reasonably relied on a statement by the person placing the advertisement that it didn't contravene the provisions of the Act. This sub-section will not allow a publisher to escape liability unless it was reasonable to rely on the statement of the person publishing the advertisement. In other words, if it was obvious that the advertisement would contravene the provisions of the act the publisher as well as the person placing the advertisement will be liable.

(5) A person who knowingly or recklessly makes a statement such as is mentioned in subsection (4)(a) which in a material respect is false or misleading commits an offence, and shall be liable on summary conviction to a fine not exceeding level 5 on the standard scale.

Section 29(5)
This provision, in relation to the making of misleading statements, is the same as in sub-section (6) of section 14 relating to employment agencies. A person who makes a misleading statement either knowing that it's misleading or not caring whether it would be misleading commits an offence and is liable to a fine on a scale which is subject to regular change.

See section 38 SDA

Instructions to discriminate.

30. It is unlawful for a person–

(a) who has authority over another person; or
(b) in accordance with whose wishes that other person is accustomed to act,

to instruct him to do any act which is unlawful by virtue of Part II or III, or procure or attempt to procure the doing by him of any such act.

Section 30
See section 39 SDA

Pressure to discriminate.

31.–(1) It is unlawful to induce, or attempt to induce, a person to do any act which contravenes Part II or III.

(2) An attempted inducement is not prevented from falling within subsection (1) because it is not made directly to the person in question, if it is made in such a way that he is likely to hear of it.

Sections 30 and 31

Apply whether or not the unlawful act actually takes place. Their intention is to prevent either instructions or pressure being applied in order to make someone else carry out a discriminatory act.

The Employment Appeals Tribunal has decided that the words 'whose wishes that other person is accustomed to act' in section 30(b) (section 39(b) SDA) meant that there had to be some relationship between the person giving the instruction and the person required to act on it. The case involved a request by a prospective employer to a local school to send along for interview people who might be employed as a filing clerk. The person at the school was asked not to send along any coloured applicants because that person would feel out of place since there were no other coloured employees. Because there was no evidence that that prospective employer had made a request either to the school or to the very person at the school who had taken a call she was not a person "in accordance with whose wishes" she was accustomed to act. The EAT went on to say that if there was evidence that that employer had made requests to the school before then the employer would be caught by sub-section (b). However, by giving a wide interpretation to the word induce or attempting to induce, the EAT found the prospective employer had contravened this section (section 40 of the SDA).

See section 40 SDA

Liability of employers and principals.

32.–(1) Anything done by a person in the course of his employment shall be treated for the purposes of this Act (except as regards offences thereunder) as done by his employer as well as by him, whether or not it was done with the employer's knowledge or approval.

Section 32(1)

Whether or not the employer knew of the act if, an employee commits a discriminatory act against another during the course of his employment the employer here is liable for that act.

(2) Anything done by a person as agent for another person with the authority (whether express or implied, and whether precedent or subsequent) of that other person shall be treated for the purposes of this Act (except as regards offences thereunder) as done by that other person as well as by him.

Section 32(2)

Under this sub-section both the principal and the person committing the act are made liable.

(3) In proceedings brought under this Act against any person in respect of an act alleged to have been done by an employee of his it shall be a defence for that

person to prove that he took such steps as were reasonably practicable to prevent the employee from doing that act, or from doing in the course of his employment acts of that description.

Section 32(3)

Providing the employer took such steps as was reasonably practicable to prevent the discriminatory act taking place he will escape liability. Ways in which this sub-section may be satisfied include showing that policies were in place to make clear that such acts were unacceptable and, for example, if proved would result in disciplinary action taking place against the offender. It can also include the provision of training to ensure that such policies are brought to the attention of managers and employees.

It would therefore be possible in proceedings brought against the employer and the individual employee, for the employer to escape liability under sub-section (3) but for the individual employee still to be held liable because he had aided the employer's unlawful act under section 33 below.

See section 41 SDA

Aiding unlawful acts.

33.–(1) A person who knowingly aids another person to do an act made unlawful by this Act shall be treated for the purposes of this Act as himself doing an unlawful act of the like description.

Section 33(1)

Whether or not an act by an employee is 'in the course of his employment' must be looked at quite liberally. It is not interpreted in the same way in which that phrase is used in an action in tort. So, even if the act by the employees would never have been authorised by the employer if the employer had known about them, it may still be 'in the course of employment' if there is a sufficient connection between those acts and the employment in question. This may even extent to social functions after normal hours and off the employer's premises.

Two police cases involving allegations of sex discrimination might serve to draw a distinction between what is and what is not 'in the course of employment'. In the first case, a probationary constable met a male officer off duty and went back to the section house in which she was living during her probationary period and in which she was sexually harassed by that other officer. The Court of Appeal held that this could not be said to be in the course of employment.

In the second case, the police constable had been sexually harrassed in two locations. The first was in a local public bar where a group of officers had gone after the end of their shifts; the second was at a leaving celebration for a colleague. In this case the EAT decided that each incident had occurred during what were, in reality, 'extensions of the workplace'.

Even if the act is committed by somebody not under the employer's control, the employer might still be liable.

In another case under this Act an hotel employing two black waitresses was found to be liable when it sent them back in to provide service at a function at which the comedian Bernard Manning was speaking. He had already made racist remarks about the women earlier in the function and, by sending them back in after that abuse, the employer was held to have subjected them to a detriment under section 4(2)(c) (section 6(2)(b) SDA).

(2) For the purposes of subsection (1) an employee or agent for whose act the employer or principal is liable under section 32 (or would be so liable but for section 32(3)) shall be deemed to aid the doing of the act by the employer or principal.

Section 33(2)

Even if the employer has a defence under section 41(3) above the employee who commits the unlawful act is made liable by this sub-section.

(3) A person does not under this section knowingly aid another to do an unlawful act if–

(a) he acts in reliance on a statement made to him by that other person that, by reason of any provision of this Act, the act which he aids would not be unlawful; and

(b) it is reasonable for him to rely on the statement.

(4) A person who knowingly or recklessly makes a statement such as is mentioned in subsection (3)(a) which in a material respect is false or misleading commits an offence, and shall be liable on summary conviction to a fine not exceeding level 5 on the standard scale.

Section 33 (3) & (4)

Provides for the same defence and penalty as in relation to discriminatory advertisements under section 29 and employment agencies under section 14

The same provisions appear at section 42 SDA.

Part V Charities

Charities.

34.–(1) A provision which is contained in a charitable instrument (whenever that instrument took or takes effect) and which provides for conferring benefits on persons of a class defined by reference to colour shall have effect for all purposes as if it provided for conferring the like benefits–

(a) on persons of the class which results if the restriction by reference to colour is disregarded; or

(b) where the original class is defined by reference to colour only, on persons generally;but nothing in this subsection shall be taken to alter the effect of any provision as regards any time before the coming into operation of this subsection.

(2) Nothing in Parts II to IV shall–

(a) be construed as affecting a provision to which this subsection applies; or
(b) render unlawful an act which is done in order to give effect to such a provision.

(3) Subsection (2) applies to any provision which is contained in a charitable instrument (whenever that instrument took or takes effect) and which provides for conferring benefits on persons of a class defined otherwise than by reference to colour (including a class resulting from the operation of subsection (1)).

(4) In this section

"charitable instrument" means an enactment or other instrument passed or made for charitable purposes, or an enactment or other instrument so far as it relates to charitable purposes, and in Scotland includes the governing instrument of an endowment or of an educational endowment as those expressions are defined in section 135(1) of the Education (Scotland) Act 1962.

In the application of this section to England and Wales,

"charitable purposes" means purposes which are exclusively charitable according to the law of England and Wales.

Section 34

Charities may discriminate on grounds of racial or ethnic origin in their treatment of beneficiaries if the trust establishing the charity permits it but they may not do so on grounds of colour. This section does not permit charities to discriminate against their employees on those grounds.

Similar provisions appear in the SDA at section 43.

Part VI General Exceptions From Parts II to IV

Special needs of racial groups in regard to education, training or welfare.

35. Nothing in Parts II to IV shall render unlawful any act done in affording persons of a particular racial group access to facilities or services to meet the special needs of persons of that group in regard to their education, training or welfare, or any ancillary benefits.

Provision of education or training for persons not ordinarily resident in Great Britain.

36. Nothing in Parts II to IV shall render unlawful any act done by a person for the benefit of persons not ordinarily resident in Great Britain in affording them access to facilities for education or training or any ancillary benefits, where it appears to him that the persons in question do not intend to remain in Great Britain after their period of education or training there.

Discriminatory training by certain bodies.

37.–(1) Nothing in Parts II to IV shall render unlawful any act done in relation to particular work by any person in or in connection with–

(a) affording only persons of a particular racial group access to facilities for training which would help to fit them for that work; or

(b) encouraging only persons of a particular racial group to take advantage of opportunities for doing that work, where it reasonably appears to that person that at any time within the twelve months immediately preceding the doing of the act–

(i) there were no persons of that group among those doing that work in Great Britain; or

(ii) the proportion of persons of that group among those doing that work in Great Britain was small in comparison with the proportion of persons of that group among the population of Great Britain.

(2) Where in relation to particular work it reasonably appears to any person that although the condition for the operation of subsection (1) is not met for the whole of Great Britain it is met for an area within Great Britain, nothing in Parts II to IV shall render unlawful any act done by that person in or in connection with–

(a) affording persons who are of the racial group in question, and who appear likely to take up that work in that area, access to facilities for training which would help to fit them for that work; or

(b) encouraging persons of that group to take advantage of opportunities in the area for doing that work.

(3) The preceding provisions of this section shall not apply to any discrimination which is rendered unlawful by section 4(1) or (2).

Section 37
i.e. acts of victimisation.

Other discriminatory training etc.

38.–(1) Nothing in Parts II to IV shall render unlawful any act done by an employer in relation to particular work in his employment at a particular establishment in Great Britain, being an act done in or in connection with–

(a) affording only those of his employees working at that establishment who are of a particular racial group access to facilities for training which would help to fit them for that work; or

(b) encouraging only persons of a particular racial group to take advantage of opportunities for doing that work at that establishment,

where any of the conditions in subsection (2) was satisfied at any time within the twelve months immediately preceding the doing of the act.

(2) Those conditions are–

(a) that there are no persons of the racial group in question among those doing that work at that establishment; or

(b) that the proportion of persons of that group among those doing that work at that establishment is small in comparison with the proportion of persons of that group–

(i) among all those employed by that employer there; or

(ii) among the population of the area from which that employer normally recruits persons for work in his employment at that establishment.

(3) Nothing in section 11 shall render unlawful any act done by an organisation to which that section applies in or in connection with–

> **Section 38(3)**
> *i.e. trade unions and employers' organisations.*

(a) affording only members of the organisation who are of a particular racial group access to facilities for training which would help to fit them for holding a post of any kind in the organisation; or

(b) encouraging only members of the organisation who are of a particular racial group to take advantage of opportunities for holding such posts in the organisation, where either of the conditions in subsection (4) was satisfied at any time within the twelve months immediately preceding the doing of the act.

(4) Those conditions are–

(a) that there are no persons of the racial group in question among persons holding such posts in that organisation; or

(b) that the proportion of persons of that group among those holding such posts in that organisation is small in comparison with the proportion of persons of that group among the members of the organisation.

(5) Nothing in Parts II to IV shall render unlawful any act done by an organisation to which section 11 applies in or in connection with encouraging only persons of a particular racial group to become members of the organisation where at any time within the twelve months immediately preceding the doing of the act–

(a) no persons of that group were members of the organisation; or

(b) the proportion of persons of that group among members of the organisation was small in comparison with the proportion of persons of that group among those eligible for membership of the organisation.

(6) Section 8 (meaning of employment at establishment in Great Britain) shall apply for the purposes of this section as if this section were contained in Part II.

Section 38(6)
Discrimination in recruitment or the treatment of persons employed is unlawful but sections 35-38 permit some forms of positive discrimination in order to provide access to employment in areas where particular groups are under-represented.

The provisions of sections 37 and 38 appear in a slightly different form in sections 47 and 48 SDA.

Sports and competitions.

39.–(1) Nothing in Parts II to IV shall render unlawful any act whereby a person discriminates against another on the basis of that other's nationality or place of birth or the length of time for which he has been resident in a particular area or place, if the act is done–

(a) in selecting one or more persons to represent a country, place or area, or any related association, in any sport or game; or
(b) in pursuance of the rules of any competition so far as they relate to eligibility to compete in any sport or game.

Section 39(1)
Selecting a sports team on the basis of nationality or place of birth or residence is permissible but selection on the basis colour, race, national or ethnic origin is not. Under this section it is lawful to select a county cricket team only from those who were born in the county but to exclude such a person on the grounds of his/her national origin is not.

Sporting facilities within the context of education is dealt with in section 18.

Section 44 SDA contains certain exemptions in relation to sport.

Indirect access to benefits etc.

40.–(1) References in this Act to the affording by any person of access to benefits, facilities or services are not limited to benefits, facilities or services provided by that person himself, but include any means by which it is in that person's power to facilitate access to benefits, facilities or services provided by any other person (the "actual provider").

Section 40(1)
Section 20 deals with the direct provision of goods, facilities or services. This section deals with the provision of such services facilities or goods indirectly. If, for example, an employer makes available membership of a sports and leisure club the employer will not escape liability by relying on the discriminatory admissions practice of the club itself

(2) Where by any provision of this Act the affording by any person of access to benefits, facilities or services in a discriminatory way is in certain circumstances prevented from being unlawful, the effect of the provision shall extend also to the liability under this Act of any actual provider.

> **Section 40(2)**
> *If the employer can lawfully discriminate under any other provision of this act, the person or body providing direct access to facilities or services will not be made liable under this sub-section.*
>
> *See also section 50 SDA*

Acts done under statutory authority etc.

41.–(1) Nothing in Parts II to IV shall render unlawful any act of discrimination done–

(a) in pursuance of any enactment or Order in Council; or
(b) in pursuance of any instrument made under any enactment by a Minister of the Crown; or
(c) in order to comply with any condition or requirement imposed by a Minister of the Crown (whether before or after the passing of this Act) by virtue of any enactment.

References in this subsection to an enactment, Order in Council or instrument include an enactment, Order in Council or instrument passed or made after the passing of this Act.

> **Section 41(1)**
> *It would normally only be possible to exclude from the ambit of this Act other statutory provisions or instruments which were already in existence at the time of the passing of this Act. This sub-section allows the exemption to extend to any instrument under an existing Act which was made after the passing of the RRA.*

(2) Nothing in Parts II to IV shall render unlawful any act whereby a person discriminates against another on the basis of that other's nationality or place of ordinary residence or the length of time for which he has been present or resident in or outside the United Kingdom or an area within the United Kingdom, if that act is done-

(a) in pursuance of any arrangements made (whether before or after the passing of this Act) by or with the approval of, or for the time being approved by, a Minister of the Crown; or
(b) in order to comply with any condition imposed (whether before or after the passing of this Act) by a Minister of the Crown.

> **Section 41(2)**
> *Under the changes which will be affected by the Race Relations Amendment Bill, Ministers of the Crown will be subject to the RRA and this exemption will no longer apply.*
>
> *The corresponding provisions of the SDA, although different in form, are in section 51A*

Acts safeguarding national security.

42. Nothing in Parts II to IV shall render unlawful an act done for the purpose of safeguarding national security.

> **Section 42**
> *Any act done for the purposes of safeguarding national security is exempted from the provisions of this act.*

PART VII THE COMMISSION FOR RACIAL EQUALITY

GENERAL

Establishment and duties of Commission.

43.–(1) There shall be a body of Commissioners named the Commission for Racial Equality consisting of at least eight but not more than fifteen individuals each appointed by the Secretary of State on a full-time or part-time basis, which shall have the following duties–

(a) to work towards the elimination of discrimination;
(b) to promote equality of opportunity, and good relations, between persons of different racial groups generally; and
(c) to keep under review the working of this Act and, when they are so required by the Secretary of State or otherwise think it necessary, draw up and submit to the Secretary of State proposals for amending it.

(1A) One of the Commissioners shall be a person who appears to the Secretary of State to have special knowledge of Scotland.

> **Section 43(1A)**
> *With the establishing of the Scottish Parliament one of the Commission's members must now have special knowledge of Scotland.*

(2) The Secretary of State shall appoint–

(a) one of the Commissioners to be chairman of the Commission; and

(b) either one or more of the Commissioners (as the Secretary of State thinks fit) to be deputy chairman or deputy chairmen of the Commission.

(3) The Secretary of State may by order amend subsection (1) so far as it regulates the number of Commissioners.

(4) Schedule 1 shall have effect with respect to the Commission.

(5) The Race Relations Board and the Community Relations Commission are hereby abolished.

> **Section 43(5)**
> *Section 53 SDA deals with the establishment of the Equal Opportunities Commission.*

Assistance to organisations.

44.–(1) The Commission may give financial or other assistance to any organisation appearing to the Commission to be concerned with the promotion of equality of opportunity, and good relations, between persons of different racial groups, but shall not give any such financial assistance out of money provided (through the Secretary of State) by Parliament except with the approval of the Secretary of State given with the consent of the Treasury.

(2) Except in so far as other arrangements for their discharge are made and approved under paragraph 13 of Schedule 1–

(a) the Commission's functions under subsection (1); and
(b) other functions of the Commission in relation to matters connected with the giving of such financial or other assistance as is mentioned in that subsection,

shall be discharged under the general direction of the Commission by a committee of the Commission consisting of at least three but not more than five Commissioners, of whom one shall be the deputy chairman or one of the deputy chairmen of the Commission.

> **Section 44**
> *Curiously, no corresponding provision appears in the SDA.*

Research and education.

45.–(1) The Commission may undertake or assist (financially or otherwise) the undertaking by other persons of any research, and any educational activities, which appear to the Commission necessary or expedient for the purposes of section 43(1).

(2) The Commission may make charges for educational or other facilities or services made available by them.

Section 45
See section 54 SDA

Annual reports.

46.–(1) As soon as practicable after the end of each calendar year the Commission shall make to the Secretary of State a report on their activities during the year (an "annual report").

(2) Each annual report shall include a general survey of developments, during the period to which it relates, in respect of matters falling within the scope of the Commission's functions.

(3) The Secretary of State shall lay a copy of every annual report before each House of Parliament, and shall cause the report to be published.

Section 46
See section 56 SDA.

CODES OF PRACTICE

Codes of practice.

47.–(1) The Commission may issue codes of practice containing such practical guidance as the Commission think fit for all or any of the following purposes, namely–

(a) the elimination of discrimination in the field of employment;
(b) the promotion of equality of opportunity in that field between persons of different racial groups.

(c) the elimination of discrimination in the field of housing;
(d) the promotion of equality of opportunity in the field of housing between persons of different racial groups.

(2) When the Commission propose to issue a code of practice, they shall prepare and publish a draft of that code, shall consider any representations made to them about the draft and may modify the draft accordingly.

(3) In the course of preparing any draft code of practice relating to the field of employment for eventual publication under subsection (2) the Commission shall consult with–

(a) such organisations or associations of organisations representative of employers or of workers; and
(b) such other organisations, or bodies,

as appear to the Commission to be appropriate.

3A. In the course of preparing any draft code of practice relating to the field of employment for eventual publication under subsection (2) the Commission shall consult with such organisations, or bodies, as appear to the Commission to be appropriate having regard to the content of the draft code.

(4) If the Commission determine to proceed with a draft code of practice, they shall transmit the draft to the Secretary of State who shall–

(a) if he approves of it, lay it before both Houses of Parliament; and

(b) if he does not approve of it, publish details of his reasons for withholding approval.

(5) If, within the period of forty days beginning with the day on which a copy of a draft code of practice is laid before each House of Parliament, or, if such copies are laid on different days, with the later of the two days, either House so resolves, no further proceedings shall be taken thereon, but without prejudice to the laying before Parliament of a new draft.

(6) In reckoning the period of forty days referred to in subsection (5), no account shall be taken of any period during which Parliament is dissolved or prorogued or during which both Houses are adjourned for more than four days.

(7) If no such resolution is passed as is referred to in subsection (5), the Commission shall issue the code in the form of the draft and the code shall come into effect on such day as the Secretary of State may by order appoint.

(8) Without prejudice to section 74(3), an order under subsection (7) may contain such transitional provisions or savings as appear to the Secretary of State to be necessary or expedient in connection with the code of practice thereby brought into operation.

(9) The Commission may from time to time revise the whole or any part of a code of practice issued under this section and issue that revised code, and subsections (2) to (8) shall apply (with appropriate modifications) to such a revised code as they apply to the first issue of a code.

(10) A failure on the part of any person to observe any provision of a code of practice shall not of itself render him liable to any proceedings; but in any proceedings under this Act before an employment tribunal, a county court or, in Scotland, a sheriff court any code of practice issued under this section shall be admissible in evidence, and if any provision of such a code appears to the tribunal or the court to be relevant to any question arising in the proceedings it shall be taken into account in determining that question.

Section 47(10)

A breach of the Code is not an offence in itself but a failure to observe one or more of its provisions may be evidence that a person has committed a breach.

(11) Without prejudice to subsection (1), a code of practice issued under this section may include such practical guidance as the Commission think fit as to what steps it is reasonably practicable for employers to take for the purpose of preventing their employees from doing in the course of their employment acts made unlawful by this Act.

> **Section 47(11)**
> *See also section 56A SDA.*

INVESTIGATIONS

Power to conduct formal investigations.

48.–(1) Without prejudice to their general power to do anything requisite for the performance of their duties under section 43(1), the Commission may if they think fit, and shall if required by the Secretary of State, conduct a formal investigation for any purpose connected with the carrying out of those duties.

(2) The Commission may, with the approval of the Secretary of State, appoint, on a full-time or part-time basis, one or more individuals as additional Commissioners for the purposes of a formal investigation.

(3) The Commission may nominate one or more Commissioners, with or without one or more additional Commissioners, to conduct a formal investigation on their behalf, and may delegate any of their functions in relation to the investigation to the persons so nominated.

> **Section 48**
> *Section 28 dealt with discriminatory practices. The note to that section made reference to situations where it may be difficult, or even impossible, to identify victims of such practices. This section gives the CRE the power to conduct investigations where it believes such discriminatory practices exist, whether or not anyone complains, although in practice such investigations may well arise from reports from aggrieved persons who are not willing to pursue a claim on their own behalf.*
>
> *See section 57 SDA*

Terms of reference.

49.–(1) The Commission shall not embark on a formal investigation unless the requirements of this section have been complied with.

(2) Terms of reference for the investigation shall be drawn up by the Commission or, if the Commission were required by the Secretary of State to conduct the investigation, by the Secretary of State after consulting the Commission.

(3) It shall be the duty of the Commission to give general notice of the holding of the investigation unless the terms of reference confine it to activities of persons named in them, but in such a case the Commission shall in the prescribed manner give those persons notice of the holding of the investigation.

(4) Where the terms of reference of the investigation confine it to activities of persons named in them and the Commission in the course of it propose to investigate any act made unlawful by this Act which they believe that a person so named may have done, the Commission shall–

(a) inform that person of their belief and of their proposal to investigate the act in question; and

(b) offer him an opportunity of making oral or written representations with regard to it (or both oral and written representations if he thinks fit);

and a person so named who avails himself of an opportunity under this subsection of making oral representations may be represented–

(i) by counsel or a solicitor; or

(ii) by some other person of his choice, not being a person to whom the Commission object on the ground that he is unsuitable.

(5) The Commission or, if the Commission were required by the Secretary of State to conduct the investigation, the Secretary of State after consulting the Commission may from time to time revise the terms of reference; and subsections (1), (3) and (4) shall apply to the revised investigation and terms of reference as they applied to the original.

Section 49
See section 58 SDA

Power to obtain information.

50.–(1) For the purposes of a formal investigation the Commission, by a notice in the prescribed form served on him in the prescribed manner–

(a) may require any person to furnish such written information as may be described in the notice, and may specify the time at which, and the manner and form in which, the information is to be furnished;

(b) may require any person to attend at such time and place as is specified in the notice and give oral information about, and produce all documents in his possession or control relating to, any matter specified in the notice.

(2) Except as provided by section 60, a notice shall be served under subsection (1) only where–

(a) service of the notice was authorised by an order made by the Secretary of State; or

(b) the terms of reference of the investigation state that the Commission believe that a person named in them may have done or may be doing acts of all or any of the following descriptions–

(i) unlawful discriminatory acts;

(ii) contraventions of section 28; and

(iii) contraventions of sections 29, 30 or 31,

> **Section 50(2)**
> *(ii) operating a discriminatory practice*
>
> *(iii) discriminatory advertisements, instructions or pressure to discriminate*

and confine the investigation to those acts.

(3) A notice under subsection (1) shall not require a person–

(a) to give information, or produce any documents, which he could not be compelled to give in evidence, or produce, in civil proceedings before the High Court or the Court of Session; or

(b) to attend at any place unless the necessary expenses of his journey to and from that place are paid or tendered to him.

> **Section 50(3)**
> *(a) This would include documents covered by legal or professional privilege such as letters between a person and his/her lawyer for the purposes of giving or receiving legal advice.*

(4) If a person fails to comply with a notice served on him under subsection (1) or the Commission have reasonable cause to believe that he intends not to comply with it, the Commission may apply to a county court or, in Scotland, a sheriff court for an order requiring him to comply with it or with such directions for the like purpose as may be contained in the order.

(5) Section 55 of the County Courts Act 1984 (penalty for neglecting witness summons) shall apply to failure without reasonable excuse to comply with an order of a county court under subsection (4) as it applies in the cases provided in the said section 55; and paragraph 73 of Schedule 1 to the Sheriff Courts (Scotland) Act 1907 (power of sheriff to grant second diligence for compelling the attendance of witnesses or havers) shall apply to an order of a sheriff court under subsection (4) as it applies in proceedings in the sheriff court.

> **Section 50(5)**
> *In other words, the Commission conducting an investigation has the same powers to compel witness to attend and/or to produce documents as the courts have…*

(6) A person commits an offence if he–

(a) wilfully alters, suppresses, conceals or destroys a document which he has been required by a notice or order under this section to produce; or
(b) in complying with such a notice or order, knowingly or recklessly makes any statement which is false in a material particular,

and shall be liable on summary conviction to a fine not exceeding level 5 on the standard scale.

Section 50(6)
...and a failure to comply is punishable.

(7) Proceedings for an offence under subsection (6) may (without prejudice to any jurisdiction exercisable apart from this subsection) be instituted–

(a) against any person at any place at which he has an office or other place of business;
(b) against an individual at any place where he resides, or at which he is for the time being.

Section 50(7)
This dispenses with the need for the CRE to discover a person's home address or the registered office of a company. In other court proceedings it would be necessary to obtain the permission of the court before service can be effected elsewhere.

See section 59 SDA

Recommendations and reports on formal investigations.

51.–(1) If in the light of any of their findings in a formal investigation it appears to the Commission necessary or expedient, whether during the course of the investigation or after its conclusion–

(a) to make to any person, with a view to promoting equality of opportunity between persons of different racial groups who are affected by any of his activities, recommendations for changes in his policies or procedures, or as to any other matters; or
(b) to make to the Secretary of State any recommendations, whether for changes in the law or otherwise, the Commission shall make those recommendations accordingly.

(2) The Commission shall prepare a report of their findings in any formal investigation conducted by them.

(3) If the formal investigation is one required by the Secretary of State–

(a) the Commission shall deliver the report to the Secretary of State; and
(b) the Secretary of State shall cause the report to be published, and, unless required by the Secretary of State, the Commission shall not publish the report.

(4) If the formal investigation is not one required by the Secretary of State, the Commission shall either publish the report, or make it available for inspection in accordance with subsection (5).

(5) Where under subsection (4) a report is to be made available for inspection, any person shall be entitled, on payment of such fee (if any) as may be determined by the Commission–

(a) to inspect the report during ordinary office hours and take copies of all or any part of the report; or
(b) to obtain from the Commission a copy, certified by the Commission to be correct, of the report.

(6) The Commission may, if they think fit, determine that the right conferred by subsection (5)(a) shall be exercisable in relation to a copy of the report instead of, or in addition to, the original.

(7) The Commission shall give general notice of the place or places where, and the times when, reports may be inspected under subsection (5).

Section 51
Reports of investigations are thus available to the public (on payment of a reasonable fee) unless the Secretary of State orders otherwise.

See section 60 SDA

Restriction on disclosure of information.

52.–(1) No information given to the Commission by any person ("the informant") in connection with a formal investigation shall be disclosed by the Commission, or by any person who is or has been a Commissioner, additional Commissioner or employee of the Commission, except–

(a) on the order of any court; or
(b) with the informant's consent; or
(c) in the form of a summary or other general statement published by the Commission which does not identify the informant or any other person to whom the information relates; or
(d) in a report of the investigation published by the Commission or made available for inspection under section 51(5); or
(e) to the Commissioners, additional Commissioners or employees of the Commission, or, so far as may be necessary for the proper performance of the functions of the Commission, to other persons; or
(f) for the purpose of any civil proceedings under this Act to which the Commission are a party, or any criminal proceedings.

(2) Any person who discloses information in contravention of subsection (1) commits an offence and shall be liable on summary conviction to a fine not exceeding level 5 on the standard scale.

(3) In preparing any report for publication or for inspection the Commission shall exclude, so far as is consistent with their duties and the object of the report, any matter which relates to the private affairs of any individual or the business interests of any person where the publication of that matter might, in the opinion of the Commission, prejudicially affect that individual or person.

Sections 49–52

These sections govern the conditions under which formal investigations under section 48 are conducted.

The restrictions on disclosure in section 52 are designed to encourage people to give evidence freely without fear that anything they may say will be published (unless, of course, they consent).

See section 61 SDA

PART VIII ENFORCEMENT

GENERAL

Restriction of proceedings for breach of Act.

53.–(1) Except as provided by this Act no proceedings, whether civil or criminal, shall lie against any person in respect of an act by reason that the act is unlawful by virtue of a provision of this Act.

Section 53(1)

This ensures that a person or body does not face double liability under this Act and under other provisions. Surprisingly, and perhaps unintentionally, this section has the effect of preventing liability attaching to a Chief Constable for the actions of his officers when dealing with members of the public. This is because section 48 of the Police Act 1948, which makes a Chief Constable liable for the torts committed by his officers in the execution of their duties, is excluded by this section.

Police officers are not employees but office holders so section 32, which makes employers liable for the acts of employees, has no application. By virtue of section 16, police officers are treated as employees but only for the purpose of giving them protection in their employment.

This is to be remedied with the proposed amendments currently before Parliament.

(2) Subsection (1) does not preclude the making of an order of certiorari, mandamus or prohibition.

Section 53(2)

Preserves the powers of the courts to issue injunctions or compelling orders to prevent unlawful acts.

(3) In Scotland, subsection (1) does not preclude the exercise of the jurisdiction of the Court of Session to entertain an application for reduction or suspension of any order or determination or otherwise to consider the validity of any order or determination, or to require reasons for any order or determination to be stated.

Section 53(3)
Preserves the same powers for the Scottish courts to make equivalent orders to those referred to in subsection (2) above.

The same limitations appear in section 62 SDA

ENFORCEMENT IN EMPLOYMENT FIELD

Jurisdiction of employment tribunals.

54.–(1) A complaint by any person ("the complainant") that another person ("the respondent")–

(a) has committed an act of discrimination against the complainant which is unlawful by virtue of Part II; or
(b) is by virtue of section 32 or 33 to be treated as having committed such an act of discrimination against the complainant,

may be presented to an employment tribunal.

Section 54(1)
Time limits within which such applications are to be made are set out in section 68 (section 76 SDA).

At the present time, the burden of proof in a race discrimination case is generally on the complainant following the general legal principle that the person who alleges must prove. However, if a respondent to a complaint complained against fails to give satisfactory answers in a questionnaire (for which, see section 65 below) or is evasive in giving evidence a tribunal is entitled to draw an inference adverse to the respondent. Where the allegation is one of indirect discrimination and the Respondent seeks to show that the requirement or condition was justifiable under section 1(1)(b)(ii), the burden is then on the respondent to prove that it is justifiable.

Similarly where an employment agency seeks to show that they were acting in reliance on a statement made by the principle employer (section 14) or a publisher seeks to rely on the same defence in relation to a discriminatory advertisement (under section 29), it is for that person to prove that they relied on the statement and that it was reasonable for them to rely on the statement.

It should be remembered that discrimination on racial grounds is less favourable treatment than the treatment that employer would have meted out to a person not of the same racial group. It is irrelevant whether or not the employer acted reasonably. A wholly unreasonable employer may have treated everyone just as badly. If that is the case then a claim that a person was discriminated against on racial grounds will fail. The claim will only succeed if a person not of that racial group would have been treated differently.

It is also important to note that there does not have to be a conscious intention to discriminate. One of the intentions of anti-discrimination legislation is to try to stop people making decisions on assumptions which have no basis in fact. An employer who decides not to give a particular job to a black person because he/she would be out of place or because there is known to be hostility to black people amongst the rest of the employer's work-force would be discriminating against him/her unlawfully even if he thought he was doing so to protect the complainant from that hostility.

The tribunal's powers to conduct the proceedings are regulated in the same way as claims for unfair dismissal under the Employment Tribunals Act 1996 and the Employment Tribunals (Constitution and Rules of Procedure) Regulations 1993 [SI 1993/2687]. The Constitution deals with the appointment of tribunal members and Chairmen so is not reproduced here.

There is a whole body of case law which is too extensive to review in a work of this kind. Apart from the differences in legal terminology, the regulations which govern tribunals in Scotland are the same (see the Employment Tribunals (Constitution and Rules of Procedure)(Scotland) Regulations 1993 [SI 1993/2688].

Brief reference will be made to those procedural matters which are more commonly, or sometimes exclusively, associated with discrimination claims:

Direct evidence of discrimination is often difficult to find. The Respondent will try to explain apparent differences in treatment as being attributable to other factors. In order to clarify the basis of the employer's defence, a complainant may submit a questionnaire in a prescribed form and the Respondent will given time in which to reply. Further reference will be made to this under section 65 below (section 74 SDA).

Unlike in other court proceedings, there is no requirement for the parties to produce lists of all documents they have or had. The parties are free to produce those documents which help their respective cases but they must not be unfairly selective in doing so. If part of a document is produced the other party is entitled to see the whole of it.

If a party knows of the existence of one or more documents the tribunal may be asked for an order compelling the other party to produce it. Before making such an order the tribunal will want to be satisfied that the document is relevant to the proceedings and that it is reasonable for them to make the order. It may be unreasonable if, for example, the documents have been destroyed or they have been archived and retrieval would be expensive or burdensome. However, the more important the document the greater the inconvenience and expense of producing it will be justified.

(2) Subsection (1) does not apply to a complaint under section 12(1) of an act in respect of which an appeal, or proceedings in the nature of an appeal, may be brought under any enactment, or to a complaint to which section 75(8) applies.

> **Section 54(2)**
> *This deals with qualification or authorisation for entry to a profession. If a statutory right of appeal exists against a refusal to confer the authorisation or qualification, that right is to be used rather than a complaint to a tribunal.*
>
> *See section 63 SDA.*

Conciliation in employment cases.

> **Section 55**
> *The provisions set out below were originally in this section but were repealed and re-enacted in section 18(2),(3), (6) and (7) of the Employment Tribunals Act 1996:–*
>
> *"Where a complaint has been presented to an employment tribunal under [. . .] section 54 and a copy of the complaint has been sent to a conciliation officer, it shall be the duty of the conciliation officer–*
>
> *(a) if he is requested to do so both by the complainant and the respondent, or*
>
> *(b) if, in the absence of requests by the complainant and the respondent, he considers that he could act under this subsection with a reasonable prospect of success,*
>
> *to endeavour to promote a settlement of the complaint without its being determined by an industrial ttribunal."*

Remedies on complaint under s. 54.

56.–(1) Where an employment tribunal finds that a complaint presented to it under section 54 is well-founded, the tribunal shall make such of the following as it considers just and equitable-

(a) an order declaring the rights of the complainant and the respondent in relation to the act to which the complaint relates;

(b) an order requiring the respondent to pay to the complainant compensation of an amount corresponding to any damages he could have been ordered by a county court or by a sheriff court to pay to the complainant if the complaint had fallen to be dealt with under section 57;

(c) a recommendation that the respondent take within a specified period action appearing to the tribunal to be practicable for the purpose of obviating or reducing the adverse effect on the complainant of any act of discrimination to which the complaint relates.

Section 56(1) (a)–(c)

(a) A declaration may be appropriate before an act of discrimination has occurred. For example, a requirement to wear a particular uniform or work on a particular day of the week may have a disproportionate effect on members of a particular racial or ethnic group because of religious or other customs. A tribunal would be entitled to declare that, if the employer were enforce that requirement, it would be indirectly discriminatory.

(b) Compensation is usually ordered to be paid where a tribunal finds that a person has been discriminated against. That compensation can include loss of earnings, which may result from a dismissal or from a failure to appoint somebody to a more highly paid post. It may include compensation for the loss of the opportunity to be appointed to a more senior post where a person was prevented from applying and will almost always include a sum for injury to feelings.

It is not possible to give guidance on the level of damages which might be awarded under this head because of the enormous variety of individual circumstances. It should be noted, however, that a tribunal does have power to award aggravated damages where an employers' conduct is held to be particularly blameworthy or the conduct complained of particularly serious. Such an award may also be appropriate where, even though the original conduct complained of is not so serious, the employers' conduct of the proceedings themselves, for example, raising spurious allegations of misconduct or incompetence, merits such an award.

There will be cases where the victim of discrimination actually suffers stress or possibly even psychiatric injury as a result of the treatment she receives. In such cases the tribunal also has the power to award damages for personal injury. Where such injury has occurred, it is important that the claim is included in the tribunal proceedings. Medical evidence will almost certainly be required as to the nature of the injury and a tribunal will probably give directions as to how and when such medical evidence should be produced.

A separate claim for personal injury pursued in the ordinary courts will not be permitted once the tribunal case has concluded because of the general rule that all matters which could have been raised in a particular set of proceedings should have been raised. A failure to raise them at the appropriate time and an attempt to raise them in separate proceedings later will be regarded as an abuse of the process of the court.

Exemplary damages, which are intended to punish the offender rather than compensate the victim, are not permitted.

As in other cases involving claims for damages, a complainant is required to take reasonable steps to mitigate any loss suffered. A tribunal must also consider whether to award interest on any damages. This is so whether or not the parties claim interest.

Interest is awarded under different heads of damage at different rates and for different periods. In a work of this kind it is not possible to set out all of the provisions for interest and detailed advice should be taken.

(c) The purpose of a recommendation is to remove the adverse consequences of the employer's action. This does not extend to a recommendation to increase the pay of a complainant. That must be covered by an order for compensation under sub-section (b).

A recommendation could include the removal of conditions for appointment to a particular post, where those conditions are held to be discriminatory. It may also include the provision of training so that the complainant is not disadvantaged in future.

It does not include the power to recommend that the complainant be appointed to the next available post.

A failure to comply with a recommendation is dealt with under subsection (4) below.

Sub-sections (2) and (3) relating to maximum amounts to be awarded have been repealed. There is no upper limit on compensation.

(4) If without reasonable justification the respondent to a complaint fails to comply with a recommendation made by an employment tribunal under subsection (1)(c), then, if it thinks it just and equitable to do so–

(a) the tribunal may increase the amount of compensation required to be paid to the complainant in respect of the complaint by an order made under subsection (1)(b); or

(b) if an order under subsection (1)(b) could have been made but was not, the tribunal may make such an order.

(5) The Secretary of State may by regulations make provision-

(a) for enabling a tribunal, where an amount of compensation falls to be awarded under sub-section (1)(b), to include in the award interest on that amount; and

(b) specifying, for cases where a tribunal decides that an award is to include an amount in respect of interest, the manner in which and the periods and rate by reference to which the interest is to be determined;

and the regulations may contain such supplementary provisions as the Secretary of State considers appropriate.

(6) The Secretary of State may by regulations modify the operation of any order made under section 14 of the Employment Tribunals Act 1996 (power to make provision as to interest on sums payable in pursuance of employment tribunal decisions) to the extent that it relates to an award of compensation under sub-section (1)(b).

Section 56(6)

With the exceptions of sub-sections (5) and (6) this section corresponds to section 65 SDA

ENFORCEMENT OF PART III

Claims under Part III.

57.–(1) A claim by any person ("the claimant") that another person ("the respondent")-

(a) has committed an act of discrimination against the claimant which is unlawful by virtue of Part III; or

(b) is by virtue of section 32 or 33 to be treated as having committed such an act of discrimination against the claimant,

may be made the subject of civil proceedings in like manner as any other claim in tort or (in Scotland) in reparation for breach of statutory duty.

(2) Proceedings under subsection (1)-

(a) shall, in England and Wales, be brought only in a designated county court; and
(b) shall, in Scotland, be brought only in a sheriff court;

but all such remedies shall be obtainable in such proceedings as, apart from this subsection and section 53(1), would be obtainable in the High Court or the Court of Session, as the case may be.

Section 57(2)

All claims other than employment claims must be made in a county court (or a sheriff court in Scotland) regardless of their potential value. The normal financial limits for starting proceedings in the High Court do not apply to discrimination claims.

Under the Civil Procedure Rules ("CPR") (Schedule 2 CCR Order 49) a person bringing such a complaint must give notice of the proceedings to the CRE and file with the court a copy of that notice. A failure to do so may result in the action being struck out.

(3) As respects an unlawful act of discrimination falling within section 1(1)(b), no award of damages shall be made if the respondent proves that the requirement or condition in question was not applied with the intention of treating the claimant unfavourably on racial grounds.

Section 57(3)

Courts and tribunals are not slow to find such intention where a requirement condition was applied with full knowledge of its discriminatory effect.

(4) For the avoidance of doubt it is hereby declared that damages in respect of an unlawful act of discrimination may include compensation for injury to feelings whether or not they include compensation under any other head

Section 57(4)
See the note to section 56(1)(b) above in relation to claims for personal injury arising out of acts of discrimination.

(5) Civil proceedings in respect of a claim by any person that he has been discriminated against in contravention of section 17 or 18 by a body to which section 19(1) applies shall not be instituted unless the claimant has given notice of the claim to the Secretary of State and either the Secretary of State has by notice informed the claimant that the Secretary of State does not require further time to consider the matter, or the period of two months has elapsed since the claimant gave notice to the Secretary of State; but nothing in this subsection applies to a counterclaim.

Section 57(5)
This sub-section relates to education and corresponds to section 66(5) SDA. It gives the Secretary of State the right to pursue the complaint since any act of discrimination in respect of the provision of education is likely to have much wider application than the individual case and it would be reasonable for the Secretary of State to take on that burden rather than leaving it to an individual.

(6) In Scotland, when any proceedings are brought under this section, in addition to the service on the defender of a copy of the summons or initial writ initiating the action a copy thereof shall be sent as soon as practicable to the Commission in a manner to be prescribed by Act of Sederunt.

Section 57(6)
The remedies available in courts are the same and compensation is calculated in exactly the same way as in employment tribunals so the reader is referred to the note to section 56 above.

While all employment tribunals are capable of hearing discrimination claims, certain county courts have been designated by the Lord Chancellor to have jurisdiction over discrimination claims. A list of such courts can be found in the County Court Directory.

A Judge hearing a claim must sit with two assessors unless each party consents to the Judge hearing the case alone (see section 67(4)).

See generally section 66 SDA

NON-DISCRIMINATION NOTICES

Issue of non-discrimination notice.

58.–(1) This section applies to–

(a) an unlawful discriminatory act; and
(b) an act contravening section 28; and

Section 58(1)(b)–(c)
(b) operating a discriminatory practice

(c) discriminatory advertisements, instructions or pressure to discriminate

(c) an act contravening section 29, 30 or 31,

and so applies whether or not proceedings have been brought in respect of the act.

Section 58(1)
This gives the CRE power to act even if no individual is willing to bring a claim.

(2) If in the course of a formal investigation the Commission become satisfied that a person is committing, or has committed, any such acts, the Commission may in the prescribed manner serve on him a notice in the prescribed form ("a non-discrimination notice") requiring him-

(a) not to commit any such acts; and
(b) where compliance with paragraph (a) involves changes in any of his practices or other arrangements-
(i) to inform the Commission that he has effected those changes and what those changes are; and
(ii) to take such steps as may be reasonably required by the notice for the purpose of affording that information to other persons concerned.

(3) A non-discrimination notice may also require the person on whom it is served to furnish the Commission with such other information as may be reasonably required by the notice in order to verify that the notice has been complied with.

(4) The notice may specify the time at which, and the manner and form in which, any information is to be furnished to the Commission, but the time at which any information is to be furnished in compliance with the notice shall not be later than five years after the notice has become final.

Sections 58 (2)–(4)
The non-discrimination notice may require the person receiving it to provide the commission with information. This is so that the Commission may be able to ascertain whether or not the discrimination has been eliminated and the person concerned can be required to furnish that information up to five years after the notice is issued and to convey that information to others, for example, those who may have been affected by the discriminatory practices which gave rise to the issue of the notice. However, there are requirements which must be complied with before the notice can be issued. See subsection

(5) The Commission shall not serve a non-discrimination notice in respect of any person unless they have first-

(a) given him notice that they are minded to issue a non-discrimination notice in his case, specifying the grounds on which they contemplate doing so; and
(b) offered him an opportunity of making oral or written representations in the matter (or both oral and written representations if he thinks fit) within a period of not less than 28 days specified in the notice; and
(c) taken account of any representations so made by him.

(6) Subsection (2) does not apply to any acts in respect of which the Secretary of State could exercise the powers conferred on him by section 19(2) and (3); but if the Commission become aware of any such acts they shall give notice of them to the Secretary of State.

Section 58(6)
The CRE cannot issue a non-discrimination notice against an education authority in the public sector since that power is reserved to the Secretary of State. If, during the course of an investigation, the CRE comes across evidence that such discrimination is taking place it must notify the Secretary of State.

In relation to Wales this function has now been transferred to the National Assembly for Wales.

(7) Section 50(4) shall apply to requirements under subsection (2)(b), (3) and (4) contained in a non-discrimination notice which has become final as it applies to requirements in a notice served under section 50(1).

Section 58(7)
This refers to the CRE's ability to apply to the court for an order that the person shall comply with an order to provide information.

See section 67 SDA.

Appeal against non-discrimination notice.

59.-(1) Not later than six weeks after a non-discrimination notice is served on any person he may appeal against any requirement of the notice-

(a) to an employment tribunal, so far as the requirement relates to acts which are within the jurisdiction of the tribunal;
(b) to a designated county court or a sheriff court, so far as the requirement relates to acts which are within the jurisdiction of the court and are not within the jurisdiction of an employment tribunal.

(2) Where the tribunal or court considers a requirement in respect of which an appeal is brought under subsection (1) to be unreasonable because it is based on an incorrect finding of fact or for any other reason, the tribunal or court shall quash the requirement.

(3) On quashing a requirement under subsection (2) the tribunal or court may direct that the non-discrimination notice shall be treated as if, in place of the requirement quashed, it had contained a requirement in terms specified in the direction.

Section 59(3)
If the appeal against the non-discrimination notice is upheld the court or tribunal may substitute its own terms.

(4) Subsection (1) does not apply to a requirement treated as included in a non-discrimination notice by virtue of a direction under subsection (3).

Section 59(4)
There is no appeal against the non-discrimination notice as substituted during the process of appeal.

The appeal must specify each of the findings of fact set out in non-discrimination notice which are appealed against and to set out the positive case which the person appealing intends to prove at the appeal.

The non-discrimination notice becomes final either when the time for lodging an appeal has passed without an appeal being lodged or on the disposal of the appeal if the court or tribunal substitutes different requirements in that notice.

See section 68 SDA

Investigation as to compliance with non-discrimination notice.

60.–(1) If-

(a) the terms of reference of a formal investigation state that its purpose is to determine whether any requirements of a non-discrimination notice are being or have been carried out, but section 50(2)(b) does not apply; and

(b) section 49(3) is complied with in relation to the investigation on a date ("the commencement date") not later than the expiration of the period of five years beginning when the non-discrimination notice became final,the Commission may within the period referred to in subsection (2) serve notices under section 50(1) for the purposes of the investigation without needing to obtain the consent of the Secretary of State.

Section 60(1)(a)–(b)
(a) i.e. there is a belief stated in the terms of reference for the investigation that a named person is doing the act made unlawful by the RRA.

(b) Such an investigation must begin within five years of the non-discriminating notice becoming final.

(2) The said period begins on the commencement date and ends on the later of the following dates–

(a) the date on which the period of five years mentioned in subsection (1)(b) expires;
(b) the date two years after the commencement date.

Section 60(2)
This means that the investigation must be completed within two years of its commencement or within five years of the date the non-discrimination notice became final.

See section 69 SDA

Register of non-discrimination notices.

61.–(1) The Commission shall establish and maintain a register ("the register") of non-discrimination notices which have become final.

(2) Any person shall be entitled, on payment of such fee (if any) as may be determined by the Commission-

(a) to inspect the register during ordinary office hours and take copies of any entry; or
(b) to obtain from the Commission a copy, certified by the Commission to be correct, of any entry in the register.

(3) The Commission may, if they think fit, determine that the right conferred by subsection (2)(a) shall be exercisable in relation to a copy of the register instead of, or in addition to, the original.

(4) The Commission shall give general notice of the place or places where, and the times when, the register or a copy of it may be inspected.

Section 61
All non-discrimination notices are accessible to members of the public on payment of a fee.

See section 70 SDA

OTHER ENFORCEMENT BY COMMISSION

Persistent discrimination.

62.-(1) If, during the period of five years beginning on the date on which any of the following became final in the case of any person, namely-

(a) a non-discrimination notice served on him; or
(b) a finding by a tribunal or court under section 54 or 57; that he has done an unlawful discriminatory act; or
(c) a finding by a court in proceedings under section 19 or 20 of the Race Relations Act 1968 that he has done an act which was unlawful by virtue of any provision of Part I of that Act, it appears to the Commission that unless restrained he is likely to do one or more acts falling within paragraph (b), or contravening section 28, the Commission may apply to a designated county court for an injunction, or to a sheriff court for an order, restraining him from doing so; and the court, if satisfied that the application is well-founded, may grant the injunction or order in the terms applied for or in more limited terms.

(2) In proceedings under this section the Commission shall not allege that the person to whom the proceedings relate has done an act falling within subsection (1)(b) or contravening section 28 which is within the jurisdiction of an employment tribunal unless a finding by an employment tribunal that he did that act has become final.

Section 62
It would be inappropriate to grant an injunction if the terms of the non-discrimination notice are being appealed.

Where there is no individual complaint, damages will not be awarded and a person who is merely served with a non-discrimination notice might be inclined not to comply with any requirement in that notice. This provision allows an application for an injunction to be made, either to the county court or to the sheriff court. If the court is satisfied that the person is likely to continue to do discriminatory acts it may grant an order in specific terms prohibiting that person from doing that act or those acts. A breach of an injunction would be a contempt of Court and is punishable, possibly by imprisonment

See section 71 SDA

Enforcement of ss. 29 to 31.

63.-(1) Proceedings in respect of a contravention of section 29, 30 or 31 shall be brought only by the Commission in accordance with the following provisions of this section.

Section 63(1)
29 deals with discriminatory advertisements, 30 with instructions to discriminate and 31 with pressure to discriminate

(2) The proceedings shall be-

(a) an application for a decision whether the alleged contravention occurred; or
(b) an application under subsection (4),

or both.

(3) An application under subsection (2)(a) shall be made-

(a) in a case based on any provision of Part II, to an employment tribunal; and
(b) in any other case, to a designated county court or a sheriff court.

(4) If it appears to the Commission-

(a) that a person has done an act which by virtue of section 29, 30 or 31 was unlawful; and
(b) that unless restrained he is likely to do further acts which by virtue of that section are unlawful, the Commission may apply to a designated county court for an injunction, or to a sheriff court for an order, restraining him from doing such acts; and the court, if satisfied that the application is well-founded, may grant the injunction or order in the terms applied for or more limited terms.

Section 63(4)
See the note to section 62 above

(5) In proceedings under subsection (4) the Commission shall not allege that the person to whom the proceedings relate has done an act which is unlawful under this Act and within the jurisdiction of an employment tribunal unless a finding by an employment tribunal that he did that act has become final.

Section 63(5)
See the note to section 62(2) above.

See generally section 72 SDA.

Preliminary action in employment cases.

64.-(1) With a view to making an application under section 62(1) or 63(4) in relation to a person the Commission may present to an employment tribunal a complaint that he has done an act within the jurisdiction of an employment tribunal, and if the tribunal considers that the complaint is well-founded it shall make a finding to that effect and, if it thinks it just and equitable to do so in the case of an act contravening any provision of Part II may also (as if the complaint had been presented by the person discriminated against) make an order such as is referred to in section 56(1)(a), or a recommendation such as is referred to in section 56(1)(c), or both.

Section 64(1)
The tribunal cannot, of course, make an award of compensation where there is no individual complainant.

(2) Subsection (1) is without prejudice to the jurisdiction conferred by section 63(2).

Section 64(2)
Exercising the right to make such an application to the tribunal does not prevent the Commission from seeking an injunction from the county court or from the sheriff court.

(3) In sections 62 and 63 and this section, the acts "within the jurisdiction of an employment tribunal" are those in respect of which such jurisdiction is conferred by sections 54 and 63.

Section 64(3)
See generally section 73 SDA but section 73(3) appears at section 69 of this Act.

HELP FOR PERSONS SUFFERING DISCRIMINATION

Help for aggrieved persons in obtaining information etc.

65.–(1) With a view to helping a person ("the person aggrieved") who considers he may have been discriminated against in contravention of this Act to decide whether to institute proceedings and,if he does so, to formulate and present his case in the most effective manner, the Secretary of State shall by order prescribe-

(a) forms by which the person aggrieved may question the respondent on his reasons for doing any relevant act, or on any other matter which is or may be relevant; and

(b) forms by which the respondent may if he so wishes reply to any questions.

Section 65(1)
These are the questionnaires which a complainant may serve on a Respondent to a claim and the forms on which the Respondent may reply.

(2) Where the person aggrieved questions the respondent (whether in accordance with an order under subsection (1) or not)-

(a) the question, and any reply by the respondent (whether in accordance with such an order or not) shall, subject to the following provisions of this section, be admissible as evidence in the proceedings;

(b) if it appears to the court or tribunal that the respondent deliberately, and without reasonable excuse, omitted to reply within a reasonable period or that his reply is evasive or equivocal, the court or tribunal may draw any inference from that fact that it considers it just and equitable to draw, including an inference that he committed an unlawful act.

Section 65(2)
This is a way of 'encouraging' a respondent to a claim to treat the questionnaires seriously and to answer reasonably promptly. Note that the tribunal is not obliged to draw an adverse inference but the replies or lack of them are part of the picture the tribunal must consider when determining the case.

(3) The Secretary of State may by order-

(a) prescribe the period within which questions must be duly served in order to be admissible under subsection (2)(a); and
(b) prescribe the manner in which a question, and any reply by the respondent, may be duly served.

(4) Rules may enable the court entertaining a claim under section 57 to determine, before the date fixed for the hearing of the claim, whether a question or reply is admissible under this section or not.

(5) This section is without prejudice to any other enactment or rule of law regulating interlocutory and preliminary matters in proceedings before a county court, sheriff court or industrial tribunal, and has effect subject to any enactment or rule of law regulating the admissibility of evidence in such proceedings

Sections 65 (4) & (5)
It may be that a respondent will consider the questions inappropriate or irrelevant. These subsections allow the court or tribunal to decide ahead of the hearing whether to order that the questions be answered or whether any reply will be admissible in the proceedings The normal rules in court or tribunal proceedings regulating the production and admissibility of documents continue to apply.

(6) In this section

"respondent" includes a prospective respondent and

"rules"-

(a) in relation to county court proceedings, means county court rules;
(b) in relation to sheriff court proceedings, means sheriff court rules.

Section 65(6)
Because the questionnaires may be submitted before the claim is made this subsection applies the rules to those who may be the subject of a claim.

See the Race Relations (Questions and Replies) Order 1977, SI 1977/842.

See section 74 SDA.

Assistance by Commission.

66.–(1) Where, in relation to proceedings or prospective proceedings under this Act, an individual who is an actual or prospective complainant or claimant applies to the Commission for assistance under this section, the Commission shall consider the application and may grant it if they think fit to do so-

(a) on the ground that the case raises a question of principle; or
(b) on the ground that it is unreasonable, having regard to the complexity of the case, or to the applicant's position in relation to the respondent or another person involved, or to any other matter, to expect the applicant to deal with the case unaided; or
(c) by reason of any other special consideration.

(2) Assistance by the Commission under this section may include-

(a) giving advice;
(b) procuring or attempting to procure the settlement of any matter in dispute;
(c) arranging for the giving of advice or assistance by a solicitor or counsel;
(d) arranging for representation by any person, including all such assistance as is usually given by a solicitor or counsel in the steps preliminary or incidental to any proceedings, or in arriving at or giving effect to a compromise to avoid or bring to an end any proceedings;
(e) any other form of assistance which the Commission may consider appropriate,

but paragraph (d) shall not affect the law and practice regulating the descriptions of persons who may appear in, conduct, defend, and address the court in, any proceedings.

Section 66 (1) & (2)
Under these sections, the Commission may give advice on pursuing a claim and help a complainant to seek a settlement or submit an application. It may go on to provide legal representation at the hearing in the case but other rules and practice govern who may appear in Court and the fact that the Commission has provided representation does not grant that person rights of audience in the courts.

Section 75(1) and (2) SDA.

(3) Where under subsection (1) an application for assistance under this section is made in writing, the Commission shall, within the period of two months beginning when the application is received-
(a) consider the application after making such enquiries as they think fit; and
(b) decide whether or not to grant it; and
(c) inform the applicant of their decision, stating whether or not assistance under this section is to be provided by the Commission and, if so, what form it will take.

(4) If, in a case where subsection (3) applies, the Commission within the period of two months there mentioned give notice to the applicant that, in relation to his application-

(a) the period of two months allowed them by that subsection is by virtue of the notice extended to three months; and

(b) the reference to two months in section 68(3) is by virtue of the notice to be read as a reference to three months,

subsection (3) and section 68(3) shall have effect accordingly.

Section 66(4)
If the CRE take longer to make a decision on whether to provide assistance, the complainant is allowed the extra time in which to file the application.

No similar time limit is contained in section 75 of the SDA.

(5) In so far as expenses are incurred by the Commission in providing the applicant with assistance under this section, the recovery of those expenses (as taxed or assessed in such manner as may be prescribed by rules or regulations) shall constitute a first charge for the benefit of the Commission-

(a) on any costs or expenses which (whether by virtue of a judgment or order of a court or tribunal or an agreement or otherwise) are payable to the applicant by any other person in respect of the matter in connection with which the assistance is given; and

(b) so far as relates to any costs or expenses, on his rights under any compromise or settlement arrived at in connection with that matter to avoid or bring to an end any proceedings.

Section 66(5)
If a person is assisted by the CRE and obtains an order at the end of the hearing that the respondent should pay her legal costs, the CRE can recover its costs from that award or from any settlement reached between the parties in order to avoid a hearing or the claim being filed with the court or tribunal. For this reason, subsection (7) below defines respondent as including prospective respondent.

See section 75(3) SDA

(6) The charge conferred by subsection (5) is subject to any charge under the Legal Aid Act 1988 *[imposed by section 10(7) of the Access to Justice Act 1999]*, or any charge or obligation forpayment in priority to other debts under the Legal Aid (Scotland) Act 1986, and is subject to any provision in, or made under, either of those Acts for payment of any sum to the Legal Aid Board *[Legal Services Commission]* or into the Scottish Legal Aid Fund.

> **Section 66(6)**
> *The words underlined are to be replaced by those in italics in square brackets from a day to be appointed.*
>
> *See section 75(4) SDA*

(7) In this section

"respondent" includes a prospective respondent and

"rules or regulations"-
(a) in relation to county court proceedings, means county court rules;
(b) in relation to sheriff court proceedings, means sheriff court rules;
(c) in relation to employment tribunal proceedings, means employment tribunal procedure regulations under Part I of the Employment Tribunals Act 1996.

> **Section 66(7)**
> *Section 75(5) SDA.*

SHERIFF COURTS AND DESIGNATED COUNTY COURTS

Sheriff courts and designated county courts.

67.–(1) For the purposes of this Act a "designated" county court is one designated for the time being for those purposes by an order made by the Lord Chancellor.

(2) An order under subsection (1) designating any county court for the purposes of this Act shall assign to that court as its district for those purposes any county court district or two or more county court districts.

> **Section 67(2)**
> *Presumably, this is so that expertise can be available to those courts so designated. The requirement for the judge to sit with two assessors (see sub-section 4 below) would otherwise require greater numbers of assessors with the requisite special knowledge and experience.*

(3) A designated county court or a sheriff court shall have jurisdiction to entertain proceedings under this Act with respect to an act done on a ship, aircraft or hovercraft outside its district, including such an act done outside Great Britain.

> **Section 67(3)**
> *See section 66(8) SDA*

(4) In any proceedings under this Act in a designated county court or a sheriff court the judge or sheriff shall, unless with the consent of the parties he sits without assessors, be assisted by two assessors appointed from a list of persons prepared

and maintained by the Secretary of State, being persons appearing to the Secretary of State to have special knowledge and experience of problems connected with relations between persons of different racial groups.

(5) The remuneration of assessors appointed under subsection (4) shall be at such rate as may, with the approval of the Minister for the Civil Service, be determined by the Lord Chancellor (for proceedings in England and Wales) or the Lord President of the Court of Session (for proceedings in Scotland).

(6) Without prejudice to section 74(3), an order for the discontinuance of the jurisdiction of any county court under this Act, whether wholly or within a part of the district assigned to it for the purposes of this Act, may include provision with respect to any proceedings under this Act commenced in that court before the order comes into operation.

Section 67(6)
If a court ceases to be so designated, any action currently in progress at that court may then be transferred to another court which is designated.

PERIOD WITHIN WHICH PROCEEDINGS TO BE BROUGHT

Period within which proceedings to be brought.

68.–(1) An employment tribunal shall not consider a complaint under section 54 unless it is presented to the tribunal before the end of the period of three months beginning when the act complained of was done.

(2) A county court or a sheriff court shall not consider a claim under section 57 unless proceedings in respect of the claim are instituted before the end of-

(a) the period of six months beginning when the act complained of was done; or
(b) in a case to which section 57(5) applies, the period of eight months so beginning.

Section 68(2)
Relates to discrimination in public sector education.

(3) Where, in relation to proceedings or prospective proceedings by way of a claim under section 57, an application for assistance under section 66 is made to the Commission before the end of the period of six or, as the case may be, eight months mentioned in paragraph (a) or (b) of subsection (2) the period allowed by that paragraph for instituting proceedings in respect of the claim shall be extended by two months.

Section 68(3)
If a potential complainant is waiting to hear whether or not assistance is to be given by the Commission in bringing the complaint, it would be unfair to require him/her to comply with the ordinary time limits. Once the time limit for a decision on assistance is past, employment the normal time limits apply.

(4) An employment tribunal, county court or sheriff court shall not consider an application under section 63(2)(a) unless it is made before the end of the period of six months beginning when the act to which it relates was done; and a county court or sheriff court shall not consider an application under section 63(4) unless it is made before the end of the period of five years so beginning.

Section 68(4)
This relates to discriminatory advertisements and to instructions and pressure to discriminate.

(5) An employment tribunal shall not consider a complaint under section 64(1) unless it is presented to the tribunal before the end of the period of six months beginning when the act complained of was done.

Section 68(5)
Preliminary action before seeking an injunction.

(6) A court or tribunal may nevertheless consider any such complaint, claim or application which is out of time if, in all the circumstances of the case, it considers that it is just and equitable to do so.

Section 68(6)
This subsection allows quite a wide discretion to extend the time limits. The discretion is much wider than that for ordinary employment tribunal claims where, in order to extend the time, the tribunal must first find that it was' not reasonably practicable' for the claim to be brought in time (section 111(2)(b) Employment Rights Act 1996).

The claim must be received by the tribunal within the time limit so a complaint about an act which took place on the 14th of February, for example, must be received by the tribunal on or before 13th May.

(7) For the purposes of this section-

(a) when the inclusion of any term in a contract renders the making of the contract an unlawful act, that act shall be treated as extending throughout the duration of the contract; and

(b) any act extending over a period shall be treated as done at the end of that period; and

(c) a deliberate omission shall be treated as done when the person in question decided upon it;

and in the absence of evidence establishing the contrary a person shall be taken for the purposes of this section to decide upon an omission when he does an act inconsistent with doing the omitted act or, if he has done no such inconsistent act, when the period expires within which he might reasonably have been expected to do the omitted act if it was to be done.

Section 68(7)(a)–(c)

(a) The complaint may therefore be made at any time up to three months after the termination of the employment.

(b) & (c). It is important to distinguish between these two provisions. A policy or rule which was operated in a discriminatory manner would be a continuing act under subsection (b). However, a refusal or an omission to provide a benefit would be dealt with under subsection (c). So if, by the operation of a rule or policy, a person was prevented from applying for promotion to a particular post by a discriminatory rule, that would be a continuing act. If the person was allowed to make the application but, for discriminatory reasons, was not appointed to the post, that would be a one off act or omission and would be dealt with under subsection (c).

Difficulty may arise in cases of repeated refusal. It may be necessary to consider whether the subsequent refusals are merely the reiteration of an earlier decision or result from reconsideration of circumstances. The repeated refusal based on an earlier decision would result in time running from the date the first decision was made. The refusal based on a reconsideration of the circumstances would mean that time ran from the date of the subsequent decision.

Where a claim is being made under a provision of European law, the time limits are usually those laid down in national law for similar claims so the above paragraphs would apply. However, if the claim is brought by an employee in the public sector or is being brought by an employee against the state for a failure to implement the provisions of European Directive, the time limit cannot begin to run until the member state has complied with its obligations under the Directive. In other words, time only begins to run once the provisions of national law comply fully with the requirements of European law. In these circumstances, a claim can be made some considerable time after the act complained of has taken place.

If the claim is being brought against the state for a failure to implement the terms of a European Directive, the claim must be made in the High Court or County Court. An employment tribunal has no jurisdiction to hear such claims.

With the exception, currently, of provisions relating to European law, see section 77.

EVIDENCE

Evidence.

69.–(1) Any finding by a court under section 19 or 20 of the Race Relations Act 1968, or by a court or employment tribunal under this Act, in respect of any act shall, if it has become final, be treated as conclusive in any proceedings under this Act.

> **Section 69(1)**
> *The person against whom the finding is made will not be permitted to re-open the matter and claim that he had not done the act which is the subject of the finding.*

(2) In any proceedings under this Act a certificate signed by or on behalf of a Minister of the Crown and certifying–

(a) that any arrangements or conditions specified in the certificate were made, approved or imposed by a Minister of the Crown and were in operation at a time or throughout a period so specified; or

(b) that an act specified in the certificate was done for the purpose of safeguarding national security, shall be conclusive evidence of the matters certified.

(3) A document purporting to be a certificate such as is mentioned in subsection (2) shall be received in evidence and, unless the contrary is proved, shall be deemed to be such a certificate.

> **Section 69(3)**
> *Thus no evidence will be heard as to whether the acts were so approved or imposed or whether there was a genuine national security issue once the certificate is signed and presented to the court or tribunal.*

PART IX

> **Section 70**
> *Repealed by the Public Order Act 1986*

PART X

Supplemental

Local authorities: general statutory duty.

71. Without prejudice to their obligation to comply with any other provision of this Act, it shall be the duty of every local authority to make appropriate arrangements with a view to securing that their various functions are carried out with due regard to the need-

(a) to eliminate unlawful racial discrimination; and

(b) to promote equality of opportunity, and good relations, between persons of different racial groups.

Section 71
It is not enough that local authorities do not commit unlawful acts. This imposes a positive duty on them to ensure that, in carrying out their functions, there are proper procedures in place to ensure, so far as possible, that there is no discrimination and to promote equality of opportunity.

No corresponding obligation exists under the SDA.

Validity and revision of contracts.

72.–(1) A term of a contract is void where–

(a) its inclusion renders the making of the contract unlawful by virtue of this Act; or
(b) it is included in furtherance of an act rendered unlawful by this Act; or
(c) it provides for the doing of an act which would be rendered unlawful by this Act.

Section 72(1)
It is not possible to include a term in a contract which permits unlawful discrimination. This section renders such a term void so as to preserve the rest of the contract.

(2) Subsection (1) does not apply to a term the inclusion of which constitutes, or is in furtherance of, or provides for, unlawful discrimination against a party to the contract, but the term shall be unenforceable against that party.

Section 72(2)
If the whole of the term were to be void, any benefit conferred on a party to a contract as part of an unlawful clause would also be rendered void. This subsection allows the party who would benefit under that clause to retain the benefit while rendering the discriminatory provisions of that clause unenforceable against him or her.

(3) A term in a contract which purports to exclude or limit any provision of this Act is unenforceable by any person in whose favour the term would operate apart from this subsection.

Section 72(3)
It is not possible under the act to prevent a person from bringing a claim in a court or tribunal under this Act unless subsection (4) applies.

(4) Subsection (3) does not apply-

(a) to a contract settling a complaint to which section 54(1) applies where the contract is made with the assistance of a conciliation officer; or
(b) to a contract settling a claim to which section 57 applies.

(4A) The conditions regulating compromise contracts under this Act are that

(a) the contract must be in writing;
(b) the contract must relate to the particular complaint;
(c) the complainant must have received advice from a relevant independent adviser as to the terms and effect of the proposed contract and in particular its effect on his ability to pursue his complaint before an employment tribunal;
(d) there must be in force, when the adviser gives the advice, a contract of insurance, or an indemnity provided for members of a profession or professional body, covering the risk of a claim by the complainant in respect of loss arising in consequence of the advice;
(e) the contract must identify the adviser; and
(f) the contract must state that the conditions regulating compromise contracts under this Act are satisfied.

Section 72(4)(a)–(f)

(a) If a conciliation officer employed by the Advisory Conciliation and Arbitration Service (ACAS) is involved in discussions between the parties for the purpose of settling a claim brought under this act or under the Equal Pay Act, any agreement reached as a consequence will be recorded on a form which ACAS produce for this purpose (called a "COT3"). The agreement recorded on that form is effective to prevent the person from bringing or pursuing the claim in the employment tribunal.

(b) It is possible in the normal way to draw up a contract which settles a claim brought under section 57. Subsection (3) above prevents a term in the original contract from operating so as to bar the assertion of the right not to be discriminated against. This subsection allows the claim, once asserted, to be settled in the normal way.

(c),(d) & (e) The combined effects of these provisions are that, if a person compromises a claim on the basis of advice from a suitable person and that advice is wrong, the complainant may then pursue a claim against the adviser.

(f) These provisions are strictly enforced so a failure to comply with any one of them will result in the claim still being permitted to proceed. Where money has been paid under such an agreement, the tribunal may take account of such payment and award nothing in addition or only such further sum as it considers just and equitable under section 65 above.

When the RRA was originally enacted it was only possible to settle a complaint through ACAS with the assistance of a conciliation officer. Subsequent amendments have permitted the settling of complaints in a variety of circumstances. Even the expanded provisions narrowly confine the circumstances in which a complaint can be settled in order to protect the rights of the complainant.

(4B) A person is a relevant independent adviser for the purposes of subsection (4A)(c)–

(a) if he is a qualified lawyer,
(b) if he is an officer, official, employee or member of an independent trade union who has been certified in writing by the trade union as competent to give advice and as authorised to do so on behalf of the trade union,
(c) if he works at an advice centre (whether as an employee or a volunteer) and has been certified in writing by the centre as competent to give advice and as authorised to do so on behalf of the centre, or
(d) if he is a person of a description specified in an order made by the Secretary of State.

Section 72(4B)(a)–(c)
Identifies the kinds of persons who can be relevant independent advisers for the purposes of this section. To date no other advisers have been specified under subsection (d).

((4BA) But a person is not a relevant independent adviser for the purposes of subsection (4A)(c) in relation to the complainant–

(a) if he is, is employed by or is acting in the matter for the other party or a person who is connected with the other party,
(b) in the case of a person within subsection (4B)(b) or (c), if the trade union or advice centre is the other party or a person who is connected with the other party,
(c) in the case of a person within subsection (4B)(c), if the complainant makes a payment for the advice received from him, or
(d) in the case of a person of a description specified in an order under subsection (4B)(d), if any condition specified in the order in relation to the giving of advice by persons of that description is not satisfied.

Section 72(4BA)
This is to ensure that the adviser is properly independent, has no connection with the other party and is not the other party to the complaint.

(4BB) In subsection (4B)(a)"qualified lawyer" means–

(a) as respects England and Wales, a barrister (whether in practice as such or employed to give legal advice), a solicitor who holds a practising certificate, or a person other than a barrister or solicitor who is an authorised advocate or authorised litigator (within the meaning of the Courts and Legal Services Act 1990), and

Section 72(4BB)
This includes, for example, Legal Executives who are members of the Institute of Legal Executives. This is designed to ensure that anyone who gives advice is properly qualified to do so. It does not include people who style themselves "Employment Law Consultants" unless they are otherwise qualified under this subsection.

(b) as respects Scotland, an advocate (whether in practice as such or employed to give legal advice), or a solicitor who holds a practising certificate.

(4BC) In subsection (4B)(b)"independent trade union" has the same meaning as in the Trade Union and Labour Relations (Consolidation) Act 1992.

Section 72(4BC)
Whether or not a trade union is "independent" can only be determined by the Certification Officer under that Act.

(4C) For the purposes of subsection (4BA) any two persons are to be treated as connected–

(a) if one is a company of which the other (directly or indirectly) has control, or
(b) if both are companies of which a third person (directly or indirectly) has control.

(4D) An agreement under which the parties agree to submit a dispute to arbitration–

(a) shall be regarded for the purposes of subsection (4)(a) and (aa) as being a contract settling a complaint if–
  (i) the dispute is covered by a scheme having effect by virtue of an order under section 21(2A) of the Trade Union and Labour Relations (Consolidation) Act 1992, and
  (ii) the agreement is to submit it to arbitration in accordance with the scheme, but
(b) shall be regarded for those purposes as neither being nor including such a contract in any other case.

Section 72(4D)
The only arbitration permitted under this subsection is that provided for in section 21(2A) of the Trade Union and Labour Relations (Consolidation) Act 1992. This provision was inserted by the Employment Rights (Dispute Resolution) Act 1998 and is effective for arbitration agreements entered into on or after 1 August 1998.

(5) On the application of any person interested in a contract to which subsection (2) applies, a designated county court or a sheriff court may make such order as it thinks just for removing or modifying any term made unenforceable by that subsection; but such an order shall not be made unless all persons affected have been given notice of the application (except where under rules of court notice may be dispensed with) and have been afforded an opportunity to make representations to the court.

> **Section 72(5)**
> *Where a discriminatory provision has been included in a term of a contract, this subsection allows the courts to modify the terms or to remove them provided all interested parties have been given an opportunity to make representations to the court.*

(6) An order under subsection (5) may include provision as respects any period before the making of the order.

> **Section 72(6)**
> *This allows the order of the Court to have retrospective effect*
>
> *See section 77 SDA.*

Power to amend certain provisions of Act.

73.–(1) The Secretary of State may by an order the draft of which has been approved by each House of Parliament-

- (a) amend or repeal section 9 (including that section as amended by a previous order under this subsection);
- (b) amend Part II, III or IV so as to render lawful an act which, apart from the amendment, would be unlawful by reason of section 4(1) or (2), 20(1), 21, 24 or 25;
- (c) amend section 10(1) or 25(1)(a) so as to alter the number of partners or members specified in that provision.

> **Section 73(1)(a)–(c)**
> *(a) Exceptions for seamen recruited abroad.*
>
> *(b) Section 4(1) and (2) – discrimination in employment;*
>
> *Section 20(1) – the provision of goods, facilities or services;*
>
> *Section 21 – the disposal or management of premises;*
>
> *Section 24 – consent for assignment or sub-letting;*
>
> *Section 25 – associations which are not trade unions or employers' organisations.*
>
> *(c) amend section 10(1) or 25(1)(a) so as to alter the number of partners or members specified in that provision.*
>
> *Section 10(1) Partnerships;*
>
> *Section 25(1)(a) – associations of 25 or more members which are not trade unions or employers organisations.*
>
> *(c) Section 10(1) Partnerships;*
>
> *Section 25(1)(a) – associations of 25 or more members which are not trade unions or employers organisations.*

(2) The Secretary of State shall not lay before Parliament the draft of an order under subsection (1) unless he has consulted the Commission about the contents of the draft.

> **Section 73(2)**
> *Similar provisions appear in section 80 SDA.*

Orders and regulations.

74.–(1) Any power of a Minister of the Crown to make orders or regulations under the provisions of this Act (except section 50(2)(a)) shall be exercisable by statutory instrument.

> **Section 74(1)**
> *The requirement to furnish information.*

(2) An order made by a Minister of the Crown under the preceding provisions of this Act (except sections 50(2)(a) and 73(1)), and any regulations made under section 56(5) or (6) or 75(5)(a), or (9A) shall be subject to annulment in pursuance of a resolution of either House of Parliament.

> **Section 74(2)**
> *Section 50(2)(a) – the requirement to furnish information;*
>
> *Section 73(1) – an amendment once it has been approved by both houses of Parliament.*

(3) An order under this Act may make different provision in relation to different cases or classes of case, may exclude certain cases or classes of case, and may contain transitional provisions and savings.

(4) Any power conferred by this Act to make orders include power (exercisable in the like manner and subject to the like conditions) to vary or revoke any order so made.

(5) Any document purporting to be an order made by the Secretary of State under section 50(2)(a) and to be signed by him or on his behalf shall be received in evidence, and shall, unless the contrary is proved, be deemed to be made by him.

> **Section 74(5)**
> *An order requiring a person to furnish information.*
>
> *Similar provisions appear in section 81 SDA.*

Application to Crown etc.

75.–(1) This Act applies-

(a) to an act done by or for purposes of a Minister of the Crown or government department; or

(b) to an act done on behalf of the Crown by a statutory body, or a person holding a statutory office, as it applies to an act done by a private person.

Section 75(1)
Wherever a Minister of the Crown, a government department, a statutory body or a person holding a statutory office exercises a discretion in the performance of their duties they cannot do so on a discriminatory basis; any such decision would therefore be liable to judicial review since, by this section, there would be no jurisdiction to exercise the discretion in that manner.

(2) Parts II and IV apply to-

(a) service for purposes of a Minister of the Crown or government department, other than service of a person holding a statutory office; or
(b) service on behalf of the Crown for purposes of a person holding a statutory office or purposes of a statutory body; or
(c) service in the armed forces,

as they apply to employment by a private person, and shall so apply as if references to a contract of employment included references to the terms of service.

Section 75(2)(a)–(c)
(a) The exclusion of those holding statutory office may be now have to disapplied, in relation to the corresponding provision of the SDA (section 85), because it is inconsistent with Article 141 of the EU Treaty guaranteeing equal pay. A decision to that effect in relation to the right of employment tribunal chairmen to claim equal pay has been made by the Northern Ireland Court of Appeal.

Until there is provision on race relations in European law this decision would not apply to this section.

(b) & (c) Part II - Discrimination in the employment field.

Part IV – other unlawful acts

(3) Subsections (1) and (2) have effect subject to section 16.

Section 75(3)
Section 16 deals with the Police

(4) Subsection (2) of section 8 and subsection (4) of section 27 shall have effect in relation to any ship, aircraft or hovercraft belonging to or possessed by Her Majesty in right of the Government of the United Kingdom as it has effect in relation to a ship, aircraft or hovercraft such as is mentioned in paragraph (a) or (b) of the subsection in question; and section 8(3) shall apply accordingly.

> **Section 75(4)**
> *8(2) – employment on board a ship etc.;*
>
> *27(4) – goods, facilities and services provided outside Great Britain.*

(5) Nothing in this Act shall-

(a) invalidate any rules (whether made before or after the passing of this Act) restricting employment in the service of the Crown or by any public body prescribed for the purposes of this subsection by regulations made by the Minister for the Civil Service to persons of particular birth, nationality, descent or residence; or

(b) render unlawful the publication, display or implementation of any such rules, or the publication of advertisements stating the gist of any such rules.

> **Section 75(5)**
> *Discrimination in relation to such employment and the advertising for such posts remain permitted in so far as they are not in conflict with the right under the EU Treaty guaranteeing freedom of movement of workers between member states.*

In this subsection

"employment" includes service of any kind, and

"public body" means a body of persons, whether corporate or unincorporate, carrying on a service or undertaking of a public nature.

(6) The provisions of Parts II to IV of the Crown Proceedings Act 1947 shall apply to proceedings against the Crown under this Act as they apply to proceedings in England and Wales which by virtue of section 23 of that Act are treated for the purposes of Part II of that Act as civil proceedings by or against the Crown, except that in their application to proceedings under this Act section 20 of that Act (removal of proceedings from county court to High Court) shall not apply.

> **Section 75(6)**
> *Thus the exclusive jurisdiction of designated county courts is preserved even in relation to proceedings against the Crown.*

(7) The provisions of Part V of the Crown Proceedings Act 1947 shall apply to proceedings against the Crown under this Act as they apply to proceedings in Scotland which by virtue of the said Part are treated as civil proceedings by or against the Crown, except that in their application to proceedings under this Act the proviso to section 44 of that Act (removal of proceedings from the sheriff court to the Court of Session) shall not apply.

Section 75(7)
See the note to (6) above.

(8) This subsection applies to any complaint by a person ("the complainant") that another person-

(a) has committed an act of discrimination against the complainant which is unlawful by virtue of section 4; or

(b) is by virtue of section 32 or 33 to be treated as having committed such an act of discrimination against the complainant,

Section 75(8)
instructions and pressure to discriminate

if at the time when the act complained of was done the complainant was serving in the armed forces and the discrimination in question relates to his service in those forces.

(9) No complaint to which sub-section (8) applies shall be presented to an employment tribunal under section 54 unless –

(a) the complainant has made a complaint to an officer under the service redress procedures applicable to him and has submitted that complaint to the Defence Council under those procedures; and

(b) the Defence Council have made a determination with respect to the complaint.

Section 75(9)
Allows members of the armed forces to present claims to employment tribunals provided they have used the internal service redress procedures first.

(9A) Regulations may make provision enabling a complainant to which subsection 9(A) applies to be presented to an employment tribunal under section 63 in such circumstances as may be specified by the regulations, notwithstanding that subsection (9B) would otherwise preclude the presentation of the complaint to an employment tribunal.

(9B) Where a complaint is presented to an employment tribunal under section 54 by virtue of regulations under subsection (9A) the service redress procedures may continue after the complaint is so presented.

Section 75(9B)
The normal time limits for presenting claims to employment tribunals apply to members of the armed forces. So a person who waited for the internal service redress procedures to be completed before presenting a claim might well be out of time.

These sections allow a claim to be presented to an employment tribunal while the service redress procedures are underway.

(10) In this section–

(a) "the armed forces" means any of the naval, military or air forces of the Crown;
(b) "statutory body" means a body set up by or in pursuance of an enactment, and "statutory office" means an office so set up; and
(c) service "for purposes of" a Minister of the Crown or government department does not include service in any office in Schedule 2 (Ministerial offices) to the House of Commons Disqualification Act 1975 as for the time being in force.

Application to House of Commons staff

75A.–(1) Parts II and IV apply to an act done by an employer of a relevant member of the House of Commons staff, and to service as such a member, as they apply to an act done by and to service for the purposes of a Minister of the Crown or government department, and accordingly apply as if references to a contract of employment included references to the terms of service of such a member.

(2) In this section "relevant member of the House of Commons staff" has the same meaning as in section 195 of the Employment Rights Act 1996; and subsections (6) to (12) of that section (person to be treated as employer of House of Commons staff) apply, with any necessary modifications, for the purposes of Parts II and IV as they apply by virtue of this section.

Section 75A

House of Commons' staff may be employed personally by the speaker, by the House of Commons' Commission or by some other person designated by the speaker or by the Commission.

This section applies the protection in relation to employment and in relation to discriminatory practices, advertisements, instructions to discriminate, pressure to discriminate, the liability of employers and aiding unlawful acts to such staff.

See Section 85A SDA.

Application to House of Lords staff

75B.–(1) Parts II and IV apply in relation to employment as a relevant member of the House of Lords staff as they apply in relation to other employment.

(2) In this section "relevant member of the House of Lords staff" has the same meaning as in section 194 of the Employment Rights Act 1996; and subsection (7) of that section applies for the purposes of this section.

Section 75B

The corresponding provisions in relation to House of Lords' staff as in section 75A above.

See section 85B SDA.

Government appointments outside s. 4.

76.–(1) This section applies to any appointment by a Minister of the Crown or government department to an office or post where section 4 does not apply in relation to the appointment.

(2) In making the appointment, and in making the arrangements for determining who should be offered the office or post, the Minister of the Crown or government department shall not do an act which would be unlawful under section 4 if the Crown were the employer for the purposes of this Act.

Financial provisions.

77.– There shall be defrayed out of money provided by Parliament-

(a) sums required by the Secretary of State for making payments under paragraph 5 or 16 of Schedule 1 or paragraph 12 of Schedule 2, and for defraying any other expenditure falling to be made by him under or by virtue of this Act;
(b) any expenses incurred by the Secretary of State with the consent of the Treasury in undertaking, or financially assisting the undertaking by other persons of, research into any matter connected with relations between persons of different racial groups;
(c) payments falling to be made under section 67(5) in respect of the remuneration of assessors; and
(d) any increase attributable to the provisions of this Act in the sums payable out of money provided by Parliament under any other Act.

General interpretation provisions.

78.–(1) In this Act, unless the context otherwise requires-

"access" shall be construed in accordance with section 40;

"act" includes a deliberate omission;

"advertisement" includes every form of advertisement or notice, whether to the public or not, and whether in a newspaper or other publication, by television or radio, by display of notices, signs, labels, showcards or goods, by distribution of samples, circulars, catalogues, price lists or other material, by exhibition of pictures, models or films, or in any other way, and references to the publishing of advertisements shall be construed accordingly;

"the Commission" means the Commission for Racial Equality;

"Commissioner" means a member of the Commission;

"designated county court" has the meaning given by section 67(1);

"discrimination" and related terms shall be construed in accordance with section 3(3);

"dispose", in relation to premises, includes granting a right to occupy the premises, and any reference to acquiring premises shall be construed accordingly;

"education" includes any form of training or instruction;

"the Education Acts" has the meaning given by section 578 of the Education Act 1996;

"employment" means employment under a contract of service or of apprenticeship or a contract personally to execute any work or labour, and related expressions shall be construed accordingly;

"employment agency" means a person who, for profit or not, provides services for the purpose of finding employment for workers or supplying employers with workers;

"estate agent" means a person who, by way of profession or trade, provides services for the purpose of finding premises for persons seeking to acquire them or assisting in the disposal of premises;

"final" shall be construed in accordance with subsection (4);

"firm" has the meaning given by section 4 of the Partnership Act 1890;

"formal investigation" means an investigation under section 48;

"further education" has for Scotland the meaning given by section 135(1) of the Education (Scotland) Act 1980;

"general notice", in relation to any person, means a notice published by him at a time and in a manner appearing to him suitable for securing that the notice is seen within a reasonable time by persons likely to be affected by it;

"genuine occupational qualification" shall be construed in accordance with section 5;

"Great Britain" includes such of the territorial waters of the United Kingdom as are adjacent to Great Britain;

"independent school" has for England and Wales the meaning given by section 463 of the Education Act 1996, and for Scotland the meaning given by section 135(1) of the Education (Scotland) Act 1980;

"managers" has for Scotland the same meaning as in section 135(1) of the Education (Scotland) Act 1980;

"Minister of the Crown" includes the Treasury and the Defence Council;

"nationality" includes citizenship;

"near relative" shall be construed in accordance with subsection (5);

"non-discrimination notice" means a notice under section 58;

"notice" means a notice in writing;

"prescribed" means prescribed by regulations made by the Secretary of State;

"profession" includes any vocation or occupation;

"proprietor", in relation to a school, has for England and Wales the meaning given by section 579 of the Education Act 1996, and for Scotland the meaning given by section 135(1) of the Education (Scotland) Act 1980.

"pupil" in Scotland includes a student of any age;

"racial grounds" and "racial group" have the meaning given by section 3(1);

"school" has for England and Wales the meaning given by section 4 of the Education Act 1996, and for Scotland the meaning given by section 135(1) of the Education (Scotland) Act 1980;

"school education" has for Scotland the meaning given by section 135(1) of the Education (Scotland) Act 1980;

"self-governing school" has the same meaning as in the Education (Scotland) Act 1980;

"trade" includes any business;

"training" includes any form of education or instruction;

"university" includes a university college and the college, school or hall of a university;

(2) It is hereby declared that in this Act "premises", unless the context otherwise requires, includes land of any description.

(3) Any power conferred by this Act to designate establishments or persons may be exercised either by naming them or by identifying them by reference to a class or other description.

(4) For the purposes of this Act a non-discrimination notice or a finding by a court or tribunal becomes final when an appeal against the notice or finding is dismissed, withdrawn or abandoned or when the time for appealing expires without an appeal having been brought; and for this purpose an appeal against a non-discrimination notice shall be taken to be dismissed if, notwithstanding that a requirement of the notice is quashed on appeal, a direction is given in respect of it under section 59(3).

(5) For the purposes of this Act a person is a near relative of another if that person is the wife or husband, a parent or child, a grandparent or grandchild, or a brother or sister of the other (whether of full blood or half-blood or by affinity), and "child" includes an illegitimate child and the wife or husband of an illegitimate child.

(6) Except so far as the context otherwise requires, any reference in this Act to an enactment shall be construed as a reference to that enactment as amended by or under any other enactment, including this Act.

(7) In this Act, except where otherwise indicated-

(a) a reference to a numbered Part, section or Schedule is a reference to the Part or section of, or the Schedule to, this Act so numbered; and

(b) a reference in a section to a numbered subsection is a reference to the subsection of that section so numbered; and

(c) a reference in a section, subsection or Schedule to a numbered paragraph is a reference to the paragraph of that section, subsection or Schedule so numbered; and

(d) a reference to any provision of an Act (including this Act) includes a Schedule incorporated in the Act by that provision.

Transitional and commencement provisions, amendments and repeals.

79.–(1) The provisions of Schedule 2 shall have effect for making transitional provision for the purposes of this Act.

(2) This Act shall come into operation on such day as the Secretary of State may by order appoint, and different days may be so appointed for different provisions and for different purposes.

(3), (4) DELETED MATTER

(5) Subject to the provisions of Schedule 2, the enactments specified in Schedule 5 are hereby repealed to the extent shown in column 3 of that Schedule.

(6) *Repealed by the Public Order Act 1986.*

(7) An order under this section may make such transitional provision as appears to the Secretary of State to be necessary or expedient in connection with the provisions thereby brought into operation, including such adaptations of those provisions, or of any provisions of this Act then in operation, as appear to the Secretary of State necessary or expedient in consequence of the partial operation of this Act.

Short title and extent.

80.–(1) This Act may be cited as the Race Relations Act 1976.

(2) This Act, except so far as it amends or repeals any provision of the House of Commons Disqualification Act 1975 or the Northern Ireland Assembly Disqualification Act 1975, does not extend to Northern Ireland.

SCHEDULES

SCHEDULE 1

Deals with the establishment of the Commission for Racial Equalities see also Schedule 1 Sex Discrimination Act for the estalishment of the Equal Opportunities Commission

SCHEDULE 2

SECTION 79. TRANSITIONAL PROVISIONS

Schedule 2

The rest of the provisions deal with the transfer of powers, property and liabilities to the CRE and are not reproduced here.

Disability Discrimination Act 1995

DISABILITY DISCRIMINATION

The protection against disability discrimination differs in a number of respects from the protection afforded by the Sex Discrimination Act 1975 and the Race Relations Act 1976. Firstly, there is no provision for indirect discrimination against people with disabilities and, secondly, there is a general defence of justification to discrimination on the grounds of a person's disability.

Instead of protection against indirect discrimination, the Act imposes a duty on employers and service providers to make reasonable adjustments. The effect of this is to impose a duty not to treat disabled persons equally with those who do not have a disability. This recognises that to treat such people equally is likely to put them at a disadvantage because of their disability.

The conceptual difficulties are tackled at the outset because the Act provides a comprehensive definition of what is a disability. In addition to Schedule 1, which describes the nature of a disability by breaking it down into four components, guidance and regulations issued under the Act offer further assistance in understanding what is, or what is not, a disability.

Because of the differences in the concept of disability discrimination when compared to sex and race discrimination, it is not always the case that the provisions of this Act can be applied in the same way as provisions of the other Acts. For this reason there will be less cross-referencing. However, where the provisions of the DDA mirror the provisions of the SDA and the RRA this will be referred to in the notes. One significant way in which the DDA now follows the structure of the SDA and the RRA is in relation to the Disability Rights Commission (the DRC). The DRC was established, not under the original Act, but under the Disability Rights Commission Act 1999 and began its work in April 2000. The DRC now has the same duties, powers and responsibilities as the EOC and CRE.

PART I DISABILITY

Meaning of "disability" and "disabled person".

1.–(1) Subject to the provisions of Schedule 1, a person has a disability for the purposes of this Act if he has a physical or mental impairment which has a substantial and long-term adverse effect on his ability to carry out normal day-to-day activities.

(2) In this Act "disabled person" means a person who has a disability.

Section 1

There are four elements each of which must be present for a person to be defined as being disabled or having a disability:

(a) does the applicant have a:

(i) physical impairment, or

(ii) mental impairment?

(b) does that impairment have an adverse effect on the person's ability to carry out normal day-to-day activities?

(c) is the adverse effect substantial?

(d) is that adverse effect long-term?

Schedule 1 provides more detail as to how each of those requirements is to be interpreted and the reader is referred to schedule 1 at page xx.

Past disabilities.

2.–(1) The provisions of this Part and Parts II and III apply in relation to a person who has had a disability as they apply in relation to a person who has that disability.

(2) Those provisions are subject to the modifications made by Schedule 2.

(3) Any regulations or order made under this Act may include provision with respect to persons who have had a disability.

(4) In any proceedings under Part II or Part III of this Act, the question whether a person had a disability at a particular time ("the relevant time") shall be determined, for the purposes of this section, as if the provisions of, or made under, this Act in force when the act complained of was done had been in force at the relevant time.

(5) The relevant time may be a time before the passing of this Act.

Section 2

A person who has had a disability continues to be protected under this section.

The section appears to be designed to cater for those situations where a person no longer suffers from the physical or mental impairment but may still be subject to irrational prejudice because they had the impairment at some time in the past. This may be particularly appropriate where a person has, in the past, suffered from a mental disability and an employer makes assumptions about the risk of that disability returning.

This section is not designed to deal with recurring conditions which may be currently in remission.

The Secretary of State for Employment and Education has issued 'Guidance on matters to be taken into account in determining questions relating to the definition of disability'

(5) Even if a person had a disability before the coming into force of this Act but no longer suffers from the disability, he/she remains protected under this sub-section.

Guidance.

3.–(1) The Secretary of State may issue guidance about the matters to be taken into account in determining–

(a) whether an impairment has a substantial adverse effect on a person's ability to carry out normal day-to-day activities; or

(b) whether such an impairment has a long-term effect.

> **Section 3(1)**
> *Referred to in the note to section 2 above.*

(2) The guidance may, among other things, give examples of–

(a) effects which it would be reasonable, in relation to particular activities, to regard for purposes of this Act as substantial adverse effects;

(b) effects which it would not be reasonable, in relation to particular activities, to regard for such purposes as substantial adverse effects;

(c) substantial adverse effects which it would be reasonable to regard, for such purposes, as long-term;

(d) substantial adverse effects which it would not be reasonable to regard, for such purposes, as long-term.

(3) A tribunal or court determining, for any purpose of this Act, whether an impairment has a substantial and long-term adverse effect on a person's ability to carry out normal day-to-day activities, shall take into account any guidance which appears to it to be relevant.

> **Section 3(3)**
> *A Court or Tribunal must consider the guidance when determining whether or not a person has a disability for the purposes of the Act.*

(4) In preparing a draft of any guidance, the Secretary of State shall consult such persons as he considers appropriate.

(5) Where the Secretary of State proposes to issue any guidance, he shall publish a draft of it, consider any representations that are made to him about the draft and, if he thinks it appropriate, modify his proposals in the light of any of those representations.

(6) If the Secretary of State decides to proceed with any proposed guidance, he shall lay a draft of it before each House of Parliament.

(7) If, within the 40-day period, either House resolves not to approve the draft, the Secretary of State shall take no further steps in relation to the proposed guidance.

(8) If no such resolution is made within the 40-day period, the Secretary of State shall issue the guidance in the form of his draft.

(9) The guidance shall come into force on such date as the Secretary of State may appoint by order.

(10) Subsection (7) does not prevent a new draft of the proposed guidance from being laid before Parliament.

(11) The Secretary of State may–

(a) from time to time revise the whole or part of any guidance and re-issue it;
(b) by order revoke any guidance.

Section 3(11)
The DRC may offer the Secretary of State advice as to how the guidance may be revised or amended.

(12) In this section–

"40-day period", in relation to the draft of any proposed guidance, means–
(a) if the draft is laid before one House on a day later than the day on which it is laid before the other House, the period of 40 days beginning with the later of the two days, and
(b) in any other case, the period of 40 days beginning with the day on which the draft is laid before each House,

no account being taken of any period during which Parliament is dissolved or prorogued or during which both Houses are adjourned for more than 4 days; and

"guidance" means guidance issued by the Secretary of State under this section and includes guidance which has been revised and re-issued.

PART II EMPLOYMENT

DISCRIMINATION BY EMPLOYERS

Discrimination against applicants and employees.

Section 4
This section prohibits discrimination against employees and potential employees on the same terms as section 4 of the RRA and section 6 of the SDA.

Employment bears the wider meaning which applies under the SDA and the RRA and includes any work which is to be carried out personally. The definition of employment appears at section 68.

4.–(1) It is unlawful for an employer to discriminate against a disabled person–

(a) in the arrangements which he makes for the purpose of determining to whom he should offer employment;
(b) in the terms on which he offers that person employment; or
(c) by refusing to offer, or deliberately not offering, him employment.

Section 4(1)
This section applies to the appointment process and the terms on which an individual is offered employment.

(2) It is unlawful for an employer to discriminate against a disabled person whom he employs–

(a) in the terms of employment which he affords him;
(b) in the opportunities which he affords him for promotion, a transfer, training or receiving any other benefit;
(c) by refusing to afford him, or deliberately not affording him, any such opportunity; or
(d) by dismissing him, or subjecting him to any other detriment.

Section 4(2)
Once employed, a person cannot be discriminated against in the terms of employment offered, the opportunities for promotion, transfer and training or any other benefits under the contract.

Unlike the SDA and the RRA, advertisements which suggest that employers will discriminate against a disabled person give rise to a presumption, under section 11, that an unsuccessful disabled applicant has been discriminated against. It is not therefore necessary under section 4(2)(d), for the disabled person to prove that he/she has suffered a detriment.

The Secretary of State for Education and Employment has issued a 'Code of Practice for the elimination of discrimination in the field of employment against disabled persons or persons who have had a disability'.

This code provides advice and guidance for employers on how to avoid discrimination in employment.

(3) Subsection (2) does not apply to benefits of any description if the employer is concerned with the provision (whether or not for payment) of benefits of that description to the public, or to a section of the public which includes the employee in question, unless–

(a) that provision differs in a material respect from the provision of the benefits by the employer to his employees; or
(b) the provision of the benefits to the employee in question is regulated by his contract of employment; or
(c) the benefits relate to training.

Section 4(3)
These provisions draw a distinction between the services provided to the person as an employee and those provided to that person, albeit by the employer, as a member of the public. If they are provided under the contract of employment, the complaint must be brought under sub-section (b) above; if it relates to those provided to members of the public generally, the complaint must be brought under section 19 in a county court.

(4) In this Part "benefits" includes facilities and services.

(5) In the case of an act which constitutes discrimination by virtue of section 55, this section also applies to discrimination against a person who is not disabled.

Section 4(5)
Section 55 below deals with victimisation. This sub-section ensures that the protection against victimisation is extended to a non-disabled person who has assisted a disabled person in formulating or presenting a complaint whether to a tribunal, a court or merely to the employer.

(6) This section applies only in relation to employment at an establishment in Great Britain.

Section 4(6)
This expression is defined in sections 68(1) to (5) and is narrower than the definition in section 10 SDA and section 8 RRA.

Even if the employee does some of the work at an establishment in Great Britain, it is not protected if it is mainly outside. Unlike the SDA and the RRA, work on board a ship, aircraft or hovercraft is excluded.

Despite this section, it is possible that this section cannot be relied upon to exclude work done in an EU member state. This is because of the effect of the EC Treaty which guarantees the freedom of movement of workers of any member state. This has already been applied in a case involving the RRA where it was held that the exclusion of employment wholly or mainly outside Great Britain must be disapplied because of the overriding application of EU law

Meaning of "discrimination".

5.–(1) For the purposes of this Part, an employer discriminates against a disabled person if–

(a) for a reason which relates to the disabled person's disability, he treats him less favourably than he treats or would treat others to whom that reason does not or would not apply; and

(b) he cannot show that the treatment in question is justified.

Section 5(1)(a)-(b)

(a) For some reason the definition under this section is different from that under section 1 SDA ("on the ground of her sex") or section 1 RRA ("on racial grounds"). It means that it must be related to the complainant's disability (unlike the RRA) but does not have to be on the ground of the disability (unlike the SDA).

The difference could be explained because of the absence of the concept of indirect discrimination under this Act. Unlike sections 39 and 40 of the SDA and sections 30 and 31 of the RRA, there is no specific provision under this Act which deals with instructions to discriminate or pressure to discriminate. The wider definition under this section would encompass such circumstances. An employer who sought to defend a claim on the grounds that the dismissal was not because the person was disabled but was instead because other employees refused to work with him or her would be caught by this definition.

Of course, in order for the treatment to be related to the person's disability, the employer must know certain things. It is not necessary for the employer to know that the condition the person suffers from amounts to a disability within the meaning of this Act. The employer must at least be aware of the symptoms from which the person suffers which might amount to a disability. So if a person is dismissed for a series of unexplained absences, it will not be for a reason related to the person's disability. If, however, the person is dismissed for a series of absences which are attributed to a particular set of symptoms where no specific diagnosis has been made, the dismissal may still be for a reason related to the person's disability when the four stage test under section 1 is considered in the light of the Guidance.

As with the other anti-discrimination legislation, the comparator may be real or hypothetical but care must be taken to ensure that the comparator is appropriate. For example, it would not be appropriate to compare a disabled person's record of absences with another employee who had a similar absence record but who was not disabled. The appropriate comparator in these circumstances is a person who did not have such a record of absences because, in this particular case, the person would not have that record of absences but for his disability. In an appropriate case it may be that the correct comparator is a person with a different kind of disability. A person with a disability relating to his or her mobility ought to be provided with proper access to office premises, for example by means of ramps or stair lifts, in order to get to his or her place of work. A blind or partially sighted person may not have the same problem in gaining access to the place of work but might need documents presented in Braille in order to be able to carry out the work. A refusal or a failure to provide such documents would be less favourable treatment for a reason related to that person's disability.

(b) Unlike the SDA and the RRA, the defence of justification is available to all kinds of disability discrimination. Whether or not discrimination is justified is a matter of fact for an employment tribunal to determine. When making such determination the tribunal must take account of the Code of Practice and the Disability Discrimination (Employment) Regulations 1996. Regulations 3, 4, 5, and 6 provide for particular circumstances where such discrimination is to be taken to be justified.

In general terms, whether or not discrimination is justified is to be determined by balancing the reasonable needs of the employer and the discriminatory effect of the treatment. This is the same general test as for indirect sex and race discrimination and it will not be justified if the same effect could have been achieved by a non-discriminatory route.

See also the further limitation under sub-section (3) below.

(2) For the purposes of this Part, an employer also discriminates against a disabled person if–

(a) he fails to comply with a section 6 duty imposed on him in relation to the disabled person; and

(b) he cannot show that his failure to comply with that duty is justified.

Section 5(2)

There is no provision for indirect discrimination under this Act and this sub-section makes direct discrimination what might otherwise be regarded as indirect discrimination, that is, treatment not directly related to the person's disability but to the fact that the person cannot overcome the effects of that disability without adjustment being made to the premises in which the person is employed or the organisation of the work which he or she is employed to do.

The general test as to whether or not that failure is justified involves a similar balancing act to the test of justification under sub-section (1) above. However, it is likely to be more restricted in its practical application because of the way in which the duty arises (see the notes to section 6 below) if, for example, the adjustment that would have to be made is inordinately expensive, the duty to make that adjustment would not arise.

(3) Subject to subsection (5), for the purposes of subsection (1) treatment is justified if, but only if, the reason for it is both material to the circumstances of the particular case and substantial.

Section 5(3)

This will prevent the defence of justification being used if the reason for the treatment has no real bearing on the particular case or if it is not 'substantial' (meaning more than minor or trivial).

(4) For the purposes of subsection (2), failure to comply with a section 6 duty is justified if, but only if, the reason for the failure is both material to the circumstances of the particular case and substantial.

Section 5(4)

See the notes to sub-sections (2) and (3) above.

(5) If, in a case falling within subsection (1), the employer is under a section 6 duty in relation to the disabled person but fails without justification to comply with that duty, his treatment of that person cannot be justified under subsection (3) unless it would have been justified even if he had complied with the section 6 duty.

> **Section 5(5)**
> *If an employer unjustifiably fails to make a reasonable adjustment under section (6) below, the general defence under sub-section (1)(b) is no longer available.*

(6) Regulations may make provision, for purposes of this section, as to circumstances in which–

(a) treatment is to be taken to be justified;
(b) failure to comply with a section 6 duty is to be taken to be justified;
(c) treatment is to be taken not to be justified;
(d) failure to comply with a section 6 duty is to be taken not to be justified.

> **Section 5(6)**
> *See the Disability Discrimination (Employment) Regulations 1996 SI 1996/1456.*

(7) Regulations under subsection (6) may, in particular–

(a) make provision by reference to the cost of affording any benefit; and
(b) in relation to benefits under occupational pension schemes, make provision with a view to enabling uniform rates of contributions to be maintained.

> **Section 5(7)**
> *See the note to sub-section (6) above.*

Duty of employer to make adjustments.

6.–(1) Where–

(a) any arrangements made by or on behalf of an employer, or
(b) any physical feature of premises occupied by the employer,

place the disabled person concerned at a substantial disadvantage in comparison with persons who are not disabled, it is the duty of the employer to take such steps as it is reasonable, in all the circumstances of the case, for him to have to take in order to prevent the arrangements or feature having that effect.

> **Section 6(1)**
> *In place of a provision rendering indirect discrimination unlawful, the DDA imposes a duty on employers to make reasonable adjustments. This takes account of the fact that treating disabled people in the same way as people without a disability may place them at a disadvantage. This section, in effect, imposes a requirement for a kind of positive discrimination, requiring the employer to take positive steps to create a level playing field so that the disabled person is no longer at a disadvantage.*

(2) Subsection (1)(a) applies only in relation to–

(a) arrangements for determining to whom employment should be offered;

(b) any term, condition or arrangements on which employment, promotion, a transfer, training or any other benefit is offered or afforded.

Section 6(2)
This limits the operation of sub-section (1)(a) to the job-related requirements, the organisation of the work etc, in relation to employing a person for the first time, appointing them to a new job or offering access to training or other benefits under the contract.

(3) The following are examples of steps which an employer may have to take in relation to a disabled person in order to comply with subsection (1)–

(a) making adjustments to premises;

(b) allocating some of the disabled person's duties to another person;

(c) transferring him to fill an existing vacancy;

(d) altering his working hours;

(e) assigning him to a different place of work;

(f) allowing him to be absent during working hours for rehabilitation, assessment or treatment;

(g) giving him, or arranging for him to be given, training;

(h) acquiring or modifying equipment;

(i) modifying instructions or reference manuals;

(j) modifying procedures for testing or assessment;

(k) providing a reader or interpreter;

(l) providing supervision.

Section 6(3)
As the section says, these are only examples of what steps an employer may be required to take and the list should not be regarded as exhaustive.

(4) In determining whether it is reasonable for an employer to have to take a particular step in order to comply with subsection (1), regard shall be had, in particular, to–

(a) the extent to which taking the step would prevent the effect in question;

(b) the extent to which it is practicable for the employer to take the step;

(c) the financial and other costs which would be incurred by the employer in taking the step and the extent to which taking it would disrupt any of his activities;

(d) the extent of the employer's financial and other resources;

(e) the availability to the employer of financial or other assistance with respect to taking the step.

This subsection is subject to any provision of regulations made under subsection (8).

Section 6(4)
This means that the duty to make the adjustments will depend on all the circumstances and a large employer may be under a duty to make adjustments which would not apply to a small employer where, for example the cost of doing so is disproportionate when compared to the size of the employer's undertaking. Sub-section (e) should be considered in relation to small employers. If money is available from other sources in order to pay for an alteration, the duty may arise even if, without such assistance, it would be regarded as being beyond the employer's means.

(5) In this section, "the disabled person concerned" means–
 (a) in the case of arrangements for determining to whom employment should be offered, any disabled person who is, or has notified the employer that he may be, an applicant for that employment;
 (b) in any other case, a disabled person who is–
  (i) an applicant for the employment concerned; or
  (ii) an employee of the employer concerned.

(6) Nothing in this section imposes any duty on an employer in relation to a disabled person if the employer does not know, and could not reasonably be expected to know–
 (a) in the case of an applicant or potential applicant, that the disabled person concerned is, or may be, an applicant for the employment; or
 (b) in any case, that that person has a disability and is likely to be affected in the way mentioned in subsection (1).

Section 6(5) & (6)
Because of the requirement for the employer to know of the person's disability, or at least its symptoms or its consequences, an employer is not to be criticised for a failure to take account of them unless he has previously been told that that person is an applicant for the employment. Once notified, the employer must then consider whether or not it is necessary to change any of the arrangements made under sub-section (1)(a) above.

(7) Subject to the provisions of this section, nothing in this Part is to be taken to require an employer to treat a disabled person more favourably than he treats or would treat others.

Section 6(7)
The ways in which an employer may be required to treat a disabled person more favourably than he treats or would treat others is limited in the ways set out in this section.

(8) Regulations may make provision, for the purposes of subsection (1)–
 (a) as to circumstances in which arrangements are, or a physical feature is, to be taken to have the effect mentioned in that subsection;

(b) as to circumstances in which arrangements are not, or a physical feature is not, to be taken to have that effect;
(c) as to circumstances in which it is reasonable for an employer to have to take steps of a prescribed description;
(d) as to steps which it is always reasonable for an employer to have to take;
(e) as to circumstances in which it is not reasonable for an employer to have to take steps of a prescribed description;
(f) as to steps which it is never reasonable for an employer to have to take;
(g) as to things which are to be treated as physical features;
(h) as to things which are not to be treated as such features.

(9) Regulations made under subsection (8) (c), (d), (e) or (f) may, in particular, make provision by reference to the cost of taking the steps concerned.

(10) Regulations may make provision adding to the duty imposed on employers by this section, including provision of a kind which may be made under subsection (8)

Section 6(8), (9) & (10)
See the Disability Discrimination (Employment) Regulations 1996 SI 1996/1456.

(11) This section does not apply in relation to any benefit under an occupational pension scheme or any other benefit payable in money or money's worth under a scheme or arrangement for the benefit of employees in respect of–

(a) termination of service;
(b) retirement, old age or death;
(c) accident, injury, sickness or invalidity; or
(d) any other prescribed matter.

Section 6(11)
An employer is thus entitled to offer retirement and death in service benefits on the same terms as to non-disabled employees without the requirement to make any adjustment. Without the adjustment this might amount to less favourable treatment but that is to be taken to be justified under regulation 4 of the Disability Discrimination (Employment) Regulations 1996.

(12) This section imposes duties only for the purpose of determining whether an employer has discriminated against a disabled person; and accordingly a breach of any such duty is not actionable as such.

Section 6(12)
In other words, the cause of action arises under section 4 and not under this section.

Exemption for small businesses.

7.–(1) Nothing in this Part applies in relation to an employer who has fewer than 15 employees.

> **Section 6(7)**
> *Sub-section (1) has already been amended. The original number of employees was 20.*

(2) The Secretary of State may by order amend subsection (1) by substituting a different number (not greater than 20) for the number for the time being specified there.

(3) Before making an order under subsection (2) the Secretary of State shall consult–

(a) the Disability Rights Commission;
(b) such organisations representing the interests of employers as he considers appropriate; and
(c) such organisations representing the interests of disabled persons in employment or seeking employment as he considers appropriate.

(4) The Secretary of State shall, before laying an order under this section before Parliament, publish a summary of the views expressed to him in his consultations.

> *Subsections (3) and (4) were inserted by the Disability Rights Commission Act 1999 and provide for a more streamlined procedure for consultation.*

ENFORCEMENT ETC.

Enforcement, remedies and procedure.

> **Section 8**
> *This section is the same as section 63 of the SDA and section 54 of the RRA.*

8.–(1) A complaint by any person that another person–

(a) has discriminated against him in a way which is unlawful under this Part, or
(b) is, by virtue of section 57 or 58, to be treated as having discriminated against him in such a way,

> **Section 8(1)(b)**
> *Sections 57 and 58 deal with aiding unlawful acts and the liability of employers and principles. Time limits within which such applications are to be made are set out in schedule 3 and generally follow the time limits set out in the SDA and the RRA.*

may be presented to an employment tribunal.

Section 8(1)
As with other anti-discrimination legislation the burden of proof is on the person bringing the complaint, subject to certain exceptions in particular, see section 11 below.

The burden shifts where an employer claims that the treatment, although discriminatory, was justified. In this case the employer has the burden of showing that the treatment was justified.

In deciding whether discrimination is proved the court or tribunal is entitled to draw inferences from the evidence where it is appropriate to do so. If the employer cannot or will not provide a credible explanation for the treatment or their replies, either in evidence or stated in the questionnaire (for which see section 56 below), are misleading or evasive adverse inferences might justifiably be drawn.

Discrimination cannot be inferred simply because the employer's behaviour is unreasonable. An employer may be so unreasonable as to treat everyone unfairly. If that is the case then a claim that a person has been discriminated against for a reason related to the disability will fail. The claim will only succeed if a person who didn't suffer from that disability would have been treated differently.

It is also important to note that there does not have to be a conscious intention to discriminate. One of the intentions of anti-discrimination legislation is to try to stop people making decisions based on assumptions which have no basis in fact. An employer who decides not to give a particular job to a person with a disability because of the belief that that person could not do the job because, for example, it would be too exhausting, would be discriminating against that person for a reason related to the disability even if the decision was made in what was believed to be the best interests of the complainant.

The tribunal's powers to conduct the proceedings are regulated in the same way as claims for unfair dismissal under the Employment Tribunals Act 1996 and the Employment Tribunals (Constitution and Rules of Procedure) Regulations 1993 [SI 1993/2687]. There is a whole body of case law which is too extensive to review in a work of this kind. Apart from the differences in legal terminology, the regulations which govern tribunals in Scotland are the same (see the Employment Tribunals (Constitution and Rules of Procedure) (Scotland) Regulations 1993)) [SI 1993/2688].

Brief reference will be made to those procedural matters which are more commonly, or sometimes exclusively, associated with discrimination claims.

Direct evidence of discrimination is often difficult to find. The Respondent will try to explain apparent differences in treatment as being attributable to other factors. In order to clarify the basis of the employer's defence, a complainant may submit a questionnaire in a prescribed form and the Respondent will be given time in which to reply. Further reference will be made to this under section 56 below.

Unlike in other Court proceedings, there is no requirement for the parties to produce lists of all documents they have or had. The parties are free to produce those documents which help their case but they must not be unfairly selective in doing so. If part of a document is produced the other party is entitled to see the whole of it. If a party knows of the existence of one or more documents the tribunal may be asked for an order compelling the other party to produce it. Before making such an order the tribunal will want to be satisfied that the document is relevant to the proceedings and that it is reasonable for them to make the order. It may be unreasonable if, for example, the documents have been destroyed or they have been archived and retrieval would be expensive or burdensome. However, the more important the document the greater the inconvenience and expense of producing it will be justified. In cases in which involve the giving of evidence of a personal nature in a disability claim, the tribunal has power to make an order that the parties are not identified. The power, under rule 14, only extends to the promulgation of the tribunal's decision but such an order does afford a degree of protection while evidence is being given.

(2) Where an employment tribunal finds that a complaint presented to it under this section is well-founded, it shall take such of the following steps as it considers just and equitable–

Section 8(2)(a)-(c)
Corresponding to section 65 of the SDA and section 56 of the RRA this section sets out the powers of a tribunal when they find a complaint is well founded.

(a) making a declaration as to the rights of the complainant and the respondent in relation to the matters to which the complaint relates;

(a) A declaration under sub-section (a) may be appropriate before an act of discrimination has occurred. For example, a mobility clause in a contract of employment may have an adverse effect on a person with a disability if he or she lives in a specially adapted house and specially adapted living accommodation might be difficult to find in the area to which the employee is to be transferred. A tribunal would be entitled to declare that if the employer were to rely on that clause in the contract and require the individual to move, it would be discriminatory.

(b) ordering the respondent to pay compensation to the complainant;

(b) Compensation under sub-section (b) is usually ordered to be paid where a tribunal finds that a person has been discriminated against. That compensation can include loss of earnings, which may result from a dismissal or from a failure to appoint a person to a more highly paid post. It may include compensation for the loss of the opportunity to be appointed to a more senior post where a person was prevented from applying and will almost always include a sum for injury to feelings.

It is not possible to give guidance on the level of damages which might be awarded under this head because of the enormous variety of individual circumstances. It should be noted, however, that a tribunal does have power to award aggravated damages where an employer's conduct is held to be particularly blameworthy or the conduct complained of particularly serious. Such an award may also be appropriate where, even though the original conduct complained of is not so serious, the employer's conduct of the proceedings themselves, for example, raising spurious allegations of misconduct or incompetence, merits such an award.

There will be cases where the victim of discrimination actually suffers stress or possibly even psychiatric injury as a result of the treatment he or she receives. In such cases the tribunal also has the power to award damages for personal injury (see sub-section (3) and (4) below).

Where such injury has occurred, it is important that the claim is included in the tribunal proceedings. Medical evidence will almost certainly be required as to the nature of the injury and the tribunal will probably give directions as to how and when such medical evidence should be produced.

A separate claim for personal injury, where that injury is sustained as a result of the employer's treatment of the complainant, will not be permitted once the tribunal case has concluded because of the general rule that all matters which could have been raised in a particular set of proceedings should have been raised. A failure to raise them at the appropriate time and an attempt to raise them in separate proceedings later will be regarded as an abuse of the process of the Court.

Exemplary damages, which are intended to punish the offender rather than compensate the victim, are not permitted.

As in other cases involving claims for damages, a complainant is required to take reasonable steps to mitigate any loss suffered. A tribunal must also consider whether to award interest on any damages. This is so whether or not the parties claim interest.

Interest is awarded under different heads of damage at different rates and for different periods. In a work of this kind it is not possible to set out all of the provisions for interest and detailed advice should be taken.

(c) recommending that the respondent take, within a specified period, action appearing to the tribunal to be reasonable, in all the circumstances of the case, for the purpose of obviating or reducing the adverse effect on the complainant of any matter to which the complaint relates.

(c) The purpose of a recommendation is to remove the adverse consequences of the employer's action. This does not extend to a recommendation to increase the pay of a complainant. That must be covered by an order for compensation under sub-section (b).

A recommendation must relate to the particular circumstances of the case being dealt with. It could include the removal of conditions for appointment to a particular post, where those conditions are held to be discriminatory. It may also include the provision of training so that the complainant is not disadvantaged in the future but it does not include the power to recommend that the complainant be appointed to the next available post.

A failure to comply with a recommendation made by a tribunal is dealt with under sub-section (5) below.

(3) Where a tribunal orders compensation under subsection (2)(b), the amount of the compensation shall be calculated by applying the principles applicable to the calculation of damages in claims in tort or (in Scotland) in reparation for breach of statutory duty.

(4) For the avoidance of doubt it is hereby declared that compensation in respect of discrimination in a way which is unlawful under this Part may include compensation for injury to feelings whether or not it includes compensation under any other head.

(5) If the respondent to a complaint fails, without reasonable justification, to comply with a recommendation made by an employment tribunal under subsection (2)(c) the tribunal may, if it thinks it just and equitable to do so–

(a) increase the amount of compensation required to be paid to the complainant in respect of the complaint, where an order was made under subsection (2)(b); or
(b) make an order under subsection (2)(b).

Section 8(5)
On a failure to comply with the recommendation, the tribunal may award additional compensation under sub-section (a) or may award compensation if it hadn't previously done so.

(6) Regulations may make provision–

(a) for enabling a tribunal, where an amount of compensation falls to be awarded under subsection (2)(b), to include in the award interest on that amount; and
(b) specifying, for cases where a tribunal decides that an award is to include an amount in respect of interest, the manner in which and the periods and rate by reference to which the interest is to be determined.

Section 8(6)
See the Employment Tribunals Interest on Awards in Discrimination Cases Regulations 1996, SI 1996/2803, as amended by the Employment Rights (Dispute Resolution) Act 1998.

(7) Regulations may modify the operation of any order made under section 14 of the Employment Tribunals Act 1996 (power to make provision as to interest on sums payable in pursuance of employment tribunal decisions) to the extent that it relates to an award of compensation under subsection (2)(b).

(8) Part I of Schedule 3 makes further provision about the enforcement of this Part and about procedure.

Validity of certain agreements.

9.–(1) Any term in a contract of employment or other agreement is void so far as it purports to–

(a) require a person to do anything which would contravene any provision of, or made under, this Part;
(b) exclude or limit the operation of any provision of this Part; or
(c) prevent any person from presenting a complaint to an employment tribunal under this Part.

Section 9(1)
A complainant or potential complainant cannot sign a contract which prevents him/her from bringing or continuing proceedings under this Act unless all of the provisions of this section are complied with.

A failure to meet any one of the conditions would allow the complainant to bring or continue with their claim. Despite this, if a complainant has received a significant sum of money in settlement of a complaint but the strict technical requirements of this section have not been complied with a tribunal may nevertheless reduce any award it is minded to make under section 8(2)(b) to take account of the amount already received.

(2) Paragraphs (b) and (c) of subsection (1) do not apply to an agreement not to institute proceedings under section 8(1), or to an agreement not to continue such proceedings, if–

(a) a conciliation officer has acted under section 18 of the Employment Tribunals Act 1996 in relation to the matter; or
(b) the conditions set out in subsection (3) are satisfied.

Section 9(2)
If a conciliation officer employed by ACAS helps the parties to reach an agreement and that agreement is recorded on a special form (called a COT3), that will be effective to prevent the claim going any further. It is to be noted, however, that a conciliation officer will not normally record on a COT3 an agreement which has been reached independently by the parties. Before an agreement can be so recorded, the conciliation officer must be involved in the discussions between the parties before the agreement is reached.

(3) The conditions are that–

(a) the complainant must have received advice from a relevant independent adviser as to the terms and effect of the proposed agreement (and in particular its effect on his ability to pursue his complaint before an employment tribunal);
(b) when the adviser gave the advice there must have been in force a contract of insurance, or an indemnity provided for members of a professional body, covering the risk of a claim by the complainant in respect of loss arising in consequence of the advice; and
(c) the agreement must be in writing, relate to the particular complaint, identify the adviser and state that the conditions are satisfied.

(4) In this section–

"independent", in relation to legal advice to the complainant, means that it is given by a lawyer who is not acting for the other party or for a person who is connected with that other party; and

"qualified lawyer" means–

(a) as respects proceedings in England and Wales, a barrister (whether in practice as such or employed to give legal advice) or a solicitor of the Supreme Court who holds a practising certificate; and
(b) as respects proceedings in Scotland, an advocate (whether in practice as such or employed to give legal advice) or a solicitor who holds a practising certificate.

(5) For the purposes of subsection (4), any two persons are to be treated as connected if–

(a) one is a company of which the other (directly or indirectly) has control, or
(b) both are companies of which a third person (directly or indirectly) has control.

Section 9(3) to (5)

These sections are designed to protect a potential complainant so that, before an agreement is reached which would prevent them from bringing or pursuing a case before an employment tribunal they have received proper advice from a person qualified to give it. It is always possible that someone giving such advice can do so negligently so that the complainant is prevented from pursuing a claim even though they have received bad advice. This is the reason for the stipulation in sub-section (3)(b) that there should be in force in respect of that advice a policy of insurance so that the complainant may then sue the adviser for negligence and obtain from the adviser all that might have been obtained from the employer if the complaint had been allowed to proceed.

Subsections (3) and (4) were inserted by the Disability Rights Commission Act 1999 and provide for a more streamlined procedure for consultation.

(6) An agreement under which the parties agree to submit a dispute to arbitration–

(a) shall be regarded for the purposes of sub-section (2) as being an agreement not to institute, or an agreement not to continue, proceedings if–

(i) the dispute is covered by a scheme having effect by virtue of an order under Section 212A of the Trade Union and Labour Relations (Consolidation) Act 1992, and

(ii) the agreement is to submit to arbitration in accordnace with the scheme, but

(b) shall be regarded as neither being nor including such an agreement in any other case.

This applies only to agreements entered into after 1 August 1998.

Section 9(6)
Instead of pursuing a complaint before a full tribunal, a complainant may now refer the matter to arbitration as an alternative means of dealing with the claim. This provision was introduced by the Employment Rights (Dispute Resolution) Act 1998. A person who agrees to refer their dispute to arbitration is prevented by this section from later pursuing the complaint in the employment tribunal.

Charities and support for particular groups of persons.

10.–(1) Nothing in this Part–

(a) affects any charitable instrument which provides for conferring benefits on one or more categories of person determined by reference to any physical or mental capacity; or

(b) makes unlawful any act done by a charity or recognised body in pursuance of any of its charitable purposes, so far as those purposes are connected with persons so determined.

(2) Nothing in this Part prevents–

(a) a person who provides supported employment from treating members of a particular group of disabled persons more favourably than other persons in providing such employment; or

(b) the Secretary of State from agreeing to arrangements for the provision of supported employment which will, or may, have that effect.

(3) In this section–

"charitable instrument" means an enactment or other instrument (whenever taking effect) so far as it relates to charitable purposes;

"charity" has the same meaning as in the Charities Act 1993;

"recognised body" means a body which is a recognised body for the purposes of Part I of the Law Reform (Miscellaneous Provisions) (Scotland) Act 1990; and "supported employment" means facilities provided, or in respect of which payments are made, under section 15 of the Disabled Persons (Employment) Act 1944.

(4) In the application of this section to England and Wales, "charitable purposes" means purposes which are exclusively charitable according to the law of England and Wales.

(5) In the application of this section to Scotland, "charitable purposes" shall be construed in the same way as if it were contained in the Income Tax Acts.

Section 10

It would be against the whole purpose of the act for charities providing support to disabled people to be prevented from providing that support in furtherance of its charitable purposes.

Note the different meaning of " "charitable purposes" " in its application to England and Wales on the one hand and Scotland on the other under sub-sections (4) and (5).

Advertisements suggesting that employers will discriminate against disabled persons.

11.–(1) This section applies where–

(a) a disabled person has applied for employment with an employer;
(b) the employer has refused to offer, or has deliberately not offered, him the employment;
(c) the disabled person has presented a complaint under section 8 against the employer;
(d) the employer has advertised the employment (whether before or after the disabled person applied for it); and
(e) the advertisement indicated, or might reasonably be understood to have indicated, that any application for the advertised employment would, or might, be determined to any extent by reference to–
 (i) the successful applicant not having any disability or any category of disability which includes the disabled person's disability; or
 (ii) the employer's reluctance to take any action of a kind mentioned in section 6.

(2) The tribunal hearing the complaint shall assume, unless the contrary is shown, that the employer's reason for refusing to offer, or deliberately not offering, the employment to the complainant was related to the complainant's disability.

(3) In this section "advertisement" includes every form of advertisement or notice, whether to the public or not.

Section 11
A person who does not succeed in obtaining employment will always be at a disadvantage in trying to prove the reason why he or she was unsuccessful. This information is always in the possession of the employer.

Under this section it is for the employer to produce that evidence in order to show that the failure or refusal to offer employment was not for a reason related to the applicant's disability where the advertisement for the post suggests that the employer did not want to appoint a disabled person.

Whether the advertisement does suggest that the employer will discriminate against a disabled person is to be looked at objectively and not according to the employer's claimed intention. An illustration of the way this section might work in practice is given in the Code of Practice at paragraph 5.7

DISCRIMINATION BY OTHER PERSONS

Discrimination against contract workers.

12.–(1) It is unlawful for a principal, in relation to contract work, to discriminate against a disabled person–

(a) in the terms on which he allows him to do that work;

(b) by not allowing him to do it or continue to do it;

(c) in the way he affords him access to any benefits or by refusing or deliberately omitting to afford him access to them; or

(d) by subjecting him to any other detriment.

Section 12(1)
The same protection is afforded to contract workers employed by a third party as is provided to those directly employed under section 4.

(2) Subsection (1) does not apply to benefits of any description if the principal is concerned with the provision (whether or not for payment) of benefits of that description to the public, or to a section of the public which includes the contract worker in question, unless that provision differs in a material respect from the provision of the benefits by the principal to contract workers.

Section 12(2)
This is the same exclusion as applies under section 4(3) in relation to employees.

(3) The provisions of this Part (other than subsections (1) to (3) of section 4) apply to any principal, in relation to contract work, as if he were, or would be, the employer

of the contract worker and as if any contract worker supplied to do work for him were an employee of his.

Section 12(3)
It is the person for whom the work is ultimately done who is liable under this section but the exclusions prevent double liability occurring under section 4.

(4) In the case of an act which constitutes discrimination by virtue of section 55, this section also applies to discrimination against a person who is not disabled.

Section 12(4)
Victimisation Claims.

(5) This section applies only in relation to contract work done at an establishment in Great Britain (the provisions of section 68 about the meaning of "employment at an establishment in Great Britain" applying for the purposes of this subsection with the appropriate modifications).

Section 12(5)
The same exclusion as operates in relation to employees under section 4(6) but with the same reservation in respect of the operation of European law (for which see the note to section 4(6) above).

(6) In this section–

"principal" means a person ("A") who makes work available for doing by individuals who are employed by another person who supplies them under a contract made with A;

"contract work" means work so made available; and

"contract worker" means any individual who is supplied to the principal under such a contract.

Section 12(6)
This applies even if the individual is two stages removed from the "principal". For example, a person is supplied by company A to an employment agency. The employment agency then provides the worker provided by company A to the principal. Even though there is no direct contractual relationship between the company which employs the complainant and the principal, the person is protected against discrimination by this section.

Discrimination by trade organisations.

13.–(1) It is unlawful for a trade organisation to discriminate against a disabled person–

(a) in the terms on which it is prepared to admit him to membership of the organisation; or

(b) by refusing to accept, or deliberately not accepting, his application for membership.

(2) It is unlawful for a trade organisation, in the case of a disabled person who is a member of the organisation, to discriminate against him–

(a) in the way it affords him access to any benefits or by refusing or deliberately omitting to afford him access to them;

(b) by depriving him of membership, or varying the terms on which he is a member; or

(c) by subjecting him to any other detriment.

(3) In the case of an act which constitutes discrimination by virtue of section 55, this section also applies to discrimination against a person who is not disabled.

> **Section 13(3)**
> *Trade organisations are under the same duty as any other employer not to discriminate against a person on grounds related to a disability under this section they have additional duties in relation to members of the organisation. This is because some trade organisations govern who can work in that profession or the terms on which they must carry out their work.*
>
> *The scope of the protection is as wide as it is for employees under sub-sections (1) and (2) and includes protection against victimisation under sub-section (3).*

(4) In this section "trade organisation" means an organisation of workers, an organisation of employers or any other organisation whose members carry on a particular profession or trade for the purposes of which the organisation exists.

> **Section 13(4)**
> *This includes trade unions, employers' associations and other professional bodies. There is no limitation on the size of membership.*
>
> *The organisation or association will usually be responsible for the actions of its employees and its members towards each other because of the vicarious liability imposed by section 58.*

Meaning of "discrimination" in relation to trade organisations.

14.–(1) For the purposes of this Part, a trade organisation discriminates against a disabled person if–

(a) for a reason which relates to the disabled person's disability, it treats him less favourably than it treats or would treat others to whom that reason does not or would not apply; and
(b) it cannot show that the treatment in question is justified.

Section 14(1)
It is probably merely deficiencies in drafting which require the meaning of discrimination to be set out separately here. In the SDA and the RRA the definition appears at section 1 and is then applied throughout the Act. The definition of discrimination here is precisely the same as that under section 5 in relation to employment and the defence of justification is also available.

(2) For the purposes of this Part, a trade organisation also discriminates against a disabled person if–

(a) it fails to comply with a section 15 duty imposed on it in relation to the disabled person; and
(b) it cannot show that its failure to comply with that duty is justified.

Section 14(2)
The duty to make reasonable adjustments also applies to trade organisations in relation to members and a failure to comply with that duty amounts to discrimination.

(3) Subject to subsection (5), for the purposes of subsection (1) treatment is justified if, but only if, the reason for it is both material to the circumstances of the particular case and substantial.

(4) For the purposes of subsection (2), failure to comply with a section 15 duty is justified if, but only if, the reason for the failure is both material to the circumstances of the particular case and substantial.

(5) If, in a case falling within subsection (1), the trade organisation is under a section 15 duty in relation to the disabled person concerned but fails without justification to comply with that duty, its treatment of that person cannot be justified under subsection (3) unless the treatment would have been justified even if the organisation had complied with the section 15 duty.

(6) Regulations may make provision, for purposes of this section, as to circumstances in which–

(a) treatment is to be taken to be justified;
(b) failure to comply with a section 15 duty is to be taken to be justified;
(c) treatment is to be taken not to be justified;
(d) failure to comply with a section 15 duty is to be taken not to be justified.

Duty of trade organisations to make adjustments

15.–(1) Where–

(a) any arrangements made by or on behalf of a trade organisation, or
(b) any physical feature of premises occupied by the organisation,

place the disabled person concerned at a substantial disadvantage in comparison with persons who are not disabled, it is the duty of the organisation to take such steps as it is reasonable, in all the circumstances of the case, for it to have to take in order to prevent the arrangements or feature having that effect.

Section 15(1) (a) – (b)

(a) From October 1999 trade organisations are subject to the "Code of Practice on duties of trade organisations to their disabled members and applicants", SI 1999/1190.

Although the duty to make adjustments only exists in relation to members and those who have notified the association that they are applying for membership, a large organisation would be well advised to take advice on what steps could be taken in order to remove any difficulty or disadvantage that a member or an applicant for membership might face. The most obvious example here is the provision of membership application forms in braille or via audio tape.

(b) The duty to make adjustments to any physical features of premises occupied by the organisation does not come into force until October 2004.

Apart from sub-section (1)(b), the duty to make adjustments is similar to that which applies to employers under section 6 and the reader is referred to the notes to that section.

(2) Subsection (1)(a) applies only in relation to–

(a) arrangements for determining who should become or remain a member of the organisation;
(b) any term, condition or arrangements on which membership or any benefit is offered or afforded.

(3) In determining whether it is reasonable for a trade organisation to have to take a particular step in order to comply with subsection (1), regard shall be had, in particular, to–

(a) the extent to which taking the step would prevent the effect in question;
(b) the extent to which it is practicable for the organisation to take the step;

(c) the financial and other costs which would be incurred by the organisation in taking the step and the extent to which taking it would disrupt any of its activities;
(d) the extent of the organisation's financial and other resources;
(e) the availability to the organisation of financial or other assistance with respect to taking the step.

This subsection is subject to any provision of regulations made under subsection (7).

(4) In this section "the disabled person concerned" means–
(a) in the case of arrangements for determining to whom membership should be offered, any disabled person who is, or has notified the organisation that he may be, an applicant for membership;
(b) in any other case, a disabled person who is–
(i) an applicant for membership; or
(ii) a member of the organisation.

(5) Nothing in this section imposes any duty on an organisation in relation to a disabled person if the organisation does not know, and could not reasonably be expected to know that the disabled person concerned–
(a) is, or may be, an applicant for membership; or
(b) has a disability and is likely to be affected in the way mentioned in subsection (1).

(6) Subject to the provisions of this section, nothing in this Part is to be taken to require a trade organisation to treat a disabled person more favourably than it treats or would treat others.

(7) Regulations may make provision for the purposes of subsection (1) as to any of the matters mentioned in paragraphs (a) to (h) of section 6(8) (the references in those paragraphs to an employer being read for these purposes as references to a trade organisation).

(8) Subsection (9) of section 6 applies in relation to such regulations as it applies in relation to regulations made under section 6(8).

(9) Regulations may make provision adding to the duty imposed on trade organisations by this section, including provision of a kind which may be made under subsection (7).

(10) This section imposes duties only for the purpose of determining whether a trade organisation has discriminated against a disabled person; and accordingly a breach of any such duty is not actionable as such.

PREMISES OCCUPIED UNDER LEASES

Alterations to premises occupied under leases.

16.–(1) This section applies where–

(a) an employer or trade organisation ("the occupier") occupies premises under a lease;
(b) but for this section, the occupier would not be entitled to make a particular alteration to the premises; and
(c) the alteration is one which the occupier proposes to make in order to comply with a section 6 duty or section 15 duty.

Section 16(1)
The employer or the trade organisation may not own the premises from which the business is conducted. This section gives the organisations limited defences under the Act for a failure to make the alterations which would be covered by the duty to make the reasonable adjustment.

(2) Except to the extent to which it expressly so provides, the lease shall have effect by virtue of this subsection as if it provided–
(a) for the occupier to be entitled to make the alteration with the written consent of the lessor;
(b) for the occupier to have to make a written application to the lessor for consent if he wishes to make the alteration;
(c) if such an application is made, for the lessor not to withhold his consent unreasonably; and
(d) for the lessor to be entitled to make his consent subject to reasonable conditions.

Section 16(2) (a) – (d)
(a) If the lease makes no express provision for the occupier to be able to make alterations, this section now provides that the lease is taken to include a term which permits the alterations provided written consent is sought beforehand.

(c) and (d) The lessor cannot just refuse to allow the alterations to be made but is entitled to impose reasonable conditions for the making of them.

If the lease contains express terms as to the conditions which will apply if alternations are made or which permit the lessor to impose conditions then the employer or the trade association is to be treated as if it was not entitled to make the alterations. This gives it a complete defence to an allegation that it has failed to comply with the duty to make the adjustment.

Under schedule 4, Part I, the organisation cannot use this defence unless it has previously made written application for consent to make the alterations. If there are other adjustments, not requiring alterations to the premises, which can be carried out under the duty to make reasonable adjustments, the defence under this section will not be available to that separate duty.

(3) In this section–

"lease" includes a tenancy, sub-lease or sub-tenancy and an agreement for a lease, tenancy, sub-lease or sub-tenancy; and

"sub-lease" and "sub-tenancy" have such meaning as may be prescribed.

(4) If the terms and conditions of a lease–

(a) impose conditions which are to apply if the occupier alters the premises, or

(b) entitle the lessor to impose conditions when consenting to the occupier's altering the premises,

the occupier is to be treated for the purposes of subsection (1) as not being entitled to make the alteration.

(5) Part I of Schedule 4 supplements the provisions of this section.

Section 16(5)

Schedule 4 makes further provisions relating to the alteration of premises, including the ability to make the lessor a party to the proceedings and giving the court or tribunal hearing the case the power to give the occupier the consent needed if the lessor has unreasonably refused consent.

OCCUPATIONAL PENSION SCHEMES AND INSURANCE SERVICES

Occupational pension schemes.

17.–(1) Every occupational pension scheme shall be taken to include a provision ("a non-discrimination rule")–

(a) relating to the terms on which–

(i) persons become members of the scheme; and

(ii) members of the scheme are treated; and

(b) requiring the trustees or managers of the scheme to refrain from any act or omission which, if done in relation to a person by an employer, would amount to unlawful discrimination against that person for the purposes of this Part.

Section 17(1)

An employer or trade association cannot exclude disabled employees or members from membership of a scheme or from treating them any differently to non-disabled employees or members.

A pension scheme is separate from the employer and/or the trustees. This sub-section subjects the trustees and/or the managers of the scheme to the same general rules prohibiting discrimination as applies to the employer or the organisation under earlier sections.

(2) The other provisions of the scheme are to have effect subject to the non-discrimination rule.

(3) Without prejudice to section 67, regulations under this Part may–

(a) with respect to trustees or managers of occupational pension schemes make different provision from that made with respect to employers; or

(b) make provision modifying the application to such trustees or managers of any regulations made under this Part, or of any provisions of this Part so far as they apply to employers.

Section 17(3)

Section 67 is the general power to make regulations by statutory instrument.

The "Disability Discrimination (Employment) Regulations 1996" do allow different terms to be applied to disabled members where the cost for providing those benefits will be substantially greater than the cost of providing them for non-disabled employees (see regulation 4.)

(4) In determining, for the purposes of this section, whether an act or omission would amount to unlawful discrimination if done by an employer, any provision made under subsection (3) shall be applied as if it applied in relation to the notional employer.

Insurance services.

18.–(1) This section applies where a provider of insurance services ("the insurer") enters into arrangements with an employer under which the employer's employees, or a class of his employees–

(a) receive insurance services provided by the insurer; or

(b) are given an opportunity to receive such services.

(2) The insurer is to be taken, for the purposes of this Part, to discriminate unlawfully against a disabled person who is a relevant employee if he acts in relation to that employee in a way which would be unlawful discrimination for the purposes of Part III if–

(a) he were providing the service in question to members of the public; and

(b) the employee was provided with, or was trying to secure the provision of, that service as a member of the public.

(3) In this section–

"insurance services" means services of a prescribed description for the provision of benefits in respect of–

(a) termination of service;

(b) retirement, old age or death;

(c) accident, injury, sickness or invalidity; or

(d) any other prescribed matter; and

"relevant employee" means–

(a) in the case of an arrangement which applies to employees of the employer in question, an employee of his;

(b) in the case of an arrangement which applies to a class of employees of the employer, an employee who is in that class.

(4) For the purposes of the definition of "relevant employee" in subsection (3), "employee", in relation to an employer, includes a person who has applied for, or is contemplating applying for, employment by that employer or (as the case may be) employment by him in the class in question.

Section 18

There would be a gaping hole in the protection afforded to employees if the kind of benefits provided under section 17 above could be provided by a third party through the employer without similar restrictions on discriminatory provision.

See the Disability Discrimination (Description of Insurance Services) Regulations 1999 (SI 1999/2114).

PART III DISCRIMINATION IN OTHER AREAS

GOODS, FACILITIES AND SERVICES

Discrimination in relation to goods, facilities and services.

19.–(1) It is unlawful for a provider of services to discriminate against a disabled person–

(a) in refusing to provide, or deliberately not providing, to the disabled person any service which he provides, or is prepared to provide, to members of the public;

(b) in failing to comply with any duty imposed on him by section 21 in circumstances in which the effect of that failure is to make it impossible or unreasonably difficult for the disabled person to make use of any such service;

(c) in the standard of service which he provides to the disabled person or the manner in which he provides it to him; or

(d) in the terms on which he provides a service to the disabled person.

Section 19(1) (b) & (c)

As with codes of practice issued under the SDA and the RRA the "Code of Practice in relation to rights of access to the provision of goods, facilities, services and premises" provides guidance on what steps can be taken to prevent discrimination against disabled people. Like the other codes, it does not have direct legal force but can be relied upon in any proceedings as evidence of the provider's general approach.

The obligations do not arise only when the provider of services is faced with a request from a disabled person. If the organisation exists to provide those services to the general public it is expected that steps will be taken to anticipate what the needs of people with disabilities might be and for steps to be taken to meet those needs.

As with employers and trade organisations, there is a general duty to make reasonable adjustments under section 21. At present that duty extends only to providing extra help or making changes to the way the services are provided. From 2004 the duty to make reasonable adjustments will extend to making physical changes to the premises where necessary to overcome physical barriers.

The duty extends to providers of voluntary services.

(2) For the purposes of this section and sections 20 and 21–

(a) the provision of services includes the provision of any goods or facilities;
(b) a person is "a provider of services" if he is concerned with the provision, in the United Kingdom, of services to the public or to a section of the public; and
(c) it is irrelevant whether a service is provided on payment or without payment.

(3) The following are examples of services to which this section and sections 20 and 21 apply–

(a) access to and use of any place which members of the public are permitted to enter;
(b) access to and use of means of communication;
(c) access to and use of information services;
(d) accommodation in a hotel, boarding house or other similar establishment;
(e) facilities by way of banking or insurance or for grants, loans, credit or finance;
(f) facilities for entertainment, recreation or refreshment;
(g) facilities provided by employment agencies or under section 2 of the Employment and Training Act 1973;
(h) the services of any profession or trade, or any local or other public authority.

Section 19(3) (a) – (h)
These are examples only and should not be taken to be exhaustive.

Protection against victimisation.

(4) In the case of an act which constitutes discrimination by virtue of section 55, this section also applies to discrimination against a person who is not disabled.

(5) Except in such circumstances as may be prescribed, this section and sections 20 and 21 do not apply to–

(a) education which is funded, or secured, by a relevant body or provided at–

(i) an establishment which is funded by such a body or by a Minister of the Crown; or

(ii) any other establishment which is a school as defined in section 4(1) and (2) of the Education Act 1996 or section 135(1) of the Education (Scotland) Act 1980;

(b) any service so far as it consists of the use of any means of transport; or

(c) such other services as may be prescribed.

Section 19(5)
Separate provision is made for these services elsewhere in the Act and this section avoids double liability.

(6) In subsection (5) "relevant body" means–

(a) a local education authority in England and Wales;
(b) an education authority in Scotland;
(c) the Funding Agency for Schools;
(d) the Schools Funding Council for Wales;
(e) the Further Education Funding Council for England;
(f) the Further Education Funding Council for Wales;
(ff) the Scottish Further Education Funding Council established by an order under section 7(1) of the Further and Higher Education (Scotland) Act 1992;
(g) the Higher Education Funding Council for England;
(h) the Scottish Higher Education Funding Council;
(i) the Higher Education Funding Council for Wales;
(j) the Teacher Training Agency;
(k) a voluntary organisation; or
(l) a body of a prescribed kind.

Meaning of "discrimination".

20.–(1) For the purposes of section 19, a provider of services discriminates against a disabled person if–

(a) for a reason which relates to the disabled person's disability, he treats him less favourably than he treats or would treat others to whom that reason does not or would not apply; and

(b) he cannot show that the treatment in question is justified.

(2) For the purposes of section 19, a provider of services also discriminates against a disabled person if–

(a) he fails to comply with a section 21 duty imposed on him in relation to the disabled person; and

(b) he cannot show that his failure to comply with that duty is justified.

Section 20 (1) & (2)
The same general definition as for employment under section 5 and trade organisations under section 14.

Under sub-section (1)(b) the general defence of justification is also available.

(3) For the purposes of this section, treatment is justified only if–
(a) in the opinion of the provider of services, one or more of the conditions mentioned in subsection (4) are satisfied; and
(b) it is reasonable, in all the circumstances of the case, for him to hold that opinion.

Section 20(3)
The conditions under sub-section (4) do not have to exist in fact. It is sufficient if the provider of the services reasonably believes that those conditions are satisfied.

(4) The conditions are that–
(a) in any case, the treatment is necessary in order not to endanger the health or safety of any person (which may include that of the disabled person);
(b) in any case, the disabled person is incapable of entering into an enforceable agreement, or of giving an informed consent, and for that reason the treatment is reasonable in that case;
(c) in a case falling within section 19(1)(a), the treatment is necessary because the provider of services would otherwise be unable to provide the service to members of the public;
(d) in a case falling within section 19(1) (c) or (d), the treatment is necessary in order for the provider of services to be able to provide the service to the disabled person or to other members of the public;
(e) in a case falling within section 19(1)(d), the difference in the terms on which the service is provided to the disabled person and those on which it is provided to other members of the public reflects the greater cost to the provider of services in providing the service to the disabled person.

(5) Any increase in the cost of providing a service to a disabled person which results from compliance by a provider of services with a section 21 duty shall be disregarded for the purposes of subsection (4)(e).

Section 20(5)
If a section 21 duty (the duty to make reasonable adjustments) arises, it is because the question of cost has already been considered and it is not unreasonable to impose that duty despite the increase in costs. Because that element of the increase in costs has already been considered it is not then available as a defence for a second time to the provider of services under sub-section (4)(e) above.

(6) Regulations may make provision, for purposes of this section, as to circumstances in which–

(a) it is reasonable for a provider of services to hold the opinion mentioned in subsection (3)(a);

(b) it is not reasonable for a provider of services to hold that opinion.

(7) Regulations may make provision for subsection (4)(b) not to apply in prescribed circumstances where–

(a) a person is acting for a disabled person under a power of attorney;

(b) functions conferred by or under Part VII of the Mental Health Act 1983 are exercisable in relation to a disabled person's property or affairs; or

(c) powers are exercisable in Scotland in relation to a disabled person's property or affairs in consequence of the appointment of a curator bonis, tutor or judicial factor.

(8) Regulations may make provision, for purposes of this section, as to circumstances (other than those mentioned in subsection (4)) in which treatment is to be taken to be justified.

(9) In subsections (3), (4) and (8) "treatment" includes failure to comply with a section 21 duty.

Duty of providers of services to make adjustments.

21.–(1) Where a provider of services has a practice, policy or procedure which makes it impossible or unreasonably difficult for disabled persons to make use of a service which he provides, or is prepared to provide, to other members of the public, it is his duty to take such steps as it is reasonable, in all the circumstances of the case, for him to have to take in order to change that practice, policy or procedure so that it no longer has that effect.

(2) Where a physical feature (for example, one arising from the design or construction of a building or the approach or access to premises) makes it impossible or unreasonably difficult for disabled persons to make use of such a service, it is the duty of the provider of that service to take such steps as it is reasonable, in all the circumstances of the case, for him to have to take in order to–

(a) remove the feature;

(b) alter it so that it no longer has that effect;

(c) provide a reasonable means of avoiding the feature; or

(d) provide a reasonable alternative method of making the service in question available to disabled persons.

(3) Regulations may prescribe–

(a) matters which are to be taken into account in determining whether any provision of a kind mentioned in subsection (2)(c) or (d) is reasonable; and

(b) categories of providers of services to whom subsection (2) does not apply.

(4) Where an auxiliary aid or service (for example, the provision of information on audio tape or of a sign language interpreter) would–

(a) enable disabled persons to make use of a service which a provider of services provides, or is prepared to provide, to members of the public, or
(b) facilitate the use by disabled persons of such a service,

it is the duty of the provider of that service to take such steps as it is reasonable, in all the circumstances of the case, for him to have to take in order to provide that auxiliary aid or service.

(5) Regulations may make provision, for the purposes of this section–

(a) as to circumstances in which it is reasonable for a provider of services to have to take steps of a prescribed description;
(b) as to circumstances in which it is not reasonable for a provider of services to have to take steps of a prescribed description;
(c) as to what is to be included within the meaning of "practice, policy or procedure";
(d) as to what is not to be included within the meaning of that expression;
(e) as to things which are to be treated as physical features;
(f) as to things which are not to be treated as such features;
(g) as to things which are to be treated as auxiliary aids or services;
(h) as to things which are not to be treated as auxiliary aids or services.

(6) Nothing in this section requires a provider of services to take any steps which would fundamentally alter the nature of the service in question or the nature of his trade, profession or business.

(7) Nothing in this section requires a provider of services to take any steps which would cause him to incur expenditure exceeding the prescribed maximum.

(8) Regulations under subsection (7) may provide for the prescribed maximum to be calculated by reference to–

(a) aggregate amounts of expenditure incurred in relation to different cases;
(b) prescribed periods;
(c) services of a prescribed description;
(d) premises of a prescribed description; or
(e) such other criteria as may be prescribed.

(9) Regulations may provide, for the purposes of subsection (7), for expenditure incurred by one provider of services to be treated as incurred by another.

(10) This section imposes duties only for the purpose of determining whether a provider of services has discriminated against a disabled person; and accordingly a breach of any such duty is not actionable as such.

Section 21
Sub-sections (2)(a) - (c) and (7) - (9) inclusive expected to be brought into force in 2004.

Otherwise see the Disability Discrimination (Services and Premises) Regulations 1996 (SI 1996/1836) and (SI 1999/1191). The Disability Discrimination (services & premises) Regulations 1999

PREMISES

Discrimination in relation to premises.

22.–(1) It is unlawful for a person with power to dispose of any premises to discriminate against a disabled person–

(a) in the terms on which he offers to dispose of those premises to the disabled person;
(b) by refusing to dispose of those premises to the disabled person; or
(c) in his treatment of the disabled person in relation to any list of persons in need of premises of that description.

(2) Subsection (1) does not apply to a person who owns an estate or interest in the premises and wholly occupies them unless, for the purpose of disposing of the premises, he–

(a) uses the services of an estate agent, or
(b) publishes an advertisement or causes an advertisement to be published.

Section 22(2)
This would apply to the private sale of any house provided the sale is managed through an estate agent or advertised. It is to be noted, however, that under this section there is no duty to make reasonable adjustments.

(3) It is unlawful for a person managing any premises to discriminate against a disabled person occupying those premises–

(a) in the way he permits the disabled person to make use of any benefits or facilities;
(b) by refusing or deliberately omitting to permit the disabled person to make use of any benefits or facilities; or
(c) by evicting the disabled person, or subjecting him to any other detriment.

Section 22(1)–(3)
Although set out slightly differently, this section corresponds to section 30(1) - (3) SDA and section 21 RRA.

(4) It is unlawful for any person whose licence or consent is required for the disposal of any premises comprised in, or (in Scotland) the subject of, a tenancy to discriminate against a disabled person by withholding his licence or consent for the disposal of the premises to the disabled person.

> **Section 22(4)**
> *See also section 31(1) SDA and section 21(3) RRA.*

(5) Subsection (4) applies to tenancies created before as well as after the passing of this Act.

(6) In this section–

"advertisement" includes every form of advertisement or notice, whether to the public or not;

"dispose", in relation to premises, includes granting a right to occupy the premises, and, in relation to premises comprised in, or (in Scotland) the subject of, a tenancy, includes–

(a) assigning the tenancy, and

(b) sub-letting or parting with possession of the premises or any part of the premises;

and "disposal" shall be construed accordingly;

"estate agent" means a person who, by way of profession or trade, provides services for the purpose of finding premises for persons seeking to acquire them or assisting in the disposal of premises; and

"tenancy" means a tenancy created–

(a) by a lease or sub-lease,

(b) by an agreement for a lease or sub-lease,

(c) by a tenancy agreement, or

(d) in pursuance of any enactment.

(7) In the case of an act which constitutes discrimination by virtue of section 55, this section also applies to discrimination against a person who is not disabled.

> **Section 22(7)**
> *Acts of victimisation.*

(8) This section applies only in relation to premises in the United Kingdom.

Exemption for small dwellings.

23.–(1) Where the conditions mentioned in subsection (2) are satisfied, subsection (1), (3) or (as the case may be) (4) of section 22 does not apply.

(2) The conditions are that–

(a) the relevant occupier resides, and intends to continue to reside, on the premises;
(b) the relevant occupier shares accommodation on the premises with persons who reside on the premises and are not members of his household;
(c) the shared accommodation is not storage accommodation or a means of access; and
(d) the premises are small premises.

(3) For the purposes of this section, premises are "small premises" if they fall within subsection (4) or (5).

(4) Premises fall within this subsection if–

(a) only the relevant occupier and members of his household reside in the accommodation occupied by him;
(b) the premises comprise, in addition to the accommodation occupied by the relevant occupier, residential accommodation for at least one other household;
(c) the residential accommodation for each other household is let, or available for letting, on a separate tenancy or similar agreement; and
(d) there are not normally more than two such other households.

(5) Premises fall within this subsection if there is not normally residential accommodation on the premises for more than six persons in addition to the relevant occupier and any members of his household.

(6) For the purposes of this section "the relevant occupier" means–

(a) in a case falling within section 22(1), the person with power to dispose of the premises, or a near relative of his;
(b) in a case falling within section 22(4), the person whose licence or consent is required for the disposal of the premises, or a near relative of his.

(7) For the purposes of this section–

"near relative" means a person's spouse, partner, parent, child, grandparent, grandchild, or brother or sister (whether of full or half blood or by affinity); and

"partner" means the other member of a couple consisting of a man and a woman who are not married to each other but are living together as husband and wife.

Section 23
This is the same exemption as applies under section 32 SDA and section 22 RRA although, in each case, the provisions are set out slightly differently.

Meaning of "discrimination" .

24.–(1) For the purposes of section 22, a person ("A") discriminates against a disabled person if–

(a) for a reason which relates to the disabled person's disability, he treats him less favourably than he treats or would treat others to whom that reason does not or would not apply; and

(b) he cannot show that the treatment in question is justified.

(2) For the purposes of this section, treatment is justified only if–

(a) in A's opinion, one or more of the conditions mentioned in subsection (3) are satisfied; and

(b) it is reasonable, in all the circumstances of the case, for him to hold that opinion.

Section 24 (1) & (2)

In broad terms, the same definition as applies under sections 5, 14 and 20 above.

(3) The conditions are that–

(a) in any case, the treatment is necessary in order not to endanger the health or safety of any person (which may include that of the disabled person);

(b) in any case, the disabled person is incapable of entering into an enforceable agreement, or of giving an informed consent, and for that reason the treatment is reasonable in that case;

(c) in a case falling within section 22(3)(a), the treatment is necessary in order for the disabled person or the occupiers of other premises forming part of the building to make use of the benefit or facility;

(d) in a case falling within section 22(3)(b), the treatment is necessary in order for the occupiers of other premises forming part of the building to make use of the benefit or facility.

Section 24(3)

A similar definition of justification as is provided in section 20(4) above in relation to the provision of goods, facilities and services.

(4) Regulations may make provision, for purposes of this section, as to circumstances in which–

(a) it is reasonable for a person to hold the opinion mentioned in subsection 2(a);

(b) it is not reasonable for a person to hold that opinion.

(5) Regulations may make provision, for purposes of this section, as to circumstances (other than those mentioned in subsection (3)) in which treatment is to be taken to be justified.

ENFORCEMENT, ETC.

Enforcement, remedies and procedure.

25.–(1) A claim by any person that another person–

(a) has discriminated against him in a way which is unlawful under this Part; or

(b) is by virtue of section 57 or 58 to be treated as having discriminated against him in such a way,

may be made the subject of civil proceedings in the same way as any other claim in tort or (in Scotland) in reparation for breach of statutory duty.

Section 25(1)

(b) Section 57 – aiding unlawful acts.

Section 58 – liability of employers and principals.

As with the SDA and the RRA, all claims other than employment claims must be made in a county court (or a sheriff court in Scotland) regardless of their potential value. The normal financial limits for starting proceedings in the High Court do not apply to discrimination claims.

This section corresponds to section 66 of the SDA and section 57 RRA. Unlike those provisions, there is no requirement under the DDA for a complainant to give notice to the DRC of the intention to bring the proceedings and the requirement under the CPR for a Judge to sit with two assessors does not apply to claims under the DDA.

Time limits within which proceedings must brought and matters of certain kinds of evidence are dealt with in part II of schedule 3 below.

(2) For the avoidance of doubt it is hereby declared that damages in respect of discrimination in a way which is unlawful under this Part may include compensation for injury to feelings whether or not they include compensation under any other head.

Section 25(2)

There will be cases where the victim of discrimination actually suffers stress or possibly psychiatric injury as a result of the treatment he/she receives. In such cases the Court or tribunal also has the power to award damages for personal injury. Where such injury has occurred, it is important that the claim is included in the Court proceedings. Medical evidence will almost certainly be required as to the nature of the injury and a Court will probably give directions as to how and when such medical evidence should be produced.

A separate claim for personal injury pursued at a later date will not be permitted once the discrimination claim has concluded because of the general rule that all matters which could have been raised in a particular set of proceedings should have been raised. A failure to raise them at the appropriate time and an attempt to raise them in separate proceedings later will be regarded as an abuse of the process of the Court.

(3) Proceedings in England and Wales shall be brought only in a county court.

(4) Proceedings in Scotland shall be brought only in a sheriff court.

(5) The remedies available in such proceedings are those which are available in the High Court or (as the case may be) the Court of Session.

(6) Part II of Schedule 3 makes further provision about the enforcement of this Part and about procedure.

Validity and revision of certain agreements.

26.–(1) Any term in a contract for the provision of goods, facilities or services or in any other agreement is void so far as it purports to–

(a) require a person to do anything which would contravene any provision of, or made under, this Part,

(b) exclude or limit the operation of any provision of this Part, or

(c) prevent any person from making a claim under this Part.

> **Section 26**
> *As with employment claims (see section 9 above) there are restrictions on the way in which the provisions of this act can be compromised or excluded. It is not possible for a term of a contract to exclude the operation of the Act but, once a claim is brought, it can be settled under sub-section (2) in the same way as any other claim before a Court. The stricter requirements relating to employment claims do not apply to claims brought under this part.*

(2) Paragraphs (b) and (c) of subsection (1) do not apply to an agreement settling a claim to which section 25 applies.

(3) On the application of any person interested in an agreement to which subsection (1) applies, a county court or a sheriff court may make such order as it thinks just for modifying the agreement to take account of the effect of subsection (1).

> **Section 26(3)**
> *If there is doubt as to the effect of a contract term, an application can be made to the court, which has the power to modify the agreement so that a person's rights are not excluded. But sub-sections (4) - (6) must be complied with before such agreement can be modified.*

(4) No such order shall be made unless all persons affected have been–

(a) given notice of the application; and

(b) afforded an opportunity to make representations to the court.

(5) Subsection (4) applies subject to any rules of court providing for that notice to be dispensed with.

(6) An order under subsection (3) may include provision as respects any period before the making of the order.

Alterations to premises occupied under leases.

27.–(1) This section applies where–

(a) a provider of services ("the occupier") occupies premises under a lease;

(b) but for this section, he would not be entitled to make a particular alteration to the premises; and

(c) the alteration is one which the occupier proposes to make in order to comply with a section 21 duty.

> **Section 27(1)**
> *This section mirrors those of section 16 in relation to an employer's or trade organisation's ability to make alterations to premises.*
>
> *It has the effect of implying terms into the lease permitting such alterations to be made with the written consent of the lessor.*

(2) Except to the extent to which it expressly so provides, the lease shall have effect by virtue of this subsection as if it provided–

(a) for the occupier to be entitled to make the alteration with the written consent of the lessor;

(b) for the occupier to have to make a written application to the lessor for consent if he wishes to make the alteration;

(c) if such an application is made, for the lessor not to withhold his consent unreasonably; and

(d) for the lessor to be entitled to make his consent subject to reasonable conditions.

> **Section 27(2)**
> *Implied terms under this section will not be permitted where they contradict or conflict with express terms of the lease.*

(3) In this section–

"lease" includes a tenancy, sub-lease or sub-tenancy and an agreement for a lease, tenancy, sub-lease or sub-tenancy; and

"sub-lease" and "sub-tenancy" have such meaning as may be prescribed.

(4) If the terms and conditions of a lease–

(a) impose conditions which are to apply if the occupier alters the premises, or

(b) entitle the lessor to impose conditions when consenting to the occupier's altering the premises,

> **Section 27(4)**
> *If the express terms of the lease impose conditions as to the alteration of the premises or give the lessor the right to impose conditions then the occupier of the premises is entitled to defend a claim that he/they have failed to make reasonable adjustments on the grounds that they are not entitled to make the alternations required.*

the occupier is to be treated for the purposes of subsection (1) as not being entitled to make the alteration.

(5) Part II of Schedule 4 supplements the provisions of this section.

Conciliation of disputes

28. (1) The Commission may make arrangements with any other person for the provision of conciliation services by, or by persons appointed by, that person in relation to disputes arising under this Part.

> **Section 28(1)**
> *Under section 18 of the Employment Tribunals Act 1996 a conciliation officer is required to take steps to promote a settlement of the proceedings without them being determined by an employment tribunal. This section deals with conciliation procedures in relation to non-employment claims.*
>
> *Since the Disability Rights Commission began its work only in April 2000, no such arrangements have yet been made in relation to non-employment claims. Proceedings will be used in evidence in any subsequent proceedings.*

(2) In deciding what arrangements (if any) to make, the Commission shall have regard to the desirability of securing, so far as reasonably practicable, that conciliation services are available for all disputes arising under this Part which the parties may wish to refer to conciliation.

(3) No member or employee of the Commission may provide conciliation services in relation to disputes arising under this Part.

(4) The Commission shall ensure that any arrangements under this section include appropriate safeguards to prevent the disclosure to members or employees of the Commission of information obtained by a person in connection with the provision of conciliation services in pursuance of the arrangements.

(5) Subsection (4) does not apply to information relating to a dispute which is disclosed with the consent of the parties to that dispute.

(6) Subsection (4) does not apply to information which–

(a) is not identifiable with a particular dispute or a particular person; and

(b) is reasonably required by the Commission for the purpose of monitoring the operation of the arrangements concerned.

(7) Anything communicated to a person while providing conciliation services in pursuance of any arrangements under this section is not admissible in evidence in any proceedings except with the consent of the person who communicated it to that person.

> **Section 28(7)**
> *The general rule in Court proceedings is that any discussions between the parties which are expressed to be "without prejudice" cannot be used as evidence in any subsequent proceedings. Because conciliation involves discussions conducted through a third party, it is important that those discussions should not be hampered by a fear that anything said to a conciliation officer as part of a genuine attempt to settle the proceedings will be used in evidence in any subsequent proceedings.*

(8) In this section "conciliation services" means advice and assistance provided by a conciliator to the parties to a dispute with a view to promoting its settlement otherwise than through the courts.

Part IV Education

Education of disabled persons.

29. (1) and (2) repealed by the Education Act 1996

(3) In section 1 of the Education Act 1994 (establishment of the Teacher Training Agency) add, at the end–

"(4) In exercising their functions, the Teacher Training Agency shall have regard to the requirements of persons who are disabled persons for the purposes of the Disability Discrimination Act 1995."

Further and higher education of disabled persons.

30.–(1) The Further and Higher Education Act 1992 is amended as set out in subsections (2) to (6).

(2) In section 5 (administration of funds by further education funding councils), in subsection (6)(b), after "may" insert ", subject to subsection (7A) below,".

(3) After section 5(7) insert–

"(7A) Without prejudice to the power to impose conditions given by subsection (6)(b) above, the conditions subject to which a council gives financial support under this section to the governing body of an institution within the further education sector–

(a) shall require the governing body to publish disability statements at such intervals as may be prescribed; and
(b) may include conditions relating to the provision made, or to be made, by the institution with respect to disabled persons.

(7B) For the purposes of subsection (7A) above–

"disability statement" means a statement containing information of a prescribed description about the provision of facilities for education made by the institution in respect of disabled persons;

"disabled persons" means persons who are disabled persons for the purposes of the Disability Discrimination Act 1995; and

"prescribed" means prescribed by regulations."

(4) In section 8 (supplementary functions) add, at the end–

"(6) As soon as is reasonably practicable after the end of its financial year, each council shall make a written report to the Secretary of State on–

(a) the progress made during the year to which the report relates in the provision of further education for disabled students in their area; and
(b) their plans for the future provision of further education for disabled students in their area.

(7) In subsection (6) above–

"disabled students" means students who are disabled persons for the purposes of the Disability Discrimination Act 1995; and

"financial year" means the period of twelve months ending with 31st March 1997 and each successive period of twelve months."

(5) In section 62 (establishment of higher education funding councils), after subsection (7) insert–

"(7A) In exercising their functions, each council shall have regard to the requirements of disabled persons.

(7B) In subsection (7A) "disabled persons" means persons who are disabled persons for the purposes of the Disability Discrimination Act 1995."

(6) In section 65 (administration of funds by higher education funding councils), after subsection (4) insert–

"(4A) Without prejudice to the power to impose conditions given by subsection (3) above, the conditions subject to which a council makes grants, loans or other payments under this section to the governing body of a higher education institution shall require the governing body to publish disability statements at such intervals as may be specified.

(4B) For the purposes of subsection (4A) above–

"disability statement" means a statement containing information of a specified description about the provision of facilities for education and research made by the institution in respect of persons who are disabled persons for the purposes of the Disability Discrimination Act 1995; and

"specified" means specified in the conditions subject to which grants, loans or other payments are made by a council under this section."

(7) – (9) *Repealed by the Education Act 1996.*

Further and higher education of disabled persons: Scotland.

31.–(1) The Further and Higher Education (Scotland) Act 1992 is amended as follows.

(2) In section 37 (establishment of Scottish Higher Education Funding Council) after subsection (4) insert–

"(4A) In exercising their functions, the Council shall have regard to the requirements of disabled persons.

(4B) In subsection (4A) above, "disabled persons" means persons who are disabled persons for the purpose of the Disability Discrimination Act 1995."

(3) In section 40 (administration of funds by the Council), after subsection (4) insert–

"(5)Without prejudice to the power to impose conditions given by subsection (3) above, the conditions subject to which the Council make grants, loans or other payments under this section to the governing body of an institution within the higher education sector shall require the governing body to publish disability statements at such intervals as may be specified.

(6) For the purposes of subsection (5) above–

"disability statement" means a statement containing information of a specified description about the provision of facilities for education and research made by the institution in respect of persons who are disabled persons for the purpose of the Disability Discrimination Act 1995; and

"specified" means specified in the conditions subject to which grants, loans or other payments are made by the Council under this section."

Section 29 – 31
These sections amend other statutes relating to education and are self explanatory.

PART V PUBLIC TRANSPORT

TAXIS

Taxi accessibility regulations.

32.–(1) The Secretary of State may make regulations ("taxi accessibility regulations") for the purpose of securing that it is possible–

(a) for disabled persons–
  (i) to get into and out of taxis in safety;
  (ii) to be carried in taxis in safety and in reasonable comfort; and
(b) for disabled persons in wheelchairs–
  (i) to be conveyed in safety into and out of taxis while remaining in their wheelchairs; and
  (ii) to be carried in taxis in safety and in reasonable comfort while remaining in their wheelchairs.

(2) Taxi accessibility regulations may, in particular–

(a) require any regulated taxi to conform with provisions of the regulations as to–
  (i) the size of any door opening which is for the use of passengers;
  (ii) the floor area of the passenger compartment;
  (iii) the amount of headroom in the passenger compartment;
  (iv) the fitting of restraining devices designed to ensure the stability of a wheelchair while the taxi is moving;
(b) require the driver of any regulated taxi which is plying for hire, or which has been hired, to comply with provisions of the regulations as to the carrying of ramps or other devices designed to facilitate the loading and unloading of wheelchairs;
(c) require the driver of any regulated taxi in which a disabled person who is in a wheelchair is being carried (while remaining in his wheelchair) to comply with provisions of the regulations as to the position in which the wheelchair is to be secured.

(3) The driver of a regulated taxi which is plying for hire, or which has been hired, is guilty of an offence if–

(a) he fails to comply with any requirement imposed on him by the regulations; or
(b) the taxi fails to conform with any provision of the regulations with which it is required to conform.

(4) A person who is guilty of such an offence is liable, on summary conviction, to a fine not exceeding level 3 on the standard scale.

(5) In this section–

"passenger compartment" has such meaning as may be prescribed;

"regulated taxi" means any taxi to which the regulations are expressed to apply;

"taxi" means a vehicle licensed under–

(a) section 37 of the Town Police Clauses Act 1847, or
(b) section 6 of the Metropolitan Public Carriage Act 1869, but does not include a taxi which is drawn by a horse or other animal.

Section 32

At present no regulations have been made under this section. It is designed to ensure that taxis are accessible to all wheelchair users and that such users can be carried in comfort and safety.

It is expected that there will be regulations in place in respect of new vehicles by 2002. The government's stated objective is that all taxis should be accessible to disabled persons by 2012.

The section covers only licensed taxis, meaning hackney or black cabs and not mini cabs and hire cars.

Designated transport facilities.

33.–(1) In this section "a franchise agreement" means a contract entered into by the operator of a designated transport facility for the provision by the other party to the contract of hire car services–

(a) for members of the public using any part of the transport facility; and
(b) which involve vehicles entering any part of that facility.

(2) The Secretary of State may by regulations provide for the application of any taxi provision in relation to–

(a) vehicles used for the provision of services under a franchise agreement; or
(b) the drivers of such vehicles.

(3) Any regulations under subsection (2) may apply any taxi provision with such modifications as the Secretary of State considers appropriate.

(4) In this section–

"designated" means designated for the purposes of this section by an order made by the Secretary of State;

"hire car" has such meaning as may be prescribed;

"operator", in relation to a transport facility, means any person who is concerned with the management or operation of the facility;

"taxi provision" means any provision of–

(a) this Act, or

(b) regulations made in pursuance of section 20(2A) of the Civic Government (Scotland) Act 1982, which applies in relation to taxis or the drivers of taxis; and

"transport facility" means any premises which form part of any port, airport, railway station or bus station.

Section 33
This gives the Secretary of State power to apply any part of the provisions in relation to taxis where the car hire company operates under a franchise with a public transport facility, such as an airport or a bus station.

New licences conditional on compliance with taxi accessibility regulations.

34.–(1) No licensing authority shall grant a licence for a taxi to ply for hire unless the vehicle conforms with those provisions of the taxi accessibility regulations with which it will be required to conform if licensed.

(2) Subsection (1) does not apply if such a licence was in force with respect to the vehicle at any time during the period of 28 days immediately before the day on which the licence is granted.

(3) The Secretary of State may by order provide for subsection (2) to cease to have effect on such date as may be specified in the order.

(4) Separate orders may be made under subsection (3) with respect to different areas or localities.

Section 34
Once the new regulations are in force, a local authority cannot grant a license to a taxi unless it complies with the regulations.

Exemption from taxi accessibility regulations.

35.–(1) The Secretary of State may make regulations ("exemption regulations") for the purpose of enabling any relevant licensing authority to apply to him for an order (an "exemption order") exempting the authority from the requirements of section 34.

(2) Exemption regulations may, in particular, make provision requiring a licensing authority proposing to apply for an exemption order–

(a) to carry out such consultations as may be prescribed;
(b) to publish the proposal in the prescribed manner;
(c) to consider any representations made to it about the proposal, before applying for the order;
(d) to make its application in the prescribed form.

(3) A licensing authority may apply for an exemption order only if it is satisfied–

(a) that, having regard to the circumstances prevailing in its area, it would be inappropriate for the requirements of section 34 to apply; and

(b) that the application of section 34 would result in an unacceptable reduction in the number of taxis in its area.

(4) After considering any application for an exemption order and consulting the Disabled Persons Transport Advisory Committee and such other persons as he considers appropriate, the Secretary of State may–

(a) make an exemption order in the terms of the application;

(b) make an exemption order in such other terms as he considers appropriate; or

(c) refuse to make an exemption order.

(5) The Secretary of State may by regulations ("swivel seat regulations") make provision requiring any exempt taxi plying for hire in an area in respect of which an exemption order is in force to conform with provisions of the regulations as to the fitting and use of swivel seats.

(6) The Secretary of State may by regulations make provision with respect to swivel seat regulations similar to that made by section 34 with respect to taxi accessibility regulations.

(7) In this section–

"exempt taxi" means a taxi in relation to which section 34(1) would apply if the exemption order were not in force;

"relevant licensing authority" means a licensing authority responsible for licensing taxis in any area of England and Wales other than the area to which the Metropolitan Public Carriage Act 1869 applies; and

"swivel seats" has such meaning as may be prescribed.

> **Section 35**
> *In order to temper the rather onerous requirements under section 32, the Secretary of State is given wide powers to grant exemption orders.*

Carrying of passengers in wheelchairs.

36.–(1) This section imposes duties on the driver of a regulated taxi which has been hired–

(a) by or for a disabled person who is in a wheelchair; or

(b) by a person who wishes such a disabled person to accompany him in the taxi.

(2) In this section–

"carry" means carry in the taxi concerned; and

"the passenger" means the disabled person concerned.

(3) The duties are–

(a) to carry the passenger while he remains in his wheelchair;
(b) not to make any additional charge for doing so;
(c) if the passenger chooses to sit in a passenger seat, to carry the wheelchair;
(d) to take such steps as are necessary to ensure that the passenger is carried in safety and in reasonable comfort;
(e) to give such assistance as may be reasonably required–
  (i) to enable the passenger to get into or out of the taxi;
  (ii) if the passenger wishes to remain in his wheelchair, to enable him to be conveyed into and out of the taxi while in his wheelchair;
  (iii) to load the passenger's luggage into or out of the taxi;
  (iv) if the passenger does not wish to remain in his wheelchair, to load the wheelchair into or out of the taxi.

(4) Nothing in this section is to be taken to require the driver of any taxi–

(a) except in the case of a taxi of a prescribed description, to carry more than one person in a wheelchair, or more than one wheelchair, on any one journey; or
(b) to carry any person in circumstances in which it would otherwise be lawful for him to refuse to carry that person.

(5) A driver of a regulated taxi who fails to comply with any duty imposed on him by this section is guilty of an offence and liable, on summary conviction, to a fine not exceeding level 3 on the standard scale.

(6) In any proceedings for an offence under this section, it is a defence for the accused to show that, even though at the time of the alleged offence the taxi conformed with those provisions of the taxi accessibility regulations with which it was required to conform, it would not have been possible for the wheelchair in question to be carried in safety in the taxi.

(7) If the licensing authority is satisfied that it is appropriate to exempt a person from the duties imposed by this section–

(a) on medical grounds, or
(b) on the ground that his physical condition makes it impossible or unreasonably difficult for him to comply with the duties imposed on drivers by this section,

it shall issue him with a certificate of exemption.

(8) A certificate of exemption shall be issued for such period as may be specified in the certificate.

(9) The driver of a regulated taxi is exempt from the duties imposed by this section if–

(a) a certificate of exemption issued to him under this section is in force; and
(b) the prescribed notice of his exemption is exhibited on the taxi in the prescribed manner.

> **Section 36**
> *As well as making sure that the vehicle is accessible, a taxi driver is under a duty to provide assistance to a disabled person in getting into or out of the taxi and helping them manage their luggage. Under sub-section (3)(b) no additional charge may be made for these services. These obligations are restricted to one wheelchair and one wheelchair user per journey.*

Carrying of guide dogs and hearing dogs.

37.–(1) This section imposes duties on the driver of a taxi which has been hired–

(a) by or for a disabled person who is accompanied by his guide dog or hearing dog, or
(b) by a person who wishes such a disabled person to accompany him in the taxi.

(2) The disabled person is referred to in this section as "the passenger".

(3) The duties are–

(a) to carry the passenger's dog and allow it to remain with the passenger; and
(b) not to make any additional charge for doing so.

(4) A driver of a taxi who fails to comply with any duty imposed on him by this section is guilty of an offence and liable, on summary conviction, to a fine not exceeding level 3 on the standard scale.

(5) If the licensing authority is satisfied that it is appropriate on medical grounds to exempt a person from the duties imposed by this section, it shall issue him with a certificate of exemption.

(6) In determining whether to issue a certificate of exemption, the licensing authority shall, in particular, have regard to the physical characteristics of the taxi which the applicant drives or those of any kind of taxi in relation to which he requires the certificate.

(7) A certificate of exemption shall be issued–

(a) with respect to a specified taxi or a specified kind of taxi; and
(b) for such period as may be specified in the certificate.

(8) The driver of a taxi is exempt from the duties imposed by this section if–

(a) a certificate of exemption issued to him under this section is in force with respect to the taxi; and
(b) the prescribed notice of his exemption is exhibited on the taxi in the prescribed manner.

(9) The Secretary of State may, for the purposes of this section, prescribe any other category of dog trained to assist a disabled person who has a disability of a prescribed kind.

(10) This section applies in relation to any such prescribed category of dog as it applies in relation to guide dogs.

(11) In this section–

"guide dog" means a dog which has been trained to guide a blind person; and

"hearing dog" means a dog which has been trained to assist a deaf person.

Section 37
Subject to the right to apply for a certificate of exemption under sub-section (6), a taxi driver is also bound to carry a guide dog or a hearing dog for a disabled passenger without making any additional charge.

Appeal against refusal of exemption certificate.

38.–(1) Any person who is aggrieved by the refusal of a licensing authority to issue an exemption certificate under section 36 or 37 may appeal to the appropriate court before the end of the period of 28 days beginning with the date of the refusal.

(2) On an appeal to it under this section, the court may direct the licensing authority concerned to issue the appropriate certificate of exemption to have effect for such period as may be specified in the direction.

(3) "Appropriate court" means the magistrates' court for the petty sessions area in which the licensing authority has its principal office.

Requirements as to disabled passengers in Scotland.

39.–(1) Part II of the Civic Government (Scotland) Act 1982 (licensing and regulation) is amended as follows.

(2) In subsection (4) of section 10 (suitability of vehicle for use as taxi)–

(a) after "authority" insert "- (a)"; and
(b) at the end add "; and
(b) as not being so suitable if it does not so comply."

(3) In section 20 (regulations relating to taxis etc.) after subsection (2) insert–

"(2A) Without prejudice to the generality of subsections (1) and (2) above, regulations under those subsections may make such provision as appears to the Secretary of State to be necessary or expedient in relation to the carrying in taxis of disabled persons (within the meaning of section 1(2) of the Disability Discrimination Act 1995) and such provision may in particular prescribe–

(a) requirements as to the carriage of wheelchairs, guide dogs, hearing dogs and other categories of dog;
(b) a date from which any such provision is to apply and the extent to which it is to apply; and

(c) the circumstances in which an exemption from such provision may be granted in respect of any taxi or taxi driver,

and in this subsection–

"guide dog" means a dog which has been trained to guide a blind person;

"hearing dog" means a dog which has been trained to assist a deaf person; and

"other categories of dog" means such other categories of dog as the Secretary of State may prescribe, trained to assist disabled persons who have disabilities of such kinds as he may prescribe."

Section 39

This section amends the Civic Government (Scotland) Act 1982.

PUBLIC SERVICE VEHICLES

PSV accessibility regulations.

40.–(1) The Secretary of State may make regulations ("PSV accessibility regulations") for the purpose of securing that it is possible for disabled persons–

(a) to get on to and off regulated public service vehicles in safety and without unreasonable difficulty (and, in the case of disabled persons in wheelchairs, to do so while remaining in their wheelchairs); and

(b) to be carried in such vehicles in safety and in reasonable comfort.

(2) PSV accessibility regulations may, in particular, make provision as to the construction, use and maintenance of regulated public service vehicles including provision as to–

(a) the fitting of equipment to vehicles;

(b) equipment to be carried by vehicles;

(c) the design of equipment to be fitted to, or carried by, vehicles;

(d) the fitting and use of restraining devices designed to ensure the stability of wheelchairs while vehicles are moving;

(e) the position in which wheelchairs are to be secured while vehicles are moving.

(3) Any person who–

(a) contravenes or fails to comply with any provision of the PSV accessibility regulations,

(b) uses on a road a regulated public service vehicle which does not conform with any provision of the regulations with which it is required to conform, or

(c) causes or permits to be used on a road such a regulated public service vehicle, is guilty of an offence.

(4) A person who is guilty of such an offence is liable, on summary conviction, to a fine not exceeding level 4 on the standard scale.

(5) In this section–

"public service vehicle" means a vehicle which is–

(a) adapted to carry more than eight passengers; and
(b) a public service vehicle for the purposes of the Public Passenger Vehicles Act 1981;

"regulated public service vehicle" means any public service vehicle to which the PSV accessibility regulations are expressed to apply.

(6) Different provision may be made in regulations under this section–

(a) as respects different classes or descriptions of vehicle;
(b) as respects the same class or description of vehicle in different circumstances.

(7) Before making any regulations under this section or section 41 or 42 the Secretary of State shall consult the Disabled Persons Transport Advisory Committee and such other representative organisations as he thinks fit.

Section 40

As with taxis, no such regulations have been made to date but it is expected that regulations in relation to new vehicles will be brought into force between 2000 and 2005. It is expected that single and double-decker buses must be accessible to all passengers by 2015 and coaches by 2020. Once the regulations are in force any person operating such a vehicle must obtain a certificate certifying that the accessibility regulations are complied with in respect of that vehicle.

The regulations will have the same purpose as those for taxis, namely to ensure that passengers can be carried in safety and comfort and providing similar obligations on drivers where necessary to provide assistance to disabled passengers.

Accessibility certificates.

41.–(1) A regulated public service vehicle shall not be used on a road unless–

(a) a vehicle examiner has issued a certificate (an "accessibility certificate") that such provisions of the PSV accessibility regulations as may be prescribed are satisfied in respect of the vehicle; or
(b) an approval certificate has been issued under section 42 in respect of the vehicle.

(2) The Secretary of State may make regulations–

(a) with respect to applications for, and the issue of, accessibility certificates;
(b) providing for the examination of vehicles in respect of which applications have been made;
(c) with respect to the issue of copies of accessibility certificates in place of certificates which have been lost or destroyed.

(3) If a regulated public service vehicle is used in contravention of this section, the operator of the vehicle is guilty of an offence and liable on summary conviction to a fine not exceeding level 4 on the standard scale.

(4) In this section "operator" has the same meaning as in the Public Passenger Vehicles Act 1981.

Approval certificates.

42.–(1) Where the Secretary of State is satisfied that such provisions of the PSV accessibility regulations as may be prescribed for the purposes of section 41 are satisfied in respect of a particular vehicle he may approve the vehicle for the purposes of this section.

(2) A vehicle which has been so approved is referred to in this section as a "type vehicle".

(3) Subsection (4) applies where a declaration in the prescribed form has been made by an authorised person that a particular vehicle conforms in design, construction and equipment with a type vehicle.

(4) A vehicle examiner may, after examining (if he thinks fit) the vehicle to which the declaration applies, issue a certificate in the prescribed form ("an approval certificate") that it conforms to the type vehicle.

(5) The Secretary of State may make regulations–

(a) with respect to applications for, and grants of, approval under subsection (1);
(b) with respect to applications for, and the issue of, approval certificates;
(c) providing for the examination of vehicles in respect of which applications have been made;
(d) with respect to the issue of copies of approval certificates in place of certificates which have been lost or destroyed.

(6) The Secretary of State may at any time withdraw his approval of a type vehicle.

(7) Where an approval is withdrawn–

(a) no further approval certificates shall be issued by reference to the type vehicle; but
(b) any approval certificate issued by reference to the type vehicle before the withdrawal shall continue to have effect for the purposes of section 41.

(8) In subsection (3) "authorised person" means a person authorised by the Secretary of State for the purposes of that subsection.

Special authorisations.

43.–(1) The Secretary of State may by order authorise the use on roads of–

(a) any regulated public service vehicle of a class or description specified by the order, or

(b) any regulated public service vehicle which is so specified,

and nothing in section 40, 41 or 42 prevents the use of any vehicle in accordance with the order.

(2) Any such authorisation may be given subject to such restrictions and conditions as may be specified by or under the order.

(3) The Secretary of State may by order make provision for the purpose of securing that, subject to such restrictions and conditions as may be specified by or under the order, provisions of the PSV accessibility regulations apply to regulated public service vehicles of a description specified by the order subject to such modifications or exceptions as may be specified by the order.

Reviews and appeals.

44.–(1) Subsection (2) applies where–

(a) the Secretary of State refuses an application for the approval of a vehicle under section 42(1); and
(b) before the end of the prescribed period, the applicant asks the Secretary of State to review the decision and pays any fee fixed under section 45.

(2) The Secretary of State shall–

(a) review the decision; and
(b) in doing so, consider any representations made to him in writing, before the end of the prescribed period, by the applicant.

(3) A person applying for an accessibility certificate or an approval certificate may appeal to the Secretary of State against the refusal of a vehicle examiner to issue such a certificate.

(4) An appeal must be made within the prescribed time and in the prescribed manner.

(5) Regulations may make provision as to the procedure to be followed in connection with appeals.

(6) On the determination of an appeal, the Secretary of State may–

(a) confirm, vary or reverse the decision appealed against;
(b) give such directions as he thinks fit to the vehicle examiner for giving effect to his decision.

Fees.

45.–(1) Such fees, payable at such times, as may be prescribed may be charged by the Secretary of State in respect of–

(a) applications for, and grants of, approval under section 42(1);
(b) applications for, and the issue of, accessibility certificates and approval certificates;

(c) copies of such certificates;

(d) reviews and appeals under section 44.

(2) Any such fees received by the Secretary of State shall be paid by him into the Consolidated Fund.

(3) Regulations under subsection (1) may make provision for the repayment of fees, in whole or in part, in such circumstances as may be prescribed.

(4) Before making any regulations under subsection (1) the Secretary of State shall consult such representative organisations as he thinks fit.

Rail vehicles

Rail vehicle accessibility regulations.

46.–(1) The Secretary of State may make regulations ("rail vehicle accessibility regulations") for the purpose of securing that it is possible–

(a) for disabled persons–

(i) to get on to and off regulated rail vehicles in safety and without unreasonable difficulty;

(ii) to be carried in such vehicles in safety and in reasonable comfort; and

(b) for disabled persons in wheelchairs–

(i) to get on to and off such vehicles in safety and without unreasonable difficulty while remaining in their wheelchairs, and

(ii) to be carried in such vehicles in safety and in reasonable comfort while remaining in their wheelchairs.

(2) Rail vehicle accessibility regulations may, in particular, make provision as to the construction, use and maintenance of regulated rail vehicles including provision as to–

(a) the fitting of equipment to vehicles;

(b) equipment to be carried by vehicles;

(c) the design of equipment to be fitted to, or carried by, vehicles;

(d) the use of equipment fitted to, or carried by, vehicles;

(e) the toilet facilities to be provided in vehicles;

(f) the location and floor area of the wheelchair accommodation to be provided in vehicles;

(g) assistance to be given to disabled persons.

(3) If a regulated rail vehicle which does not conform with any provision of the rail vehicle accessibility regulations with which it is required to conform is used for carriage, the operator of the vehicle is guilty of an offence.

(4) A person who is guilty of such an offence is liable, on summary conviction, to a fine not exceeding level 4 on the standard scale.

(5) Different provision may be made in rail vehicle accessibility regulations–

(a) as respects different classes or descriptions of rail vehicle;
(b) as respects the same class or description of rail vehicle in different circumstances;
(c) as respects different networks.

(6) In this section–

"network" means any permanent way or other means of guiding or supporting rail vehicles or any section of it;

"operator", in relation to any rail vehicle, means the person having the management of that vehicle;

"rail vehicle" means a vehicle–

(a) constructed or adapted to carry passengers on any railway, tramway or prescribed system; and
(b) first brought into use, or belonging to a class of vehicle first brought into use, after 31st December 1998;

"regulated rail vehicle" means any rail vehicle to which the rail vehicle accessibility regulations are expressed to apply; and

"wheelchair accommodation" has such meaning as may be prescribed.

(7) In subsection (6)–

"prescribed system" means a system using a prescribed mode of guided transport

"guided transport" having the same meaning as in the (1992 c.42.)Transport and Works Act 1992); and

"railway" and "tramway" have the same meaning as in that Act.

(8) The Secretary of State may by regulations make provision as to the time when a rail vehicle, or a class of rail vehicle, is to be treated, for the purposes of this section, as first brought into use.

(9) Regulations under subsection (8) may include provision for disregarding periods of testing and other prescribed periods of use.

(10) For the purposes of this section and section 47, a person uses a vehicle for carriage if he uses it for the carriage of members of the public for hire or reward at separate fares.

(11) Before making any regulations under subsection (1) or section 47 the Secretary of State shall consult the Disabled Persons Transport Advisory Committee and such other representative organisations as he thinks fit.

Section 46

The Rail Vehicle Accessibility Regulations 1998, SI 1998\2456 came into force on 1st November 1998 and apply to all new railway vehicles, trams, monorail systems and magnetic levitation systems. There is no final date by which all such vehicles have to comply with the regulations.

The regulations provide for the design of vehicles including the width of doors, the way in which doors are opened and closed, including audible devices warning that doors are about to close. They also include provision for toilet facilities and space within carriages for wheelchairs to be accommodated.

Exemption from rail vehicle accessibility regulations.

47.–(1) The Secretary of State may by order (an "exemption order") authorise the use for carriage of any regulated rail vehicle of a specified description, or in specified circumstances, even though that vehicle does not conform with the provisions of the rail vehicle accessibility regulations with which it is required to conform.

(2) Regulations may make provision with respect to exemption orders including, in particular, provision as to–

(a) the persons by whom applications for exemption orders may be made;
(b) the form in which such applications are to be made;
(c) information to be supplied in connection with such applications;
(d) the period for which exemption orders are to continue in force;
(e) the revocation of exemption orders.

(3) After considering any application for an exemption order and consulting the Disabled Persons Transport Advisory Committee and such other persons as he considers appropriate, the Secretary of State may–

(a) make an exemption order in the terms of the application;
(b) make an exemption order in such other terms as he considers appropriate;
(c) refuse to make an exemption order.

(4) An exemption order may be made subject to such restrictions and conditions as may be specified.

(5) In this section "specified" means specified in an exemption order.

Section 47

As with other provisions in relation to public service vehicles it is also possible for rail vehicle operators to apply for exemption certificates from the requirements of the regulations.

Supplemental

Offences by bodies corporate etc.

48.–(1) Where an offence under section 40 or 46 committed by a body corporate is committed with the consent or connivance of, or is attributable to any neglect on the part of, a director, manager, secretary or other similar officer of the body, or a person purporting to act in such a capacity, he as well as the body corporate is guilty of the offence.

(2) In subsection (1) "director", in relation to a body corporate whose affairs are managed by its members, means a member of the body corporate.

(3) Where, in Scotland, an offence under section 40 or 46 committed by a partnership or by an unincorporated association other than a partnership is committed with the consent or connivance of, or is attributable to any neglect on the part of, a partner in the partnership or (as the case may be) a person concerned in the management or control of the association, he, as well as the partnership or association, is guilty of the offence.

Section 48

Companies or corporate bodies will, of course be liable for any failure to comply with their obligations under sections 40 and 46. This section also imposes personal liabilities on any directors or managers who are responsible for ensuring that their company complies with those obligations and the liabilities of such persons is in addition to the liability of their employing company.

Forgery and false statements.

49.–(1) In this section "relevant document" means–

(a) a certificate of exemption issued under section 36 or 37;
(b) a notice of a kind mentioned in section 36(9)(b) or 37(8)(b);
(c) an accessibility certificate; or
(d) an approval certificate.

Section 49(1)

A person who misuses an approval certificate or an accessibility certificate or allows such a document in his possession to be misused by another person commits a criminal offence in so doing and may face imprisonment.

(2) A person is guilty of an offence if, with intent to deceive, he–

(a) forges, alters or uses a relevant document;
(b) lends a relevant document to any other person;
(c) allows a relevant document to be used by any other person; or
(d) makes or has in his possession any document which closely resembles a relevant document.

(3) A person who is guilty of an offence under subsection (2) is liable–

(a) on summary conviction, to a fine not exceeding the statutory maximum;
(b) on conviction on indictment, to imprisonment for a term not exceeding two years or to a fine or to both.

(4) A person who knowingly makes a false statement for the purpose of obtaining an accessibility certificate or an approval certificate is guilty of an offence and liable on summary conviction to a fine not exceeding level 4 on the standard scale.

Section 49(4)
A person who obtains an accessibility certificate or seeks to do so by making false statements also commits an offence for which the penalty would be a fine.

Part VI Sections 50–53 are repealed by the Disability Rights Commission Act 1999.

Part VII Supplemental

Codes of Practice

53A.–(1) The Disability Rights Commission may prepare and issue codes of practice giving practical guidance –

(a) to employers, service providers or other persons to whom provisions of this Part II or Part III apply on how to avoid discrimination or any other matter relating to the operating of those provisions in relation to them; or
(b) to any persons on any other matter, with a view to–
(i) promoting the equalisation of opportunities for disabled persons and persons who have had a disability, or
(ii) encouraging good practice regarding the treatment of such persons, in any field of activity regulated by any provision of Part II or Part III.

(2) The Commission shall, when requested to do so by the Secretary of State, prepare a code of practice dealing with the matters specified in the request.

(3) In preparing a code of practice the Commission shall carry out such consultations as it considers appropriate (which shall include the publication for public consultation of proposals relating to the code).

(4) The Commission may not issue a code of practice unless–

(a) a draft of it has been submitted to and approved by the Secretary of State and laid by him before both Houses of Parliament; and
(b) the 40 day period has elapsed without either House resolving not to approve the draft.

(5) If the Secretary of State does not approve a draft code of practice submitted to him he shall give the Commission a written statement of his reasons.

(6) A code of practice issued by the Commission–

(a) shall come into effect on such day as the Secretary of State made by order;
(b) may be revised in whole or in part, and re-issued, by the Commission; and (c) may be revoked by an order made by the Secretary of State at the request of the Commission.

(7) Where the Commission proposes to revise a code of practice–

(a) it shall comply with sub-section (iii) in relation to the revisions; and
(b) the other provisions of this section apply to revised code of practice as they apply to a new code of practice.

(8) Failure to observe any provision of a code of practice does not of itself make a person liable to any proceedings, but any provision of a code which appears to a Court or tribunal to be relevant to any question arising in any proceedings under Part II or Part III shall be taken into account in determining that question.

(9) In this section–

"Code of Practice" means a code of practice under this section;

"Discrimination" means anything which is unlawful discrimination for the purposes of any provision of Part II or Part III; and

"40 day period" has the same meaning in relation to a draft code of practice as it has in section 3 in relation to draft guidance.

Section 53A
Codes of practice in relation to disability, issued before the DRC began its work become the Commission's responsibility.
It is the DRC which will monitor the application of the codes already issued and suggest any amendments and the Commission which will consult before issuing any further codes.

Victimisation.

55.–(1) For the purposes of Part II or Part III, a person ("A") discriminates against another person ("B") if–

(a) he treats B less favourably than he treats or would treat other persons whose circumstances are the same as B's; and
(b) he does so for a reason mentioned in subsection (2).

(2) The reasons are that–

(a) B has–

(i) brought proceedings against A or any other person under this Act; or
(ii) given evidence or information in connection with such proceedings brought by any person; or

(iii) otherwise done anything under this Act in relation to A or any other person; or

(iv) alleged that A or any other person has (whether or not the allegation so states) contravened this Act; or

(b) A believes or suspects that B has done or intends to do any of those things.

(3) Where B is a disabled person, or a person who has had a disability, the disability in question shall be disregarded in comparing his circumstances with those of any other person for the purposes of subsection (1)(a).

(4) Subsection (1) does not apply to treatment of a person because of an allegation made by him if the allegation was false and not made in good faith.

Section 55

The protection against victimisation is not limited to the disabled person but includes anyone who makes an allegation that someone else has been discriminated against or supports or assists a disabled person in making or pursuing a complaint. Under subsection (2)(b) the protection is extended even to those who are only suspected of taking such action or providing such support or assistance.

This is the same protection as is provided under section 4 of the SDA and section 2 of the RRA.

Help for persons suffering discrimination.

56.–(1) For the purposes of this section–

(a) a person who considers that he may have been discriminated against, in contravention of any provision of Part II, is referred to as "the complainant"; and

(b) a person against whom the complainant may decide to make, or has made, a complaint under Part II is referred to as "the respondent".

(2) The Secretary of State shall, with a view to helping the complainant to decide whether to make a complaint against the respondent and, if he does so, to formulate and present his case in the most effective manner, by order prescribe–

(a) forms by which the complainant may question the respondent on his reasons for doing any relevant act, or on any other matter which is or may be relevant; and

(b) forms by which the respondent may if he so wishes reply to any questions.

(3) Where the complainant questions the respondent in accordance with forms prescribed by an order under subsection (2)–

(a) the question, and any reply by the respondent (whether in accordance with such an order or not), shall be admissible as evidence in any proceedings under Part II;

(b) if it appears to the tribunal in any such proceedings–
   (i) that the respondent deliberately, and without reasonable excuse, omitted to reply within a reasonable period, or
   (ii) that the respondent's reply is evasive or equivocal,

it may draw any inference which it considers it just and equitable to draw, including an inference that the respondent has contravened a provision of Part II.

(4) The Secretary of State may by order prescribe–

(a) the period within which questions must be duly served in order to be admissible under subsection (3)(a); and
(b) the manner in which a question, and any reply by the respondent, may be duly served.

(5) This section is without prejudice to any other enactment or rule of law regulating interlocutory and preliminary matters in proceedings before an employment tribunal, and has effect subject to any enactment or rule of law regulating the admissibility of evidence in such proceedings.

Section 56

This is the same "questionnaire" procedure which is provided under section 74 SDA and section 65 RRA.

No such order has been issued to date but it is likely that, when provision is made, probably by the DRC, it will closely follow the scheme set down in the SDA and the RRA.

As with the sex and race provisions the questionnaire may be submitted to a potential respondent before the proceedings are commenced. A failure to answer or an evasive response can be taken into account by a court or tribunal when considering whether or not discrimination has occurred.

Aiding unlawful acts.

57.–(1) A person who knowingly aids another person to do an act made unlawful by this Act is to be treated for the purposes of this Act as himself doing the same kind of unlawful act.

(2) For the purposes of subsection (1), an employee or agent for whose act the employer or principal is liable under section 58 (or would be so liable but for section 58(5)) shall be taken to have aided the employer or principal to do the act.

(3) For the purposes of this section, a person does not knowingly aid another to do an unlawful act if–

(a) he acts in reliance on a statement made to him by that other person that, because of any provision of this Act, the act would not be unlawful; and
(b) it is reasonable for him to rely on the statement.

(4) A person who knowingly or recklessly makes such a statement which is false or misleading in a material respect is guilty of an offence.

(5) Any person guilty of an offence under subsection (4) shall be liable on summary conviction to a fine not exceeding level 5 on the standard scale.

Section 57

Employers and principals are made liable for the actions of people acting on their behalf of with their authority under section 58 below. This section prevents the employee from passing on liability to the employer under section 58 and escaping responsibility for his own discriminatory conduct.

Under this section the offender would be separately liable from any liability attaching to the employer under section 58 below.

Liability of employers and principals.

58.–(1) Anything done by a person in the course of his employment shall be treated for the purposes of this Act as also done by his employer, whether or not it was done with the employer's knowledge or approval.

(2) Anything done by a person as agent for another person with the authority of that other person shall be treated for the purposes of this Act as also done by that other person.

(3) Subsection (2) applies whether the authority was–

(a) express or implied; or
(b) given before or after the act in question was done.

(4) Subsections (1) and (2) do not apply in relation to an offence under section 57(4).

(5) In proceedings under this Act against any person in respect of an act alleged to have been done by an employee of his, it shall be a defence for that person to prove that he took such steps as were reasonably practicable to prevent the employee from–

(a) doing that act; or
(b) doing, in the course of his employment, acts of that description.

Section 58

Whether or not an act by an employee is 'in the course of his employment' must be looked at quite liberally. It is not interpreted in the same way in which that phrase is used in an action in tort. So, even if the act by the employees would never have been authorised by the employer if the employer had known about them, it may still be 'in the course of employment' if there is a sufficient connection between those acts and the employment in question. This may even extent to works' functions after normal hours and off the employer's premises.

Two police cases might serve to draw a distinction between what is and what is not 'in the course of employment'. In the first case, a probationary constable met a male officer off duty and went back to the section house in which she was living during her probationary period and in which she was sexually harassed by that other officer. The Court of Appeal held that this could not be said to be in the course of employment.

In the second case, the police constable had been sexually harrassed in two locations. The first was in a local public bar where a group of officers had gone after the end of their shifts; the second was at a leaving celebration for a colleague. In this case the EAT decided that each incident had occurred during what were, in reality, 'extensions of the workplace'.

Even if the act is committed by somebody not under the employer's control, the employer might still be liable.

In another case under the RRA the hotel employing two black waitresses was found to be liable when it sent them back in to provide service at a function at which the comedian Bernard Manning was speaking. He had already made racist remarks about the women earlier in the function and, by sending them back in after that abuse, the employer was held to have subjected them to a detriment under section 4(2)(c) RRA (section 6(2)(b) SDA).

This section is broadly the same provision as appears in section 41 SDA and section 32 RRA and it is to be expected that the same principles would apply under this Act.

Statutory authority and national security etc.

59.–(1) Nothing in this Act makes unlawful any act done–

- (a) in pursuance of any enactment; or
- (b) in pursuance of any instrument made by a Minister of the Crown under any enactment; or
- (c) to comply with any condition or requirement imposed by a Minister of the Crown (whether before or after the passing of this Act) by virtue of any enactment.

(2) In subsection (1) "enactment" includes one passed or made after the date on which this Act is passed and "instrument" includes one made after that date.

(3) Nothing in this Act makes unlawful any act done for the purpose of safeguarding national security.

Section 59
Broadly similar to sections 51A and 52 of the SDA and sections 41 and 42 of the RRA. This section provides exemption for acts done in pursuance of statutory authority and those done for the purposes of safeguarding national security.

PART VIII MISCELLANEOUS

Appointment by Secretary of State of advisers.

60.–(1) The Secretary of State may appoint such persons as he thinks fit to advise or assist him in connection with matters relating to the employment of disabled persons and persons who have had a disability.

(2) Persons may be appointed by the Secretary of State to act generally or in relation to a particular area or locality.

(3) The Secretary of State may pay to any person appointed under this section such allowances and compensation for loss of earnings as he considers appropriate.

(4) The approval of the Treasury is required for any payment under this section.

(5) In subsection (1) "employment" includes self-employment.

(6) The Secretary of State may by order–

(a) provide for section 17 of, and Schedule 2 to, the Disabled Persons (Employment) Act 1944 (national advisory council and district advisory committees) to cease to have effect–

(i) so far as concerns the national advisory council; or

(ii) so far as concerns district advisory committees; or

(b) repeal that section and Schedule.

(7) At any time before the coming into force of an order under paragraph (b) of subsection (6), section 17 of the Act of 1944 shall have effect as if in subsection (1), after "disabled persons" in each case there were inserted ", and persons who have had a disability," and as if at the end of the section there were added–

"(3) For the purposes of this section–

(a) a person is a disabled person if he is a disabled person for the purposes of the Disability Discrimination Act 1995; and

(b) "disability" has the same meaning as in that Act."

(8) At any time before the coming into force of an order under paragraph (a)(i) or (b) of subsection (6), section 16 of the Chronically Sick and Disabled Persons Act 1970 (which extends the functions of the national advisory council) shall have effect as if after "disabled persons" in each case there were inserted ", and persons who have had a disability," and as if at the end of the section there were added–

"(2) For the purposes of this section–

(a) a person is a disabled person if he is a disabled person for the purposes of the Disability Discrimination Act 1995; and

(b) "disability" has the same meaning as in that Act."

Section 60

The Secretary of State has the power to appoint advisers in relation to employment matters either nationally or on a regional basis, provided that he has at first obtained the approval of the treasury for any salary or allowances to be paid to such persons.

It may be that the Secretary of State may still require specialist advisers from time to time but, now that the DRC has begun its work, it is more likely that it will be the Commission that is asked to provide such advice or guidance.

Amendment of Disabled Persons (Employment) Act 1944.

61.–(1) Section 15 of the Disabled Persons (Employment) Act 1944 (which gives the Secretary of State power to make arrangements for the provision of supported employment) is amended as set out in subsections (2) to (5).

(2) In subsection (1)–

(a) for "persons registered as handicapped by disablement" substitute "disabled persons";
(b) for "their disablement" substitute "their disability"; and
(c) for "are not subject to disablement" substitute "do not have a disability".

(3) In subsection (2), for the words from "any of one or more companies" to "so required and prohibited" substitute "any company, association or body".

(4) After subsection (2) insert–

"(2A) The only kind of company which the Minister himself may form in exercising his powers under this section is a company which is–

(a) required by its constitution to apply its profits, if any, or other income in promoting its objects; and
(b) prohibited by its constitution from paying any dividend to its members."

(5) After subsection (5) insert–

"(5A) For the purposes of this section–

(a) a person is a disabled person if he is a disabled person for the purposes of the Disability Discrimination Act 1995; and
(b) "disability" has the same meaning as in that Act."

(6) The provisions of section 16 (preference to be given under section 15 of that Act to ex-service men and women) shall become subsection (1) of that section and at the end insert–

"and whose disability is due to that service.

(2) For the purposes of subsection (1) of this section, a disabled person's disability shall be treated as due to service of a particular kind only in such circumstances as may be prescribed."

(7) The following provisions of the Act of 1944 shall cease to have effect–
- (a) section 1 (definition of "disabled person");
- (b) sections 6 to 8 (the register of disabled persons);
- (c) sections 9 to 11 (obligations on employers with substantial staffs to employ a quota of registered persons);
- (d) section 12 (the designated employment scheme for persons registered as handicapped by disablement);
- (e) section 13 (interpretation of provisions repealed by this Act);
- (f) section 14 (records to be kept by employers);
- (g) section 19 (proceedings in relation to offences); and
- (h) section 21 (application as respects place of employment, and nationality).

(8) Any provision of subordinate legislation in which "disabled person" is defined by reference to the Act of 1944 shall be construed as if that expression had the same meaning as in this Act.

(9) Subsection (8) does not prevent the further amendment of any such provision by subordinate legislation.

> **Section 61(9)**
> *Since there was legislation relating to disability prior to the DDA being enacted, this section applies the definition under this Act to earlier statutes.*

> *Sections 62 and 63 now appear as sections 12 and 32 respectively of the Employment Tribunals Act 1996 and deal with the tribunals' power (section 12) and the Employment Appeals Tribunal's power (section 32) to make a restricted reporting order in a case where a claim brought under this Act involves the giving of evidence of a personal nature. The sections also deal with the penalties for breaching such orders.*

Application to Crown etc.

64.–(1) This Act applies–
- (a) to an act done by or for purposes of a Minister of the Crown or government department, or
- (b) to an act done on behalf of the Crown by a statutory body, or a person holding a statutory office,

as it applies to an act done by a private person.

(2) Subject to subsection (5), Part II applies to service–
- (a) for purposes of a Minister of the Crown or government department, other than service of a person holding a statutory office, or
- (b) on behalf of the Crown for purposes of a person holding a statutory office or purposes of a statutory body,

as it applies to employment by a private person.

(3) The provisions of Parts II to IV of the 1947 Act apply to proceedings against the Crown under this Act as they apply to Crown proceedings in England and Wales; but section 20 of that Act (removal of proceedings from county court to High Court) does not apply.

(4) The provisions of Part V of the 1947 Act apply to proceedings against the Crown under this Act as they apply to proceedings in Scotland which by virtue of that Part are treated as civil proceedings by or against the Crown; but the proviso to section 44 of that Act (removal of proceedings from the sheriff court to the Court of Session) does not apply.

(5) Part II does not apply to service–

(a) as a member of the Ministry of Defence Police, the British Transport Police, the Royal Parks Constabulary or the United Kingdom Atomic Energy Authority Constabulary;
(b) as a prison officer; or
(c) for purposes of a Minister of the Crown or government department having functions with respect to defence as a person who is or may be required by his terms of service to engage in fire fighting.

(6) Part II does not apply to service as a member of a fire brigade who is or may be required by his terms of service to engage in fire fighting.

(7) It is hereby declared (for the avoidance of doubt) that Part II does not apply to service in any of the naval, military or air forces of the Crown.

(8) In this section–

"the 1947 Act" means the Crown Proceedings Act 1947;

"British Transport Police" means the constables appointed, or deemed to have been appointed, under section 53 of the British Transport Commission Act 1949;

"Crown proceedings" means proceedings which, by virtue of section 23 of the 1947 Act, are treated for the purposes of Part II of that Act as civil proceedings by or against the Crown;

"fire brigade" means a fire brigade maintained in pursuance of the Fire Services Act 1947;

"Ministry of Defence Police" means the force established under section 1 of the Ministry of Defence Police Act 1987;

"prison officer" means a person who is a prison officer within the meaning of section 127 of the Criminal Justice and Public Order Act 1994, apart from those who are custody officers within the meaning of Part I of that Act;

"Royal Parks Constabulary" means the park constables appointed under the Parks Regulation Act 1872;

"service for purposes of a Minister of the Crown or government department" does not include service in any office for the time being mentioned in Schedule 2 (Ministerial offices) to the House of Commons Disqualification Act 1975;

"statutory body" means a body set up by or under an enactment;

"statutory office" means an office so set up; and

"United Kingdom Atomic Energy Authority Constabulary" means the special constables appointed under section 3 of the Special Constables Act 1923 on the nomination of the United Kingdom Atomic Energy Authority.

Application to Parliament.

65.–(1) This Act applies to an act done by or for purposes of the House of Lords or the House of Commons as it applies to an act done by a private person.

(2) For the purposes of the application of Part II in relation to the House of Commons, the Corporate Officer of that House shall be treated as the employer of a person who is (or would be) a relevant member of the House of Commons staff for the purposes of section 195 of the Employment Rights Act 1996.

(3) Except as provided in subsection (4), for the purposes of the application of sections 19 to 21, the provider of services is–

(a) as respects the House of Lords, the Corporate Officer of that House; and
(b) as respects the House of Commons, the Corporate Officer of that House.

(4) Where the service in question is access to and use of any place in the Palace of Westminster which members of the public are permitted to enter, the Corporate Officers of both Houses jointly are the provider of that service.

(5) Nothing in any rule of law or the law or practice of Parliament prevents proceedings being instituted before an employment tribunal under Part II or before any court under Part III.

Sections 64 – 65

As with sections 85A and 85B of the SDA and sections 75A and 75B of the RRA, this Act applies to those acting pursuant to statutory powers and employees of Members of Parliament, Parliament itself or the House of Lords.

Government appointments outside Part II.

66.–(1) Subject to regulations under subsection (3), this section applies to any appointment made by a Minister of the Crown or government department to an office or post where Part II does not apply in relation to the appointment.

(2) In making the appointment, and in making arrangements for determining to whom the office or post should be offered, the Minister of the Crown or government department shall not act in a way which would contravene Part II if he or the department were the employer for the purposes of this Act.

(3) Regulations may provide for this section not to apply to such appointments as may be prescribed.

Section 66

Many appointments made by government ministers are not within the definition of employment. This would include people appointed to area health authorities, other statutory bodies and "quangos".

This makes such appointments subject to the provisions of this Act. It corresponds to section 86 of the SDA and section 76 of the RRA.

Regulations and orders.

67.–(1) Any power under this Act to make regulations or orders shall be exercisable by statutory instrument.

(2) Any such power may be exercised to make different provision for different cases, including different provision for different areas or localities.

(3) Any such power includes power–

(a) to make such incidental, supplemental, consequential or transitional provision as appears to the Secretary of State to be expedient; and

(b) to provide for a person to exercise a discretion in dealing with any matter.

(4) No order shall be made under section 50(3) unless a draft of the statutory instrument containing the order has been laid before Parliament and approved by a resolution of each House.

(5) Any other statutory instrument made under this Act, other than one made under section 53A(6)(a) or 70(3), shall be subject to annulment in pursuance of a resolution of either House of Parliament.

(6) Subsection (1) does not require an order under section 43 which applies only to a specified vehicle, or to vehicles of a specified person, to be made by statutory instrument but such an order shall be as capable of being amended or revoked as an order which is made by statutory instrument.

(7) Nothing in section 34(4), 40(6) or 46(5) affects the powers conferred by subsections (2) and (3).

Section 67

The general power to make statutory instruments.

Interpretation.

68.–(1) In this Act–

"accessibility certificate" means a certificate issued under section 41(1)(a);

"act" includes a deliberate omission;

"approval certificate" means a certificate issued under section 42(4);

"benefits", in Part II, has the meaning given in section 4(4);

"conciliation officer" means a person designated under section 211 of the Trade Union and Labour Relations (Consolidation) Act 1992;

"employment" means, subject to any prescribed provision, employment under a contract of service or of apprenticeship or a contract personally to do any work, and related expressions are to be construed accordingly;

"employment at an establishment in Great Britain" is to be construed in accordance with subsections (2) to (5);

"enactment" includes subordinate legislation and any Order in Council;

"licensing authority" means–

(a) in relation to the area to which the Metropolitan Public Carriage Act 1869 applies, the Secretary of State or the holder of any office for the time being designated by the Secretary of State; or

(b) in relation to any other area in England and Wales, the authority responsible for licensing taxis in that area;

"mental impairment" does not have the same meaning as in the Mental Health Act 1983 or the Mental Health (Scotland) Act 1984 but the fact that an impairment would be a mental impairment for the purposes of either of those Acts does not prevent it from being a mental impairment for the purposes of this Act;

"Minister of the Crown" includes the Treasury;

"occupational pension scheme" has the same meaning as in the Pension Schemes Act 1993;

"premises" includes land of any description;

"prescribed" means prescribed by regulations;

"profession" includes any vocation or occupation;

"provider of services" has the meaning given in section 19(2)(b);

"public service vehicle" and "regulated public service vehicle" have the meaning given in section 40;

"PSV accessibility regulations" means regulations made under section 40(1);

"rail vehicle" and "regulated rail vehicle" have the meaning given in section 46;

"rail vehicle accessibility regulations" means regulations made under section 46(1);

"regulations" means regulations made by the Secretary of State;

"section 6 duty" means any duty imposed by or under section 6;

"section 15 duty" means any duty imposed by or under section 15;

"section 21 duty" means any duty imposed by or under section 21;

"subordinate legislation" has the same meaning as in section 21 of the Interpretation Act 1978;

"taxi" and "regulated taxi" have the meaning given in section 32;

"taxi accessibility regulations" means regulations made under section 32(1);

"trade" includes any business;

"trade organisation" has the meaning given in section 13;

"vehicle examiner" means an examiner appointed under section 66A of the Road Traffic Act 1988.

(2) Where an employee does his work wholly or mainly outside Great Britain, his employment is not to be treated as being work at an establishment in Great Britain even if he does some of his work at such an establishment.

(3) Except in prescribed cases, employment on board a ship, aircraft or hovercraft is to be regarded as not being employment at an establishment in Great Britain.

(4) Employment of a prescribed kind, or in prescribed circumstances, is to be regarded as not being employment at an establishment in Great Britain.

(5) Where work is not done at an establishment it shall be treated as done–

(a) at the establishment from which it is done; or
(b) where it is not done from any establishment, at the establishment with which it has the closest connection.

Financial provisions.

69. There shall be paid out of money provided by Parliament–

(a) any expenditure incurred by a Minister of the Crown under this Act;
(b) any increase attributable to this Act in the sums payable out of money so provided under or by virtue of any other enactment.

Section 69

This grants the power of a Minister of the Crown to spend public money in order to carry out functions under this act.

Short title, commencement, extent etc.

70.–(1) This Act may be cited as the Disability Discrimination Act 1995.

(2) This section (apart from subsections (4), (5) and (7)) comes into force on the passing of this Act.

(3) The other provisions of this Act come into force on such day as the Secretary of State may by order appoint and different days may be appointed for different purposes.

(4) Schedule 6 makes consequential amendments.

(5) The repeals set out in Schedule 7 shall have effect.

(6) This Act extends to Northern Ireland, but in their application to Northern Ireland the provisions of this Act mentioned in Schedule 8 shall have effect subject to the modifications set out in that Schedule.

(7) In Part II of Schedule 1 to the House of Commons Disqualification Act 1975 and in Part II of Schedule 1 to the Northern Ireland Assembly Disqualification Act 1975 (bodies whose members are disqualified) in each case insert at the appropriate places–

"The National Disability Council."

"The Northern Ireland Disability Council.

(8) Consultations which are required by any provision of this Act to be held by the Secretary of State may be held by him before the coming into force of that provision.

Section 70

The Disability Rights Commission replaces the National Disability Council as from April 2000.

The Act gives the Commission the same powers as the Equal Opportunities Commission under section 53 of the SDA and the Commission for Racial Equality under section 43 of the RRA.

The DRC has the same powers as the EOC and the CRE in relation to carrying out formal investigations where it believes that discrimination is taking place or has taken place. It may issue non-discrimination notices or may conclude agreements with alleged offenders under the Act by which such offenders agree to take certain courses of action in order to avoid proceedings being commenced against them.

The Commission may also provide assistance to individuals in order to assist them in bringing or pursuing their complaints.

Under section 8, if a person obtains an award having succeeded in their complaint the commission is entitled to recover from any award or costs recovered any expenses it has incurred in providing that assistance.

Section 9 amends the DDA by inserting section 53A which is set out in that Act and, for this reason, is not repeated here. Section 10 inserts a new section 28 of the DDA and is set out in that part.

SCHEDULES

Section 70(4)
Consequential Amendments

SCHEDULE 1

SECTION 1(1). PROVISIONS SUPPLEMENTING SECTION 1

Impairment

1.–(1) "Mental impairment" includes an impairment resulting from or consisting of a mental illness only if the illness is a clinically well-recognised illness.

(2) Regulations may make provision, for the purposes of this Act–

(a) for conditions of a prescribed description to be treated as amounting to impairments;
(b) for conditions of a prescribed description to be treated as not amounting to impairments.

(3) Regulations made under sub-paragraph (2) may make provision as to the meaning of "condition" for the purposes of those regulations.

Long-term effects

2.–(1) The effect of an impairment is a long-term effect if–

(a) it has lasted at least 12 months;
(b) the period for which it lasts is likely to be at least 12 months; or
(c) it is likely to last for the rest of the life of the person affected.

(2) Where an impairment ceases to have a substantial adverse effect on a person's ability to carry out normal day-to-day activities, it is to be treated as continuing to have that effect if that effect is likely to recur.

(3) For the purposes of sub-paragraph (2), the likelihood of an effect recurring shall be disregarded in prescribed circumstances.

(4) Regulations may prescribe circumstances in which, for the purposes of this Act–

(a) an effect which would not otherwise be a long-term effect is to be treated as such an effect; or
(b) an effect which would otherwise be a long-term effect is to be treated as not being such an effect.

Severe disfigurement

3.–(1) An impairment which consists of a severe disfigurement is to be treated as having a substantial adverse effect on the ability of the person concerned to carry out normal day-to-day activities.

(2) Regulations may provide that in prescribed circumstances a severe disfigurement is not to be treated as having that effect.

(3) Regulations under sub-paragraph (2) may, in particular, make provision with respect to deliberately acquired disfigurements.

Normal day-to-day activities

4.–(1) An impairment is to be taken to affect the ability of the person concerned to carry out normal day-to-day activities only if it affects one of the following–

(a) mobility;
(b) manual dexterity;
(c) physical co-ordination;
(d) continence;
(e) ability to lift, carry or otherwise move everyday objects;
(f) speech, hearing or eyesight;
(g) memory or ability to concentrate, learn or understand; or
(h) perception of the risk of physical danger.

(2) Regulations may prescribe–

(a) circumstances in which an impairment which does not have an effect falling within sub-paragraph (1) is to be taken to affect the ability of the person concerned to carry out normal day-to-day activities;
(b) circumstances in which an impairment which has an effect falling within sub-paragraph (1) is to be taken not to affect the ability of the person concerned to carry out normal day-to-day activities.

Substantial adverse effects

5. Regulations may make provision for the purposes of this Act–

(a) for an effect of a prescribed kind on the ability of a person to carry out normal day-to-day activities to be treated as a substantial adverse effect;
(b) for an effect of a prescribed kind on the ability of a person to carry out normal day-to-day activities to be treated as not being a substantial adverse effect.

Effect of medical treatment

6.–(1) An impairment which would be likely to have a substantial adverse effect on the ability of the person concerned to carry out normal day-to-day activities, but for the fact that measures are being taken to treat or correct it, is to be treated as having that effect.

(2) In sub-paragraph (1) "measures" includes, in particular, medical treatment and the use of a prosthesis or other aid.

(3) Sub-paragraph (1) does not apply–

(a) in relation to the impairment of a person's sight, to the extent that the impairment is, in his case, correctable by spectacles or contact lenses or in such other ways as may be prescribed; or

(b) in relation to such other impairments as may be prescribed, in such circumstances as may be prescribed.

Persons deemed to be disabled

7.–(1) Sub-paragraph (2) applies to any person whose name is, both on 12th January 1995 and on the date when this paragraph comes into force, in the register of disabled persons maintained under section 6 of the Disabled Persons (Employment) Act 1944.

(2) That person is to be deemed–

(a) during the initial period, to have a disability, and hence to be a disabled person; and

(b) afterwards, to have had a disability and hence to have been a disabled person during that period.

(3) A certificate of registration shall be conclusive evidence, in relation to the person with respect to whom it was issued, of the matters certified.

(4) Unless the contrary is shown, any document purporting to be a certificate of registration shall be taken to be such a certificate and to have been validly issued.

(5) Regulations may provide for prescribed descriptions of person to be deemed to have disabilities, and hence to be disabled persons, for the purposes of this Act.

(6) Regulations may prescribe circumstances in which a person who has been deemed to be a disabled person by the provisions of sub-paragraph (1) or regulations made under sub-paragraph (5) is to be treated as no longer being deemed to be such a person.

(7) In this paragraph–

"certificate of registration" means a certificate issued under regulations made under section 6 of the Act of 1944; and

"initial period" means the period of three years beginning with the date on which this paragraph comes into force.

Progressive conditions

8.–(1) Where–

(a) a person has a progressive condition (such as cancer, multiple sclerosis or muscular dystrophy or infection by the human immunodeficiency virus),

(b) as a result of that condition, he has an impairment which has (or had) an effect on his ability to carry out normal day-to-day activities, but

(c) that effect is not (or was not) a substantial adverse effect,

he shall be taken to have an impairment which has such a substantial adverse effect if the condition is likely to result in his having such an impairment.

(2) Regulations may make provision, for the purposes of this paragraph–

(a) for conditions of a prescribed description to be treated as being progressive;
(b) for conditions of a prescribed description to be treated as not being progressive.

SCHEDULE 2

SECTION 2(2). PAST DISABILITIES

1. The modifications referred to in section 2 are as follows.
2. References in Parts II and III to a disabled person are to be read as references to a person who has had a disability.
3. In section 6(1), after "not disabled" insert "and who have not had a disability".
4. In section 6(6), for "has" substitute "has had".
5. For paragraph 2(1) to (3) of Schedule 1, substitute–

"(1) The effect of an impairment is a long-term effect if it has lasted for at least 12 months.

(2) Where an impairment ceases to have a substantial adverse effect on a person's ability to carry out normal day-to-day activities, it is to be treated as continuing to have that effect if that effect recurs.

(3) For the purposes of sub-paragraph (2), the recurrence of an effect shall be disregarded in prescribed circumstances."

SCHEDULE 3

SECTIONS 8(8) AND 25(6). ENFORCEMENT AND PROCEDURE

PART I EMPLOYMENT

Conciliation

1. This part now appears as section 18(1) – (3), (6) and (7) of the Employment Tribunals Act 1996. It deals with the duty of a conciliation officer to endeavour to promote a settlement of the claim

(1) Where a complaint is presented to an industrial tribunal under section 8 and a copy of it is sent to a conciliation officer, he shall–

(a) if requested to do so by the complainant and respondent, or

(b) if he considers that he has a reasonable prospect of success,

try to promote a settlement of the complaint without its being determined by an industrial tribunal.

(2) Where a person is contemplating presenting such a complaint, a conciliation officer shall, if asked to do so by the potential complainant or potential respondent, try to promote a settlement.

(3) The conciliation officer shall, where appropriate, have regard to the desirability of encouraging the use of other procedures available for the settlement of grievances.

(4) Anything communicated to a conciliation officer in a case in which he is acting under this paragraph shall not be admissible in evidence in any proceedings before an industrial tribunal except with the consent of the person who communicated it.

Restriction on proceedings for breach of Part II

2.–(1) Except as provided by section 8, no civil or criminal proceedings may be brought against any person in respect of an act merely because the act is unlawful under Part II.

(2) Sub-paragraph (1) does not prevent the making of an application for judicial review.

Period within which proceedings must be brought

3.–(1) An industrial tribunal shall not consider a complaint under section 8 unless it is presented before the end of the period of three months beginning when the act complained of was done.

(2) A tribunal may consider any such complaint which is out of time if, in all the circumstances of the case, it considers that it is just and equitable to do so.

(3) For the purposes of sub-paragraph (1)–

(a) where an unlawful act of discrimination is attributable to a term in a contract, that act is to be treated as extending throughout the duration of the contract;
(b) any act extending over a period shall be treated as done at the end of that period; and
(c) a deliberate omission shall be treated as done when the person in question decided upon it.

(4) In the absence of evidence establishing the contrary, a person shall be taken for the purposes of this paragraph to decide upon an omission–

(a) when he does an act inconsistent with doing the omitted act; or
(b) if he has done no such inconsistent act, when the period expires within which he might reasonably have been expected to do the omitted act if it was to be done.

Evidence

4.–(1) In any proceedings under section 8, a certificate signed by or on behalf of a Minister of the Crown and certifying–

(a) that any conditions or requirements specified in the certificate were imposed by a Minister of the Crown and were in operation at a time or throughout a time so specified, or

(b) that an act specified in the certificate was done for the purpose of safeguarding national security,

shall be conclusive evidence of the matters certified.

(2) A document purporting to be such a certificate shall be received in evidence and, unless the contrary is proved, be deemed to be such a certificate.

PART II DISCRIMINATION IN OTHER AREAS

Restriction on proceedings for breach of Part III

5.–(1) Except as provided by section 25 no civil or criminal proceedings may be brought against any person in respect of an act merely because the act is unlawful under Part III.

(2) Sub-paragraph (1) does not prevent the making of an application for judicial review.

Period within which proceedings must be brought

6.–(1) A county court or a sheriff court shall not consider a claim under section 25 unless proceedings in respect of the claim are instituted before the end of the period of six months beginning when the act complained of was done.

(2) Where, in relation to proceedings or prospective proceedings under section 25, the dispute concerned is referred to conciliation in pursuance of arrangements under section 28 before the end of the period of six months mentioned in sub-paragraph (1), the period allowed by that sub-paragraph shall be extended by two months.

(3) A court may consider any claim under section 25 which is out of time if, in all the circumstances of the case, it considers that it is just and equitable to do so.

(4) For the purposes of sub-paragraph (1)–

(a) where an unlawful act of discrimination is attributable to a term in a contract, that act is to be treated as extending throughout the duration of the contract;
(b) any act extending over a period shall be treated as done at the end of that period; and
(c) a deliberate omission shall be treated as done when the person in question decided upon it.

(5) In the absence of evidence establishing the contrary, a person shall be taken for the purposes of this paragraph to decide upon an omission–

(a) when he does an act inconsistent with doing the omitted act; or
(b) if he has done no such inconsistent act, when the period expires within which he might reasonably have been expected to do the omitted act if it was to be done.

Compensation for injury to feelings

7. In any proceedings under section 25, the amount of any damages awarded as compensation for injury to feelings shall not exceed the prescribed amount.

Evidence

8.–(1) In any proceedings under section 25, a certificate signed by or on behalf of a Minister of the Crown and certifying–

(a) that any conditions or requirements specified in the certificate were imposed by a Minister of the Crown and were in operation at a time or throughout a time so specified, or

(b) that an act specified in the certificate was done for the purpose of safeguarding national security,

shall be conclusive evidence of the matters certified.

(2) A document purporting to be such a certificate shall be received in evidence and, unless the contrary is proved, be deemed to be such a certificate.

SCHEDULE 4

SECTIONS 16(5) AND 27(5). PREMISES OCCUPIED UNDER LEASES

PART I OCCUPATION BY EMPLOYER OR TRADE ORGANISATION

Failure to obtain consent to alteration

1. If any question arises as to whether the occupier has failed to comply with the section 6 or section 15 duty, by failing to make a particular alteration to the premises, any constraint attributable to the fact that he occupies the premises under a lease is to be ignored unless he has applied to the lessor in writing for consent to the making of the alteration.

Joining lessors in proceedings under section 8

2.–(1) In any proceedings under section 8, in a case to which section 16 applies, the complainant or the occupier may ask the tribunal hearing the complaint to direct that the lessor be joined or sisted as a party to the proceedings.

(2) The request shall be granted if it is made before the hearing of the complaint begins.

(3) The tribunal may refuse the request if it is made after the hearing of the complaint begins.

(4) The request may not be granted if it is made after the tribunal has determined the complaint.

(5) Where a lessor has been so joined or sisted as a party to the proceedings, the tribunal may determine–

(a) whether the lessor has–
(i) refused consent to the alteration, or
(ii) consented subject to one or more conditions, and
(b) if so, whether the refusal or any of the conditions was unreasonable,

(6) If, under sub-paragraph (5), the tribunal determines that the refusal or any of the conditions was unreasonable it may take one or more of the following steps–

(a) make such declaration as it considers appropriate;
(b) make an order authorising the occupier to make the alteration specified in the order;
(c) order the lessor to pay compensation to the complainant.

(7) An order under sub-paragraph (6)(b) may require the occupier to comply with conditions specified in the order.

(8) Any step taken by the tribunal under sub-paragraph (6) may be in substitution for, or in addition to, any step taken by the tribunal under section 8(2).

(9) If the tribunal orders the lessor to pay compensation it may not make an order under section 8(2) ordering the occupier to do so.

Regulations

3. Regulations may make provision as to circumstances in which–

(a) a lessor is to be taken, for the purposes of section 16 and this Part of this Schedule to have–
(i) withheld his consent;
(ii) withheld his consent unreasonably;
(iii) acted reasonably in withholding his consent;

(b) a condition subject to which a lessor has given his consent is to be taken to be reasonable;

(c) a condition subject to which a lessor has given his consent is to be taken to be unreasonable.

Sub-leases etc.

4. The Secretary of State may by regulations make provision supplementing, or modifying, the provision made by section 16 or any provision made by or under this Part of this Schedule in relation to cases where the occupier occupies premises under a sub-lease or sub-tenancy.

PART II OCCUPATION BY PROVIDER OF SERVICES

Failure to obtain consent to alteration

5. If any question arises as to whether the occupier has failed to comply with the section 21 duty, by failing to make a particular alteration to premises, any constraint attributable to the fact that he occupies the premises under a lease is to be ignored unless he has applied to the lessor in writing for consent to the making of the alteration.

Reference to court

6.–(1) If the occupier has applied in writing to the lessor for consent to the alteration and–

(a) that consent has been refused, or
(b) the lessor has made his consent subject to one or more conditions,

the occupier or a disabled person who has an interest in the proposed alteration to the premises being made, may refer the matter to a county court or, in Scotland, to the sheriff.

(2) In the following provisions of this Schedule "court" includes "sheriff".

(3) On such a reference the court shall determine whether the lessor's refusal was unreasonable or (as the case may be) whether the condition is, or any of the conditions are, unreasonable.

(4) If the court determines–

(a) that the lessor's refusal was unreasonable, or
(b) that the condition is, or any of the conditions are, unreasonable,

it may make such declaration as it considers appropriate or an order authorising the occupier to make the alteration specified in the order.

(5) An order under sub-paragraph (4) may require the occupier to comply with conditions specified in the order.

Joining lessors in proceedings under section 25

7.–(1) In any proceedings on a claim under section 25, in a case to which this Part of this Schedule applies, the plaintiff, the pursuer or the occupier concerned may ask the court to direct that the lessor be joined or sisted as a party to the proceedings.

(2) The request shall be granted if it is made before the hearing of the claim begins.

(3) The court may refuse the request if it is made after the hearing of the claim begins.

(4) The request may not be granted if it is made after the court has determined the claim.

(5) Where a lessor has been so joined or sisted as a party to the proceedings, the court may determine–

(a) whether the lessor has–
   (i) refused consent to the alteration, or
   (ii) consented subject to one or more conditions, and

(b) if so, whether the refusal or any of the conditions was unreasonable.

(6) If, under sub-paragraph (5), the court determines that the refusal or any of the conditions was unreasonable it may take one or more of the following steps–

(a) make such declaration as it considers appropriate;
(b) make an order authorising the occupier to make the alteration specified in the order;
(c) order the lessor to pay compensation to the complainant.

(7) An order under sub-paragraph (6)(b) may require the occupier to comply with conditions specified in the order.

(8) If the court orders the lessor to pay compensation it may not order the occupier to do so.

Regulations

8. Regulations may make provision as to circumstances in which–

(a) a lessor is to be taken, for the purposes of section 27 and this Part of this Schedule to have–
   (i) withheld his consent;
   (ii) withheld his consent unreasonably;
   (iii) acted reasonably in withholding his consent;

(b) a condition subject to which a lessor has given his consent is to be taken to be reasonable;

(c) a condition subject to which a lessor has given his consent is to be taken to be unreasonable.

Sub-leases etc.

9. The Secretary of State may by regulations make provision supplementing, or modifying, the provision made by section 27 or any provision made by or under this Part of this Schedule in relation to cases where the occupier occupies premises under a sub-lease or sub-tenancy.

Index

NOTE
In the index, the following abbreviations have been used in subheadings:

CRE = Commission for Racial Equality
DDA = Disability Discrimination Act 1995
EOC = Equal Opportunities Commission
RRA = Race Relations Act 1976
SDA = Sex Discrimination Act 1975